TWENTY TO THE MILE
The Overland Telegraph Line

Derek Pugh OAM

With a foreword by
His Excellency the Honourable Hieu Van Le, AC
35th Governor of South Australia

Derek Pugh OAM: Author.
Twenty to the Mile: The Overland Telegraph Line.
Text and original photographs © Derek Pugh 2021, unless otherwise attributed.

Sesquicentenary (1872–2022) Edition.
First published January 2022.

ISBN: 978-0-6481421-9-5
All rights reserved. No part of this publication may be reproduced, stored in a retrieval system, or transmitted in any form by any means, electronic, mechanical, photocopying, recording, or otherwise, without the prior written permission of the author.

Design and layout by Michael Pugh: michael.pugh@bigpond.com

Notes: Includes bibliographical references and index.

Subjects:
Overland Telegraph Line, Port Augusta—Port Darwin 1872.
Palmerston: Darwin, Port Darwin, Northern Territory.
South Australia: History of communication.
Pioneers in Northern Australia.
Australian Aborigines.

Front Cover: O.T.L. pole, Flinders Ranges. Derek Pugh, 2021.

Contact: derekpugh1@gmail.com
www.derekpugh.com.au

This publication was supported by the History Trust of South Australia's South Australian History Fund.

A catalogue record for this book is available from the National Library of Australia

Acknowledgements

An outgoing state governor must have a million things to do in his or her last few weeks in office. Nevertheless, His Excellency Governor Hieu Van Le still found time to consider this project and write an insightful foreword for the text. He therefore has my everlasting appreciation.

Others who have contributed their time and advice include Andrew Bleby, Peter Whelan, Michael Pugh, and Lon Wallis. The latter three are regular aides in my projects, and special thanks go to them. Thanks also to Julian Todd, Richard Venus, Simmone Croft, Natalia and Arthur Yandell, my family, and everyone else who has offered help and advice.

Particular thanks also go to staff of the Library and Archives of the Northern Territory (LANT), The State Library of South Australia (SLSA), and trove.nla.gov.au, without whom the research tasks would become insurmountable.

The author acknowledges the Traditional Owners and their custodianship of the lands through which the O.T.L. ran and pays respects to their Ancestors and descendants, and those who continue cultural and spiritual connections to Country. Indigenous readers are advised that this book contains names and photographs of people who have died.

Some of the historical quotes reproduced in this book contain language now considered offensive. I apologise for repeating them, but I believe it is appropriate to quote these words for historical accuracy, without judging the users.

Contents

Acknowledgements	iii
Contents	iv
Maps	v
Timeline	vii
Foreword	xiii
Preface	xvii
1. Telegraph Lines	1
2. Port Darwin	15
3. The Route	19
Gallery: O.T.L. Workers	26
4. The Southern Section	29
5. The Central Section	39
6. The Northern Section	57
Gallery: Adelaide and Palmerston	102
7. Life On The O.T.L.	109
Gallery: Alice Springs	168
8. Explorers	171
9. Along The O.T.L.	193
Appendix: Telegraph Line Construction Parties	271
Bibliography	279
Index	287

Maps

Map 1: The Northern Territory of South Australia lasted from 1863 until 1911.   vi
When the Commonwealth Government resumed control, the name was
changed, simply, to Northern Territory. The Overland Telegraph Line followed
John McDouall Stuart's track through the centre of Australia (1903, Johnson).

Map 2: This map, produced by the Surveryor General's department, c. 1871, shows   24
exploration tracks taken by Stuart, Sturt, McKinlay, Gregory and Leichhardt.
It was used by an O.T.L. manager, possibly Todd, who annotated it in pencil
and red ink. The work sections, the route of the telegraph lines, and details of
natural features are marked. Details of each section A–E are reproduced in
Chapter 5 (SLSA, map C54).

Map 3: Detail of Map 2. Section A, from the end of Bagot's contract. Also shows   41
Stuart's exploration routes, c. 1871 (SLSA, C54).

Map 4: Detail of Map 2. Section B, Finke and Hugh Rivers, Chambers Pillar.   43
The Finke Depot is marked with a cross. Also shows Stuart's exploration
routes, c. 1871 (SLSA, C54).

Map 5: Detail of Map 2. Section C, through the MacDonnell Ranges. Also shows   46
Stuart's exploration routes, c. 1871 (SLSA, C54).

Map 6: Detail of Map 2. Section D, Central Mount Stuart. Also shows Stuart's   51
exploration routes, c. 1871 (SLSA, C54).

Map 7: Detail of Map 2. Section E, Davenport and Murchison Ranges, and   55
Tennant Creek (Attack Creek is north of the section). Also shows Stuart's
exploration routes, c. 1871 (SLSA, C54).

Map 8: Richard Knuckey's hand-drawn map showing the cart track from the   84
Roper River to the line, dated 3 March 1871 (SLSA, C34).

Map 9: Detail of Richard Knuckey's hand-drawn map showing Roper River Depot   885
area, dated 3 March 1871 (SLSA, C34).

Map 10: The eastern section of Giles's map of his expedition from the O.T.L.,   180
departing from Chambers Pillar in 1872, and returning to Ross's Waterhole
in August 1873 (Giles, 1877).

Twenty to the Mile

Map 11: Ernest Giles returned to The Peake from Western Australia on his 5th expedition in 1876 (Giles, 1877).   184

Map 12: The route of the Overland Telegraph Line and the original stations, c. 1900 (NT Heritage).   192

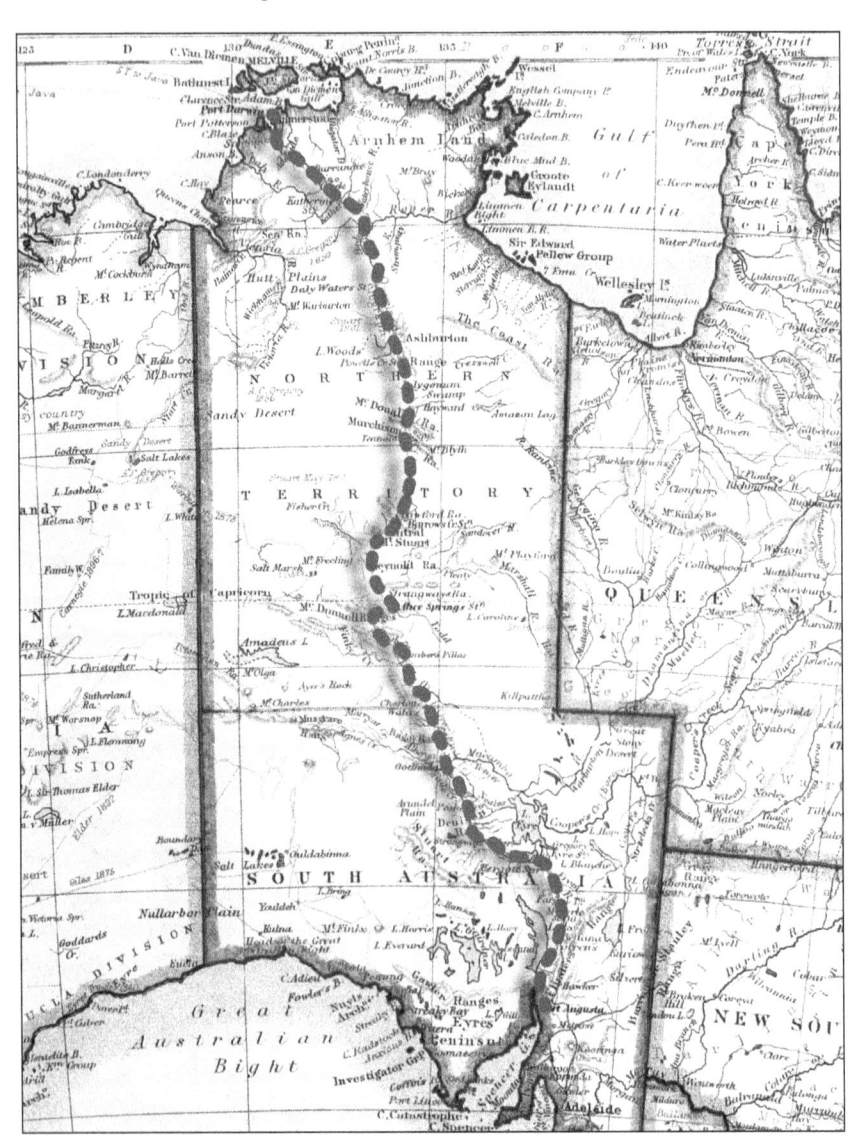

Map 1: The Northern Territory of South Australia lasted from 1863 until 1911. When the Commonwealth Government resumed control, the name was changed, simply, to Northern Territory. The Overland Telegraph Line followed John McDouall Stuart's track through the centre of Australia (1903, Johnson).

vi

Timeline

1837	American artist Samuel Morse and friends invent a simple code for numbers that can transmit marks to paper via an electrical telegraph system.
1840	Co-inventor Alfred Vail expands Morse's code to include letters.
1844	The first telegram is sent by Morse on 24 May 1844, over an experimental line from Washington, D.C., to Baltimore. The message says: 'What hath God wrought?'
1853	The first telegraph line in Australia is installed. It is 17 kilometres long and stretches from Melbourne to Williamstown. It is extended to Geelong in 1854. The first news transmitted concerned the rebellion at the Eureka Stockade.
November 1855	Charles Todd arrives in Adelaide from England.
November 1855	South Australia's first government telegraph line opens.
30 December 1857	In N.S.W. the 32 km line between Sydney and Liverpool opens.
July 1858	Adelaide–Melbourne telegraph line opens.
18 August 1859	Victoria and Tasmania are connected by an undersea telegraph line.
1862	John McDouall Stuart and party cross Australia from coast to coast and return. A route across the continent for the O.T.L. is then known to be possible.
5 February 1869	The Second Northern Territory Expedition arrives at Port Darwin on the *Moonta*, under George Goyder. The survey takes 8 months.

27 March 1869	The *Gulnare* arrives in Port Darwin under Captain Samuel White Sweet with stores and equipment. Sweet is also a photographer and he and Robert Brooks record the early settlement.
January 1870	The *Kohinoor* arrives in Port Darwin bringing new settlers and some families.
24 June 1870	Captain William Bloomfield Douglas arrives on the *Gulnare* as the first permanent Government Resident.
24 June 1870	*Bengal* arrives in Port Darwin with news that the B.A.T. Company would build an overland telegraph line from Port Darwin to Normanton.
23 July 1870	McLachlan and a survey team survey a route to the Roper River in preparation for the line being constructed to Normanton.
9 September 1870	The S.S. *Omeo* arrives in Port Darwin with the Northern O.T.L. construction team, and the news that the South Australia would build the line from Port Darwin to Port Augusta. Normanton is no longer the destination.
15 September 1870	The first telegraph pole of the O.T.L. is 'planted' by Harriet Douglas.
September 1870	Edward Meade Bagot and the southern construction party begin building the O.T.L. from Port Augusta.
1871	The first telegraph office is built in Palmerston using logs cut from the bush and thatching.
11 March 1871	William Mills finds Atherreyurre, a waterhole he names the Alice Spring after Todd's wife. It is not a spring at all, but a part of the Todd River.
1871	Gilbert McMinn and his team begin the construction of the Alice Springs Telegraph Station.
1871	First telegraph office is built in Palmerston (see Figure 22).
1 August 1871	John Little is appointed as the officer in charge of the telegraph in the Northern Territory.
24 September 1871	Robert Patterson takes over building the northern section.
7 November 1871	Undersea telegraph cable is hauled on shore and cable is laid from Port Darwin to Banyuwangi, Java.
20 November 1871	First telegram arrives in Palmerston from Captain Robert Halpin in Java: 'Advance Australia'.

Timeline

December 1871	The *Bengal* arrives in the Roper River to establish a depot.
30 December 1871	Benjamin Clarke sends the first telegraph message south from Alice Springs.
July 1872	Alice Springs Telegraph Station building completed.
1871–72	Two separate exploration parties led by William Gosse and Peter Warburton camp at Alice Springs Telegraph Station for the summer.
20 June 1872	First telegram from Port Darwin is received in Adelaide, dated 22 May. It travelled by telegraph and horse express. It is addressed by Mr C. Todd to the Chief Secretary (Hon. H. Ayers).
22 June 1872	The undersea cable breaks and it takes until October to repair.
25 June 1872	First message from Adelaide to London is transmitted by overland telegraph and horse express service.
July 1872	Alice Springs Telegraph Station building completed.
22 August 1872	First through telegram is sent from Palmerston to Adelaide after the O.T.L. is connected at Frew's Ironstone Ponds (*Warlirra*). Numerous complimentary messages are sent to Mr. C. Todd, then at Central Mount Stuart.
August 1872	Ernest Giles begins his first exploration west of the O.T.L., starting at Chambers Pillar.
11 October 1872	The S.S. *Omeo* collects workers from Roper River and returns them to Adelaide.
21 October 1872	The undersea cable to Banyuwangi is repaired at midnight.
22 October 1872	First direct telegram from England is received in the Adelaide Telegraph Office.
30 October 1872	Mr C. Todd returns from the Northern Territory overland.
15 November 1872	A public holiday in celebration of the completion of the Overland Telegraph is declared. A banquet for Mr C. Todd, officers and men is held in the town hall. There are athletics, fireworks and a ball held in the Exhibition Grounds.
30 December 1872	Steam tug *Young Australian* sinks on a rock bar in the Roper River and is abandoned.
1873	Telegraph stations begin recording meteorological information.

24 February 1873	Kaytetye warriors attack the telegraph station at Barrow Creek—James Lawrence Stapleton and John Frank are killed.
From April 1873	Richard Knuckey and a team of 60 men replace wooden poles with metal Oppenheimer poles using the Roper River Depot.
15 April 1873	Peter Warburton and party depart Alice Springs to explore westwards to the W.A. coast.
20 April 1873	William Gosse and party also depart westwards from Alice Springs. Gosse 'discovers' Uluru and other central Australian landmarks.
4 August 1873	Ernest Giles begins his 2nd expedition from the O.T.L. to the Musgrave Ranges.
2 November 1873	George Byng Scott arrives as the new Government Resident in the Northern Territory.
30 September 1874	John Forrest reaches Peake Telegraph Station after crossing the continent from Perth.
24 February 1875	The *Gothenburg* is wrecked in Queensland, taking 88 lives (about a seventh of the Palmerston population), including at least five O.T.L. workers such as C. Musgrave.
14 July 1875	Charles Johnston is murdered, and a revenge expedition is led by John Little and Constable Montagu.
September 1876	Ernest Giles returns to The Peake from Western Australia on his 5th expedition.
19 January 1876	Thomas Ferguson dies at the Alice Springs Telegraph Station.
October 1877	First Coolies are brought in directly from southern China to northern Australia.
January 1878	Alice Springs Telegraph Station becomes a post office. Mail is delivered every six weeks.
1878	The construction of the Port Augusta to Government Gums (Farina) railway begins.
November 1878	Ernest Ebenezer Flint takes over as telegraph station master from John Mueller, at Alice Springs.
June 1879	Springvale (near the Katherine Telegraph Station) and Glencoe Cattle Stations are established.

Timeline

April 1879	Mounted Constable John Shirley sets up a police post near Alice Springs Telegraph Station.
21 February 1882	The South Australian Parliamentary Party, 1882, visit and tour the gold fields and assess agricultural and pastoral opportunities, under Education Minister John Langdon Parsons.
1882	MC John Shirley transfers to Barrow Creek and MC William Willshire takes his place in Alice Springs.
6 March 1883	Edward Price leaves Port Darwin on the *Bowen*. Gilbert Rotherdale McMinn stands in as acting-Government Resident for 14 months.
1 June 1883	*North Australian*, Palmerston's second newspaper begins.
4 July 1883	David Lindsay leaves the O.T.L. line at Katherine to begin an exploration of Arnhem Land.
1884	The new town of Burrundie is established on the gold fields.
January 1887	Ernest Ebenezer Flint marries Florence Madely. She is the first woman to live at the Alice Springs Telegraph Station. Unfortunately, Ebenezer dies of rheumatic fever in July.
1888	David Lindsay surveys a town site near Alice Springs. The town of Stuart is named on 28 November.
10 December 1888	Railway service between Palmerston and Burrundie begins.
1889	The Stuart Arms Hotel is opened in the town of Stuart by Bill Benstead (It is destroyed by fire in June 1960). Wesley Turton builds a brewery nearby.
30 September 1889	Rail service between Palmerston and Pine Creek (145 miles) begins.
January 1891	The southern railway, known as the Ghan, reaches Oodnadatta, which become the railhead for the next 30 years.
June 1893	Charles Todd is knighted Knight Commander of the Order of St Michael and St George (KNMG).
March 1898	The government starts to replace the No. 8 steel wire of the O.T.L. with copper wire.
1901	Post and telegraph responsibilities are transferred from the states to the Commonwealth Government.

1911	The Northern Territory becomes a Commonwealth responsibility.
5 August 1929	Passenger trains arrive in Alice Springs for the first time.
25 January 1932	The Alice Springs Post Office opens, and the Telegraph Station is closed, after 60 years of service. It becomes a children's home.
1946	Public telephones are installed in Alice Springs.
1955	Frank Clune publishes *Overland Telegraph: An epic feat of adventure and courage,* and describes the O.T.L. as 'one of the greatest events in Australian history, an epic of triumph and tragedy …'
26 November 1980	The last Ghan of the original narrow-gauge railway departs from Alice Springs and the track to Oodnadatta is decommissioned. In October, the new Ghan starts via Tarcoola.
1982	The O.T.L. poles and cable are removed from the old rail side. Little can be seen of it now, except broken insulators and the base of poles still in the ground.
2021	150 years after the undersea cable is laid from Darwin a $500m system of high-capacity data cables is proposed between Darwin, Jakarta, and Singapore.
2022	The O.T.L. sesquicentenary year.

Foreword by
His Excellency, the Honourable Hieu Van Le, AC, 35th Governor of South Australia

The Overland Telegraph Line is one of our nation's greatest engineering feats of the nineteenth century.

I was pleased to be invited to provide a foreword for this book, as my predecessors Sir Richard Graves MacDonnell, Sir Dominick Daly, and The Right Honourable Sir James Fergusson were strong supporters of the project and have landmarks on the line named after them.

To mark the importance of completing the line, Governor Fergusson declared Friday, 15 November 1872, to be a public holiday in South Australia! Such was the community pride in its success.

The Governor also hosted a grand banquet at the Adelaide Town Hall, which was preceded by a grand procession from the Post Office to the Exhibition Hall on North Terrace, honouring the Superintendent of Telegraphs, the revered Charles Todd, and his officers and staff.

The knowledge and experience gained by the series of inland expeditions in the mid-1800s by explorer John McDouall Stuart from Adelaide through the central interior and finally to the north coast, paved the way for the Overland Telegraph route.

Rivalry between the colonies was intense, with Queensland and New South Wales competing to carry out the monumental project.

The Northern Territory was part of New South Wales from 1770 until 1862. South Australia, with the acquisition of the Northern Territory following the Stuart expedition, was in a prime position, both geographically and expertly, to build the line and become the hub for the telegraph network.

Harnessing the interior and a north-south corridor across the continent 150 years ago is an impressive feat.

The continent had been criss-crossed for thousands of years by Aboriginal people, yet to the European settlers in a new and harsh land, the journey was largely unknown and infrastructure non-existent.

The distance involved is staggering, even today.

My wife Lan and I first encountered the vastness of Australia from North to South from the window of an aeroplane more than four decades ago. We had arrived in Darwin in a ramshackle fishing boat after a long and perilous journey as some of the early boat people from Vietnam.

After a short time in a quarantine centre, we were relocated to Adelaide. We had no idea where Adelaide was or how long it would take us to get there. Outside the window we could see only darkness. After several hours, Lan became worried, her eyes filled with trepidation. She turned to me saying: 'This is taking so long; we've been flying for a long time. Do you think they are sending us back to Vietnam?'

Seeing our anxiety, the crew kindly took us to the flight deck and the pilot took time to show us where we were on the radar and how far away we were from Adelaide.

We landed in Adelaide in the early morning after many hours flying.

We had indeed come to a huge continent; one that people today can traverse from Adelaide to Darwin in a few hours by plane or, still, several days by vehicle.

We can only admire those who took the same journey 150 years ago in mere bullock and horse-drawn carts or camel trains, taking their own provisions with them, to build the Overland Telegraph Line.

Let us too, honour the role of the rugged Afghan Cameleers who provided essential support for desert exploration, including hauling supplies and basic infrastructure, including the poles for the Overland Telegraph.

Their camels were well suited to the harsh environment the men experienced, in traversing similarly mesmerising but unforgiving terrain. They are but one of the many examples of how migrants have always been an important part of our nation building. Their contribution is honoured in the name of the Ghan passenger train that runs between Adelaide and Darwin.

The Overland Telegraph project's statistics are astounding: 36,000 poles placed 80 metres apart, with associated insulators and pins, countless tons of wire and 11 repeater stations.

The line traversed a staggering 3,200 kilometres across some of the most rugged, diverse, and inhospitable landscapes—from arid deserts to lands inundated by tropical deluges.

It was completed in two years, and only seven months behind schedule.

But behind these facts and figures are the stories of fortitude, determination, and back-breaking work.

In many ways the Overland Telegraph was the internet of its time; such was the immense impact it had, enabling the fledgling colonies at the far reaches of the globe to communicate and connect with Europe and our near neighbours.

Before then, news and information to and from home took months to arrive. Now, the tyranny of distance was being conquered. Business and commerce could be conducted more easily. Banking information, market information, the data to predict trends and build businesses took hours to arrive, rather than months.

The rest of the world was now that much closer.

Through this book, Derek Pugh weaves a tale of overcoming rivalry, seizing opportunity, and mind-boggling ingenuity, through which the interior was opened up to connect the colonies to the world.

I congratulate Derek for his painstaking research in telling the tale of the Overland Telegraph and producing a book written with heart and admiration for those who brought the project to fruition. The book is a lasting tribute to the inventiveness and tenacity of the people behind the planning, building and execution of the Overland Telegraph.

A true nation-building endeavour.

His Excellency,
The Honourable Hieu Van Le, AC,
35th Governor of South Australia

Preface

One hundred and fifty years ago, a small group of talented technicians and bushmen gathered under a tall pole near Frew's Ironstone Ponds, deep in the Northern Territory bush. At 12 noon, their leader, Robert Patterson, climbed a ladder and grasped the two ends of the telegraph line in order to join them.

He promptly received an electric shock*.

This delayed the joining by a few minutes. Patterson found a handkerchief and tried again. Wrapping the wire with the cloth, he soldered the southward facing line of wire to its mate. The O.T.L. then stretched 2,839 kilometres† as a single wire from Palmerston on the north coast to Port Augusta on the south, and 300 kilometres more to Adelaide. It joined a network of telegraph wires spread across the eastern states from far Northern Queensland to Tasmania.

In Palmerston‡, John Archibald Graham Little, the Senior Telegraph Officer, waited in the log hut that was his telegraph office.

---

* Many Aboriginal people became very wary of the 'bite' of the line and, as Jeannie Gunn suggested, this may be why it was mostly left alone by people in the bush (Gunn, 1907).

† The exact length of the O.T.L. is difficult to determine. This number comes from a simple adding of Charles Todd's stated section lengths in miles between Port Augusta and Port Darwin and converting to kilometres. Some sources round the distance to 3,000 km. Others measure the line from Adelaide to Port Darwin and call it 3,200 km (for example see Australian Museum, *Australian Geographic*). Engineers Australia agree and use 3,178 km on their commemorative plaque on the joining pole at Frew's Ponds but the NT Government, on one website, enthusiastically claim 3,600 km! Charles Todd said the distance from Adelaide to Port Darwin is 1,973 miles or 3,175.2 kilometres.

‡ Palmerston was usually called Port Darwin after Darwin Harbour. Its name was officially changed to Darwin in 1911.

Twenty to the Mile

The importance of the occasion must have impressed him. Dr James Stokes Millner, then acting Government Resident, had written out a congratulatory message to be sent to the Governor of South Australia. Little tested his Morse key, and double checked. The 'dashes and dots' of Morse code would travel at electric speed to telegraph repeater stations across the continent to his south. Then, powered by large banks of batteries, operators at each of eleven stations on the line would keep the message moving*. Each operator needed to record the message exactly as it was sent, and then resend it. They were well trained.

Messages had been flying back and forth along the south and north wires for months as they grew further north from Port Augusta and further south from Palmerston and, as the lines drew closer, excitement grew. The first message from Alice Springs to Adelaide was sent on 30 December 1871. Eight months later, field operator and future stationmaster, Charles Johnston, sent a telegram from the end of the wire on the southern side:

> … wired yesterday 4½ miles; to-day 6½ miles. If the other parties are making as good speed as is reported, it will not be long before the gap is closed, and daily communication opened between Palmerston and Adelaide.†

A week before the joining of the line, Postmaster-General Charles Todd set up a camp at Barrow's Creek Telegraph Station near Central Mount Stuart. By Morse code, he kept the government informed of the line's progress, and they in turn fed the news to the newspapers:

> … The line is working splendidly. I feel assured the Government will acknowledge that since the work was resumed at the end of the wet season no time has been lost, and that with even all the vexatious delays and mishaps in the Northern Territory, the erection of 2,000 miles of telegraph through the centre of Australia in less than two years is not

---

* The stations were separated by no more than about 200 miles (321 kilometres), because the electrical current that carried the telegraphic signals would travel about 350 kms along the iron wire before fading.
† *Express and Telegraph*, 3 August 1872.

bad work, especially when it is remembered that we have had to procure our materials from England. It is to be hoped the cable will be repaired by the time our wire joins ...*

The overland line was going to be fine, but the undersea cable to Java had problems. Three days later:

... We have now only two short wire gaps; one will close on Monday or Tuesday, the other most probably on Wednesday or Thursday at latest. The cable unfortunately is still interrupted. The *Investigator* is trying to pick it up near the coast of Java; but the prevailing monsoon, which will soon moderate, has probably hitherto retarded operations.†

In the last few weeks before the lines met, a horse express run by John Lewis could cross the gap in ever lessening time. This had allowed the first message from Adelaide to London to be transmitted on 25 June 1872. Messages were transferred by hand to each end of the wire and communication between Darwin and London and Adelaide was live. It was a slow but effective solution that worked well until the undersea cable broke.

In the meantime, Todd could sit and calculate when the lines would meet. It finally happened near John McDouall Stuart's old camp at Frew's Ironstone Ponds. As the ends closed together, John Little in Darwin, and Charles Todd at Central Mount Stuart, prepared to send their first messages. The repeater stations were manned and ready.

At ten past twelve Patterson joined the wire and the messaging started. As promised in the days before, at 1 p.m. precisely, the first official electric telegram arrived in Adelaide from Port Darwin. Following that, a string of congratulatory messages was transmitted from consuls and vice-consuls, politicians, and senior public servants. All were gathered and published the next day in the newspapers‡ and the words thrilled the people of Adelaide. The most quoted text came from Todd:

---

* *Express and Telegraph*, 15 August 1872. The 'cable' he referred to, was the undersea cable to Java. It broke on 22 June 1872.
† Todd, Barrow's Creek, 18 August 1872.
‡ *Express and Telegraph*, 23 August 1872.

... We have this day or within two years from the date it was commenced, completed a line of 2,000 miles long through the very centre of Australia a few years ago a terra incognita and supposed to be a desert, and I have the satisfaction of seeing the successful completion of a scheme I officially advanced 14 years ago.*

The newspapers were enthusiastic, and the telegraph departments partied. A public holiday was announced, and banquets were planned.

The O.T.L. is held by many, even these days, as no less significant for nineteenth-century Australia as that 'giant leap' event was to the world in the twentieth century. Indeed, many claim it was the greatest engineering achievement of the nineteenth century.

The men gathered around the pole in the bush celebrated too. They fired 21 shots from their revolvers and smashed a brandy bottle against the pole. The bottle, it is said, was filled, frugally, with tea—no one was about to waste good brandy, even for such a momentous occasion.

Communication between the cities of the eastern seaboard, through Adelaide to Darwin and back, now took minutes, instead of weeks. And, after the undersea cable was repaired by men on the *Investigator* at midnight on 19 October, the line opened at 9 a.m. the next morning for communication with London. Just imagine what a difference that made for business investors, war watchers, news hounds, and English patriots keeping in touch with 'Old Blighty'. Australia's geographic isolation from the rest of the world and the 'tyranny of distance' were immediately and forever ameliorated. News now arrived from London within seven hours, rather than two or three months. It was then picked up and broadcast by the newspapers. Businessmen placed orders, did their banking, and gathered market information. Colonial governments received directives directly from the British parliament. Prosperity and wealth blossomed.

They were exciting times.

---

* *Express and Telegraph*, 23 August 1872.

This book celebrates the sesquicentenary of the joining of the wires on 22 August 1872. It tells stories of the hundreds of men, and occasional women, who worked on the line, used it, relied on it for survival—or died on it—during the nineteenth century.

The names of the men in the construction teams appear in the Appendix. No doubt some are missing, as are the unrecorded names of most of the Aboriginal men and women who also appear in the story. The full history of the greatest engineering feat of nineteenth-century Australia is yet to be finished, but I offer this tome as a step on the way.

Figure 1: Sir Charles Todd KCMG (SLSA, B-12209).

Chapter 1
Telegraph lines

The first telegraph line in Australia was installed in 1853. It was 17 kilometres long and stretched from Melbourne to Williamstown. In 1854, it was extended to Geelong, just in time to transmit the first news of the rebellion at Eureka Stockade*. By 1857, the Victorian network was already extensive, growing to 2,697 kilometres of line in the following decade, and transmitting more than 100,000 messages annually.

The South Australian government was aware of the potential value of the telegraph and were quick to respond, recruiting Charles Todd†, an experienced telegraph professional, from England in 1854.

Todd was a 28-year-old meteorologist and astronomer from Cambridge University. His career was already bright. He was, for example, the first to take daguerreotype photographs of the moon, and among the first to observe Neptune‡. He became interested in the electric telegraph when he learned that it allowed the accurate calculation of time in different areas, and the prediction of weather events. Using the telegraph allowed astronomers to control clocks and standardise time across Britain, and eventually the world. It also allowed the writing of accurate train timetables.

---

* Thompson, 2008.
† There is a persistent error concerning Charles Todd's name. Todd never had a middle name, but since 1949 he has been known as Charles Heavitree Todd (J. Todd, 2021). Heavitree was, in fact, the school attended by W.W. Mills (Venus, 2013).
‡ Symes, 1976b.

Todd was a personable and quick-witted leader, leading his men with good humour and care. Several writers mentioned his bad jokes—the 'dad jokes' of the day:

> ... during the progress of this work [Todd] would ride or drive out to the linesmen's camps, to encourage and cheer up the men and prevent them becoming lonely or disheartened. How welcome he would be, full of jokes, often such bad ones, but always optimistic and cheerful*.

Stephen King, who worked for Todd as a surveyor, recalled:

> ... Everyone liked old Charley. He was the funniest man you could have met travelling. He was the life of the party all the time, but once a joke nearly cost him his life. It was a blistering day, one of those real northern scorchers, in which a man would give all he possessed for the luxury of a bath, and Charley, coming on a bucket of water, decided to take a dive. He dived without anyone noticing him but plunged so hard that the bucket stuck to his head. He was held fast and was slowly drowning when someone noticed his plight and rescued him†.

Todd arrived in Adelaide in November 1855 accompanied by his wife, Alice Gillam Bell. His position was titled 'Astronomical and Meteorological Observer‡, and Head of the Electric Telegraph

---

* *Chronicle*, Lorna Todd, 11 December 1952, see also *Advertiser* 29 July 1873.
† *The Mail*, 10 Jan 1914
‡ Sir Charles Todd is mostly remembered for his contribution to the telegraph system connecting Australia and New Zealand to the world. However, his work in meteorology, survey and astronomy was also outstanding, and he used the telegraph to construct accurate synoptic charts and identified what is now known as the 'Southern Oscillation' climate driver. In 1862, he wrote 'I hope to be able to arrange ... for the transmission of weather reports between Sydney, Melbourne, and Adelaide, based on the reports from the different stations in each colony, by which means I think reliable information could be conveyed of approaching storms, &c.' (*Register*, 4 February 1862). Weather reports were very quickly a regular product of the O.T.L. For example, this weather report on the whole line in 1877: 'Beltana, light, clear, fine; Strangways Springs, light, clear, fine; Peake, calm, clear, pleasant; Charlotte Waters, calm, clear, pleasant; Alice Springs, light clear, pleasant; Barrow Creek, moderate, clear; Tennant Creek, fresh, clear fine; Powell Creek, moderate, dull; Daly Waters, strong, clear, pleasant; Katherine, light, very fine; Pine Creek, calm, fine; Yam Creek, light, clear, warm; Southport, calm, clear, fine; Port Darwin,

Department in South Australia'. Wasting no time, South Australia's first government telegraph line was organised almost immediately. It replaced a rudimentary amateur attempt and stretched 14 kilometres from Adelaide to Semaphore, where a government signal station was built to inform Adelaide of the arrival of ships. Unfortunately, it was an underground line and it failed due to poor insulation. Todd decided that Australian conditions required lines to be strung through the air.

Todd quickly became the driving force for telegraph lines from South Australia to the eastern states. In 1857, he met with his Victorian counterpart, Samuel McGowan, and together they planned a uniform system, compatible to both states, that would quickly put them in telegraphic communication. The Adelaide to Melbourne connection was opened in July 1858 and was so heavily used that a second line was strung in 1861.

In the meantime, lines were also being stretched across Tasmania, New South Wales, and Queensland. In 1858, Tasmania and Victoria agreed to share the costs of an undersea cable and opened it the next year. Unfortunately, the cable proved easily damaged, and was out of commission so often it was abandoned in 1861. It took another eight years before another, more reliable cable, was laid.

New South Wales constructed their first telegraph line between Sydney and Liverpool in 1857. Sydney and Melbourne were connected in October 1858 and a direct Sydney and Adelaide line was constructed in 1867.

Queensland separated from New South Wales and became a state in June 1859. Sydney was connected to the new capital of Brisbane in 1860 and telegraph lines reached Bowen in 1866, Cardwell in 1869 and Normanton in 1871*.

---

very light, clear, fine, very hot' (*Express and Telegraph*, 5 September 1877). Todd also used the telegraph to provide data for the true alignment of the Victorian-South Australian border to the 141st meridian, took measurements of the transit of Venus, and, with his wife Alice, raised six children.

* *Queenslander*, 7 October 1871.

Western Australia was last to join the telegraph. The state's first line ran between Perth and Fremantle, opening on 21 June 1869. Albany was linked in 1870 and the line across the Nullarbor Palin, connecting the state to the eastern capitals, was built in 1874.

Telegraph lines criss-crossed the British Empire, but telegrams sent from London to Sydney needed to be written on paper in Galle[*] (Ceylon) or Singapore, and then carried by ship. Messages could then be repeated on the local network in Adelaide or Brisbane and sent to their final destinations. This was slow but was quicker than sea travel direct from Europe.

As early as 1856, Todd was talking of a telegraph line connecting Adelaide with London. Lorna Todd, his daughter, wrote that he had even promised he would connect London and Australia by telegraph in his farewell speech at a dinner in London, before he emigrated[†]. His idea was to connect Java and the Gulf of Carpentaria with a submarine cable, and Java with Singapore, which already had a cable overland to Europe. He wrote to the South Australian governor, Sir Richard G. MacDonnell, suggesting the project in 1859, but discussions about a telegraphic connection with Europe went on for years. MacDonnell had already expressed the same idea in 1858[‡]. Perhaps he realised that Todd was the right man to put such ideas into practice.

Not everyone was impressed—in 1860 there were those who acknowledged that 'a flash of news from England to Australia by electric telegraph would no doubt be a very fine thing' but who would pay for it? And:

> … of what special advantage would this telegraph be to us? And who would reap the largest share of the benefit? Whether a message to England and back occupies sixty minutes or

---

[*] Even after the O.T.L. was opened, the efficient mail service still required the alignment of ships' departures and arrivals: for example, 'P. & O. Company's steamer *Golconda* sailed on Friday the 21st instant for Galle with the European mail. She left before the arrival of the *Aldinga* [from Melbourne]; our English correspondence will therefore have to wait till next mail' (*NTTG*, 22 May 1875).

[†] *Chronicle*, Lorna Todd, 11 December 1952, see also *Advertiser* 29 July 1873.

[‡] Manser, 1966.

Figure 2: John McDouall Stuart (SLSA, B-501).

sixty days is not of the least consequence to us in the management of our ordinary affairs. But supposing it were, who among us would be in a position to avail themselves of its professed advantages except our first mercantile houses? And what would be its effect on the rest? With a monopoly of intelligence, a monopoly of trade would follow. And those not able to afford two or three messages a week? at £7 to £8 a message, each way, would have to retire before those who could*.

The voices of the naysayers fell on empty ears. International telegraphy was an obvious boon to anyone interested in business or world affairs, and as the technology improved, it became inevitable. The problem was Adelaide's location on the southern side of Australia, thousands of kilometres away from the northern coast—and in the 1860s the British were still yet to discover what lay in the middle of the continent. In fact, many still believed in an inland sea, even though expeditions into the desert had failed to find one, and the difficulties of exploration seemed insurmountable.

Then, at last, on his fourth attempt, John McDouall Stuart and a small party of explorers made it to the north coast and back in one of Australia's greatest exploration expeditions. Stuart arrived in Chambers Bay, east of the current city of Darwin, on 24 July 1862, and dipped his feet, 'and washed [his] face and hands in the sea, as [he] promised the late Governor Sir Richard MacDonnell [he] would'†.

---

* *South Australian Advertiser*, 10 May 1860.
† Stuart, 1862.

To Charles Todd, Stuart's success meant that an overland route to the north coast from Adelaide was possible. In 1870 he was appointed Postmaster General and determined that, on behalf of South Australia, he would install an overland telegraph line across Australia. That same year, the Telegraph Office built a line 300 kilometres north from Adelaide to Port Augusta. Part of the overland line had therefore already been completed—there were 2,839 kilometres left to go.

But others were still interested in the prize. Western Australians thought they could run an undersea cable from Ceylon to Perth, or to the Cambridge Gulf from Timor. One suggestion was:

> … 'to lay cables from Rangoon to Singapore and Batavia, to use the Dutch line to the east end of Java, and thence to lay a cable to North West Cape, Australia, and then join the land line, proposed by a colonial company, through Western Australia to Perth, King George's Sound, to Port Lincoln, and across Spencer's and St. Vincent Gulfs, to Adelaide, where a connection with the other Australian colonies already exists'*.

The British, of course, distrusted the use of lines belonging to foreigners, and the South Australians were not keen on the line going to Western Australia first, so the idea never gathered much steam.

Victoria also considered constructing a line across the continent and, when Burke and Wills set out on their fateful expedition, one of their aims was to establish a route for the electric telegraph. When the expedition failed, the state was out of the race, even though John McKinlay travelled across the continent to the Gulf of Carpentaria, where he arrived on 22 May 1862, two months before Stuart washed his face and hands in Chambers Bay.

A direct result of Stuart's successful crossing was the colonial government's transfer of the Northern Territory to South Australian administration in 1863. The Southerners then moved quickly, and the First Northern Territory Expedition settled on Escape Cliffs, at

---

* *The Age*, 29 October 1869.

the mouth of the Adelaide River, in 1864. It was South Australia's first attempt at colonisation, but it was under-resourced, poorly planned, badly led, and completely in the wrong place. It struggled through two tortuous years before being abandoned*. South Australia took a knock—but they were not out yet.

Queensland provided the most serious competition. A new state with a small population, they envisaged an undersea cable to the Gulf of Carpentaria from Singapore and Java that would travel overland to the towns south of Cape York. This seemed the obvious route, and the Queensland Government installed a telegraph cable as far west as they could in preparation. A new town named after the Norman River had been settled in 1867. Now known as Normanton, it enjoyed a short-lived gold mining boom, and later became a pastoral supply town for the local cattle stations (Burketown was abandoned during this time because of fever and flooding). The Norman River Post Office opened in 1868 and the 1871 connection with the Queensland telegraph system meant that Queensland was ready to accept an international cable—either from under the sea, or across the Top End as soon as it reached them. Communications between the Queensland Government and London concerning the cable came thick and fast during 1870. They were not shy in expressing their competitive nature. For example, Colonial Secretary Arthur Hunter Palmer guaranteed the eastern states' cooperation, and a five per cent contribution to cable costs, as long as South Australia was left out of the loop:

> … In the event of any branch line from South Australia being allowed to join the cable, so as to cut out any portion of the line guaranteed, the guarantee on the part of this colony will cease. In order to avoid the possibility of any complication with the Government of South Australia, the proposed extension cable must not be allowed, if possible, to touch any point within their northern Territory†.

---

* Pugh, 2018a.
† Palmer, 11 June 1870.

Palmer doubted the ability of the South Australians to undertake such a big project—and have it delivered on time—anyway:

> ... The delay that would be incurred in waiting for the completion of the South Australian line would be most vexatious, and productive of the greatest inconvenience, not just to the colonies but to the company themselves ...

Palmer made a last-ditch attempt to secure the line in a telegram to his agent in London:

> ... we will guarantee to them, or any other good company, at same rate and same terms for cable from Coepang to Norman, irrespective of any arrangement company may have made with South Australia as to Port Darwin line. You are fully authorised to secure cable without delay. We will not, under any circumstances, connect with South Australian landline to Darwin ...[*]

The British Australia Telegraph Company was formed in 1869. Known by its acronym, the B.A.T.'s first idea was, indeed, to take their cable to Normanton, although the top end of the Northern Territory could hardly be avoided. An undersea cable was suggested from:

> ... Cape Van Diemen, Melville Island, to the mouth of the Norman River ... instead of constructing a land line ... from Port Darwin to Burketown, should the Queensland Government agree to guarantee five per cent per annum on the outlay for the additional length of cable[†].

At the time, most of Melville Island was unexplored. It was the home of the Tiwi people, and it was well-known that they were unwelcoming to colonial invaders and had been since the 1824 settlement attempt of Fort Dundas[‡]. A telegraph repeater station placed on the island would have been vulnerable indeed. However, the year-old colony of Palmerston at Port Darwin, on friendly Larrakia land, would more safely be the receiver of the cable[§]. An overland cable from Port Darwin to Burketown, and then 730 kilometres

---

[*] Palmer, 12 July 1870.
[†] Cracknell, 6 June 1870.
[‡] Pugh, 2017.
[§] Pugh, 2018b.

further to Normanton, could join the Queensland network. It was the obvious and most economically sensible choice for the B.A.T.—so Queenslanders thought they had the prize in the bag. In 1870, the B.A.T. were preparing to land the undersea cable at Port Darwin, and George McLachlan, the senior surveyor in Palmerston, had been sent out to explore the country to the Roper River. The telegraph's route to Normanton seemed assured[*].

But they had not reckoned on the tenacity of Charles Todd.

Despite the 'revolving door' turmoil in the South Australian government at the time, Todd was able to garner bipartisan support from the politicians for a radical plan. They offered to fund the telegraph line from Adelaide to Port Darwin, and perhaps in folly, also agree to onerous penalties if it was not built on time. It was a huge risk for the struggling state—but if Adelaide could be the entry and exit point for all news and information between Europe and Australia, South Australia's economy would swell. Even better for the tiny colony, they would have the larger states of New South Wales and Victoria paying to use it! If an international link to Queensland's telegraph system went through, Adelaide's advantage would be lost, and it would remain little more than a supply town for sheep stations. Todd understood that the O.T.L. would give Adelaide power and prestige, and he was fiercely loyal to his new home. Todd managed to convince Commander Noel Osborn, a visiting representative of the company, that the B.A.T. could save money by signing with the South Australians. He:

> … pointed out the great advantages such a line would possess over that of Queensland. He also showed that our line would be much shorter, and that Queensland could easily tap it by an extension from Normanton. Mr. Strangways, who was then Attorney-General, and in whom the overland line had found one of its earliest promoters in connection with Stuart's explorations, then took the matter up very warmly, and on receiving an official report from him, a Bill authorising the necessary loan was drafted

---

[*]   Symes, 1976b.

and laid before Parliament, and notwithstanding a Ministerial crisis, the Bill was passed by a large majority ...[*]

Henry Strangways' bill passed in June 1870 and the approved loan stood at £120,000. The government also had the assurance from the B.A.T. chairman, Viscount Charles Monck[†] that the company would, indeed, deliver the undersea cable to Port Darwin:

... Company assures landing of cable at Port Darwin as required in Under Secretary's letter of 23rd April to Osborn. Hope land line will be commenced without delay. Monck, Chairman.[‡]

Lord Monck also suggested that Queensland would be wise to connect to South Australia's line, because, if 'the whole line between Port Darwin and Port Augusta not be complete by the time of landing the cable, there would still be a connection between the cable end and the centres of government and commerce via Queensland'. The South Australians were pleased that this did not occur for years, and they held their monopoly.

Queenslanders had put a great deal of effort into building the Cardwell to Normanton telegraph line[§], but they were out-manoeuvred and gazumped—the B.A.T. signed with South Australia. Normanton is less than 2,000 kilometres from Port Darwin, Adelaide is more than 3,000. Nevertheless, the South Australia government promised the line would be completed within 18 months.

Monck and the B.A.T. board members were no fools. The route through Queensland was obviously easier but South Australia's offer was financially attractive—the costs would not be borne by the company, and the terms of the contract meant that the B.A.T. would be well compensated if the government failed to complete the line on time. The compensation penalties were significant, so failure was not an option:

---

[*] *Advertiser*, 29 July 1873.
[†] Lord Monck had recently returned from Canada, where he had been Governor General for eight years.
[‡] *Advertiser*, 29 July 1873, cable dated 23 April 1870.
[§] Langford, 2008.

... the work is to be completed so as to admit of messages being uninterruptedly transmitted from end to end by the 1st of September 1871, under a penalty of £10 per diem for each section, or £30 per diem for the whole line*.

Planting the first pole in Palmerston on 15 September 1870 was a significant event that put the tiny new settlement on the map. The first settlers had arrived on the *Kohinoor* just eight months earlier, and the government resident, Captain William Bloomfield Douglas, and his family, had only been in town for three months.

Travel from Port Darwin to Adelaide took at least six weeks by sail or two or three weeks by steamships. It thus took weeks to receive replies to letters, but a telegraph system connecting Adelaide to Palmerston would potentially carry messages and receive replies within hours. The message could then head northwest under the sea to join other telegraph networks then being spread across the world. Telegrams would travel to London and back through the repeater stations already in service across the globe. Hours-old news is much more valuable than months-old news, so control of the system was a prize worth fighting for.

Communications between London and Australia, up to then, all arrived by sea—either directly from London, or by telegram to Galle in Ceylon, or Singapore, and then by steam ship. A few ships went to Brisbane through the Torres Straits from Singapore, but most went south to Adelaide. South Australia therefore already received the mail before the eastern capitals, and the state was already linked by telegraph lines to Melbourne and Sydney. South Australian telegraph operators would tap out the news stories in Morse code, and they would appear the next day in *The Argus*, *The Herald*, and any number of newspapers in the eastern states.

As well, government and business telegrams, often coded, would be transferred at an electric speed that made a mockery of the weeks or months they had already taken to arrive in Australia by ship. It

---

* *South Australian Register*, 10 Sept 1870.

was big business, and South Australia needed it: the vagaries of the wool industry, upon which the economy was based, demanded stable industries to keep the state in business during hard times.

The success of the new Overland Telegraph Line linking Adelaide with London was paramount to the future of South Australia. Failure would have been a disaster for the South Australian government, and it was a tremendous task before them. The only white men ever to travel the country through which the line would pass were John McDouall Stuart and his team a decade earlier. The contractors were thus also explorers*. Todd suddenly realised the magnitude of the task before him:

> … And then perhaps for the first time I fully realised the vastness of the undertaking I had pledged myself to carry out. Understand me, I was as sanguine as ever as to the practicability of the thing, but the short space of time allotted to me, only eighteen months, greatly increased my difficulties. The Bill was passed in June 1870 and under the contract I had to open the communication with Port Darwin by the first of January 1872.
>
> Only a few months before, the duties of Postmaster General in addition to the management of the Telegraph Department had been transferred to me. Now I had to carry a line of telegraph 1,800 miles in length through the very centre of Australia, 1,300miles of which was uninhabited by white man—through a country of which I knew positively nothing except what Stuart had told us of the narrow strips he had traversed, and the whole had to be accomplished in the short space of eighteen months.
>
> The wire had to be procured from England, the insulators from Berlin, these on arrival, as well as the stores for the men, had to be carried over many hundreds of miles of rough country, some from Port Augusta northwards, others, after re-shipping, from Port Darwin southwards.
>
> I knew that much of the country north of Port Augusta was destitute of timber, and further acquaintance showed me I had something like 400 miles of timberless country to trudge

---

* Harcus, 1876.

over. Need I tell you how many sleepless nights and anxious hours I spent, as all these apparently insuperable difficulties stared me in the face. It was my life's ambition which I had eagerly looked forward to, but now that its weight really rested upon me, I must confess, it, at times, seemed too heavy to bear[*].

Lord Monck was worried that his company had made the wrong choice. The *Brisbane Courier* quoted his letter of November 1871 to the government, admitting to:

> … a grave apprehension that the Government lines would not be completed within anything like the time stipulated. In fact, we have been informed that the land lines cannot be completed for six months from this date.

He also suggested:

> … that the South Australian Government should guarantee to the British and Australian Telegraph Company by way of compensation, 5 per cent per annum on the capital expended by them between Singapore and Port Darwin, from the 1st of January 1872, till the completion of the land line[†].

In the end it was not only the overland line that was delayed, and no penalty was ever called for.

---

[*] *Chronicle*, Lorna Todd, 11 December 1952, see also *Advertiser*, 29 July 1873.
[†] *Brisbane Courier*, 2 September 1872.

Twenty to the Mile

Chapter 2
Port Darwin

Government Resident Douglas

Two ships arrived in Port Darwin together on 24 June 1870. The smaller, *Gulnare*, under Captain Samuel White Sweet, carried the new government resident, Captain William Bloomfield Douglas, and his family of seven. The other, the barque *Bengal*, under Captain Hummel, was a much larger ship. On board were a group of new settlers, land-order holders, and land agents come to view the land that had been bought, sight unseen, by investors in Adelaide and London. The *Bengal* had been delayed by running onto a sand bank near the entrance to Darwin Harbour. Captain Sweet had the *Gulnare* wait with her until she floated free with the tide, and then escorted the larger ship into the port.

Captain Hummel carried news that put Government Resident Douglas immediately to work, even as he and his family settled into the log and canvas hut vacated for them on the edge of 'The Camp'. He was informed that the British Australian Telegraph Company would soon be arriving to build an overland telegraph line to Normanton in Queensland. Douglas knew that the B.A.T. was preparing to lay an undersea cable from Java to Darwin but thought his role in the project would be limited because it was a private company. He was reluctant to be involved at all.

He did, however, immediately send government surveyor George McLachlan to survey a route for the telegraph line to the Roper

River. Douglas knew that the river would be useful because it was known to be navigable for many kilometres inland—Ludwig Leichhardt and Augustus Gregory had both explored and mapped sections of it during their journeys*.

Captain Douglas was a retired naval officer and his experience included time in Sarawak fighting pirates on behalf of his aunt's husband, Sir James Brooke, known as the first 'White Rajah of Sarawak'. Douglas had visions of himself as a white rajah too, so had mixed feelings about the overland telegraph—his preference was to build a comfortable Government House, and then focus on developing the gardens and a future agricultural industry. He was keen to import Coolie† labourers to do the heavy work. Coolies, he felt, were much hardier and cheaper than white workers. With abundant Coolie labour, a small compliant community, and his government bosses six weeks or more away by sail, he looked forward to building an empire.

Figure 3: Capt. Bloomfield Douglas 1858 (SLSA, PRG 280-1-40-330).

To his displeasure, Douglas soon found he actually possessed little authority to make any real decisions. The two most senior public servants were not even under his command: Sub-Inspector Foelsche and his six troopers answered to the Commissioner of Police in Adelaide, and the Senior Surveyor, George McLachlan—who had lived in Palmerston since it was first settled—worked for the surveyor-

---

* Carruthers and Stiebel, 2012.
† The term 'coolie' is a derogatory term for unskilled Asian labourers from India and China. In the 19th century, a system of Coolie trade was established in direct response to the end of slavery in European colonies. In this text, Coolie is capitalised as a measure of respect for these vital, but low paid, workers brought to Australia in a time of great need for a workforce.

general in Adelaide. Both of these men were happy to inform Douglas where he stood, so it was little wonder Douglas was accused of quarrelling*. His authority over his subordinates was limited to the mundane, and he quickly became bored. Months went by between the arrival of ships, and the inactivity led Douglas to drink heavily and become quarrelsome. It was in sad contrast to the time he 'landed in great state', as the wife of the *Gulnare's* captain, Elizabeth Sweet, described it. 'There were seven guns fired from shore, and returned from the *Gulnare*, and troopers and men arranged on the shore as guard of honour'†.

Then the *Omeo* arrived in September with the news that plans had changed, and the South Australian Government was now building the O.T.L. to Port Augusta, not Queensland, and Douglas was told that the line was now his top priority. But even in that it was others who took the lead. Everything else in the Territory was to be downplayed until the line was up and running‡. Douglas was frustrated. To make it worse, several investors from Adelaide were on his back looking for government help to start a gold mining industry. Though this intrigued Douglas, the government's answer was:

> … As the discovery of a goldfield at this time would greatly interfere with the very important work at present in hand, it is considered undesirable to take any steps in that direction until the telegraph line is completed§.

When gold was actually discovered by men digging holes for the telegraph poles near Yam Creek, Douglas's frustration grew. He grew morose and increasingly bitter. It didn't help that he disliked John Little intensely. On 2 May 1872, he complained in his diary of the arrogance of the telegraph office manager, and his own seemingly low role to play in the settlement:

---

* de la Rue, 2004.
† Sweet, 1870.
‡ Cross, 2011.
§ *Advertiser*, 26 April 1870.

> ... Mr Little's manner is most offensive and dictatorial so much so that his requisitions take the form of orders as if I were a mere storekeeper to the OT and that I am not allowed to have an opinion on my own requirements. His manner and bearing form a very great contrast to the gentlemanly and courteous conduct toward my staff and myself ...*.

Others knew about their disagreements. Charles Johnston, a telegraph operator, and Little's brother-in-law, noted in his diary that Little was:

> ... having paper war with Govt. Resdt. about *Bengal*. G.R. refusing to discharge *Bengal* & endorse Little's order on Mr. Todd, for amount of charter which would be taken by Capt. of *Bengal* and which he wished to discount at Batavia or Java—G.R. obstructing L in performance of duties—I fitting out party to start on line repair to KN—Revolvers refused from armoury & refused *Bengal* carry mail†.

---

* Bloomfield Douglas, 1872.
† Johnston, 30 May 1872.

Chapter 3
The route

Todd divided the work of constructing the 2,839 km (1,765 miles) line into three sections as follows:

Southern section: 804 km (500 miles) north from Port Augusta.

Central Section: 1,007 km (626 miles) in Central Australia.

Northern section: 1,028 km (639 miles) south of Port Darwin.

The southern section stretched from Port Augusta north to near the Northern Territory border. The contract to build it was won by Edward Meade Bagot, a South Australian pastoralist used to conditions in the bush. Bagot owned The Peake Station, where a supply depot was established, and a telegraph station would be built.

The northern section was contracted by William Trevett Dalwood and Joseph Darwent. They had some good men to help them: W. A. Paqualin was the superintendent, and the chief surveyor was Stephen King*. The latter was one of the most experienced surveyors

---

* Stephen King (Jnr) was an active member of the First Northern Territory Expedition at Escape Cliffs. He was among the six men appointed as the first policeman in the Territory by Colonel Finniss, explored with Litchfield on two occasions, returning after the second very ill with malaria. He was also a fine sketch artist (Pugh, 2018a). King returned north with Goyder in 1869 as a surveyor class 2. Strangely, that year he refused to go into the field and Goyder wrote that 'Mr King excused himself on plea that he had expected only to have survey work to do & not to have to camp out anywhere at night' (Goyder, 1869). It is likely he was fearful of the return of malaria. The 'ague' that afflicted him severely towards the end of 1872 at Powell's Creek may have been its feared return. An obituary for Stephen King can be found in *The Mail* of 10 January 1914.

in the north. He had been a part of Stuart's 1862 exploration across the continent and a part of Finniss's expedition to Escape Cliffs—including exploring from there with Fred Litchfield in 1865*. King had also been a member of the Second Northern Territory Expedition in 1869.

Todd himself led the work in the central section, with government labour, because it was considered the hardest. He had the late John McDouall Stuart's journals, and Stephen King could advise the surveyors about conditions there, but there was little other information about what lay in the centre of Australia†. More exploration was needed. In the hope of ensuring the straightest possible route for the central section of the O.T.L., Charles Todd employed a 53-year-old experienced bushman, drover, and grazier named John Ross, to head out into the desert and find it‡. He was joined in the grandly named 'Adelaide–Port Darwin Overland Telegraph Line Exploring Party' by William Harvey, surveyor, and second-in-command; Alfred Giles, third officer; Thomas Crispe§; and William Hearne. They set

Figure 4: William Trevett Dalwood, with his partner Joseph Darwent, won the contract to build the northern section of the Overland Telegraph Line (Sweet, SLSA, B-4638).

---

* Pugh, 2018a.

† Stuart had passed through several times on his expeditions north. Stuart made six expeditions into central Australia. He is most famous for his final journey when he reached the north coast in 1862.

‡ *South Australian Parliamentary Papers* 191/1884 (Todd C., 1884). Ross was on a salary of £450 per annum.

§ Thomas Bagnold Crispe was a part of John McKinlay's failed exploration party from Escape Cliffs in 1866. In January he became lost and was found after four days 'delirious, hallucinating and suffering from heat stress and dehydration' (Pugh, 2018a).

out from Mount Margaret on 14 August 1870 before the overlanding teams arrived, and Ross's instructions were clear—he was to return by mid-October to meet the construction parties 'so as to avoid delays in deciding the route to be followed by the telegraph'.

Ross was happy to explore country visited by no white men before, and he was also keen to see where John McDouall Stuart had passed nearly a decade earlier. His was the second team of white men to enter the centre of Australia, and he felt the gravity of it keenly.

Some of the time they followed Stuart's path. Alfred Giles recalled fifty years later that the tracks of Stuart's horses were still visible on the approach to Central Mount Stuart*:

> … Right along our course was a distinct pad made by Stuart's horses. We could follow it quite easily for more than a mile. When it is remembered that Stuart used this track on each occasion both backwards and forwards, and that in his last expedition in 1862 he had 70 horses, it was quite feasible that they should have been visible in portions of high ground free from flood waters, although eight or nine years had passed since they were made, and that they should appear as only having been made in as many months†.

Stuart's horses were the first hard-hooved animals to walk through central Australia. Even if the horses and white men had not been seen personally by local Aborigines as they passed by, they must have been astonished to see strange new tracks through their country‡.

---

*   Central Mount Stuart is in Anmatyerre Country. It was first named 'Sturt' by Stuart after Charles Sturt, but it was renamed Central Mount Stuart to remember its European discoverer before his diary was published.

†   Alfred Giles, 1925. Alfred's book, *Exploring in the Seventies*, is an excellent read, written after five decades and more in the Territory. Alfred Giles died aged 84 in 1931. His obituary appears in the *Chronicle* of 2 April 1931.

‡   When the white men were followed by others with horses, cattle, camels, sheep, and a wondrous metal wire strung across their lands, the Aborigines witnessed substantial and unimaginable changes to their environment and ancestral lifestyles. As Lewis (2004) discovered, in areas such as the Victoria River region, the environment changed so dramatically after cattle and sheep arrived that it was no longer possible for Aboriginal people to find enough food to live their traditional lives.

Within days, Ross's party entered the Simpson Desert, but they backtracked out again after about 100 kilometres to search further west. They entered the Fergusson Ranges but found it impassable, and then returned to report to Todd at Strangways Springs.

But a route was essential. Ross was sent out again with instructions to find a northerly way between the Fergusson and Strangways Ranges to Mount Gwynn, but this way was also impassable to wagons and construction teams. Ross failed again, despite riding over 1100 kilometres in 10 weeks. He and his team returned south to the new depot on the Hugh River, arriving on 24 January 1871 in the summer heat, utterly exhausted and bad-tempered, with Ross and Harvey's relationship at its lowest ebb. However, finding a route through the MacDonnell Ranges was still imperative, so he was sent out again in March 1871 for a third exploration. This time he passed through a gap between the MacDonnell and Fergusson Ranges, only to find that William Mills had already been there, named the gap 'Heavitree' and discovered the springs that became known as Alice.

Nevertheless, Ross's reputation was saved by making a substantial contribution to the central section of the line by finding and mapping a straight route through to the Katherine River. On the way, he passed Central Mount Stuart.

As the geographical centre of Australia, the place was a point of great interest to him as his was only the second party to reach it. It was also where the party were pleasantly surprised by Surveyor Harvey, who had a secret. Alfred Giles told the story:

> … When packing that morning our genial surveyor, Mr. Harvey, gave us an agreeable surprise. He said, 'Well, comrades, you see yonder mountain. That is Central Mount Sturt, discovered and named by John McDouall Stuart, who led the first exploring party across Australia from south to north and back again. Our party is the second to sight it since he named it 10 years ago. Tonight, or tomorrow we shall reach it, and I think that this being a very special occasion we ought to celebrate it by drinking some one's health and one another's,

too. He then, to our intense surprise, went to his swag and
unrolled from a flannel shirt a bottle of O.P. rum.

We drank Mr. Ross's health, and each other's. None of us
had the slightest suspicion that such a beverage was within
1,000 miles of us, and it certainly was a marvel to us how
Mr. Harvey had carried it safely all those hundreds of miles,
through dense scrubs, rocky gorges, and bumping against trees
and anthills without smashing it. It certainly must have been
the first rum to reach Central Australia[*].

John Ross climbed Central Mount Stuart on 4 January 1871. He found there a stone cairn built by Stuart, a copy of *The Adelaide Observer*, dated 5 January 1860[†], and a French capers bottle that contained a note written by the great explorer. Ross collected the bottle to forward to Charles Todd, while the men stood on the mountain and marvelled at where they were:

... standing on this historic mountain, and within a few
feet of Stuart's Cairn, we knew that from each point of the
compass for 1,000 miles there existed not a single white
human being, not a city, house, fence, or sign of civilization.

Stuart's note was later presented to the Public Library in Adelaide by Charles Todd. It reads:

... John McDouall Stuart and party, consisting of two men
and himself, arrived from Adelaide in the Centre of Australia
on Saturday evening, the twenty-first day of April 1860,
and have built this cairn of stones and raised this flag, to
commemorate the event, on the top of Mount Sturt. The
centre is about two miles south-south-west, at a small gum
creek, where there is a tree marked, facing the south.
John McDouall Stuart, Leader; William Darton Kekwick,
Benjamin Head[‡].

The party continued mapping the route to Katherine until Ross developed a severe attack of scurvy. They then travelled on to Port Darwin to see a doctor and once there, celebrated being the second

---

[*] Alfred Giles, 1925.
[†] The *Observer* of 7 January 1860 was 8 pages long.
[‡] *Observer*, 14 October 1905.

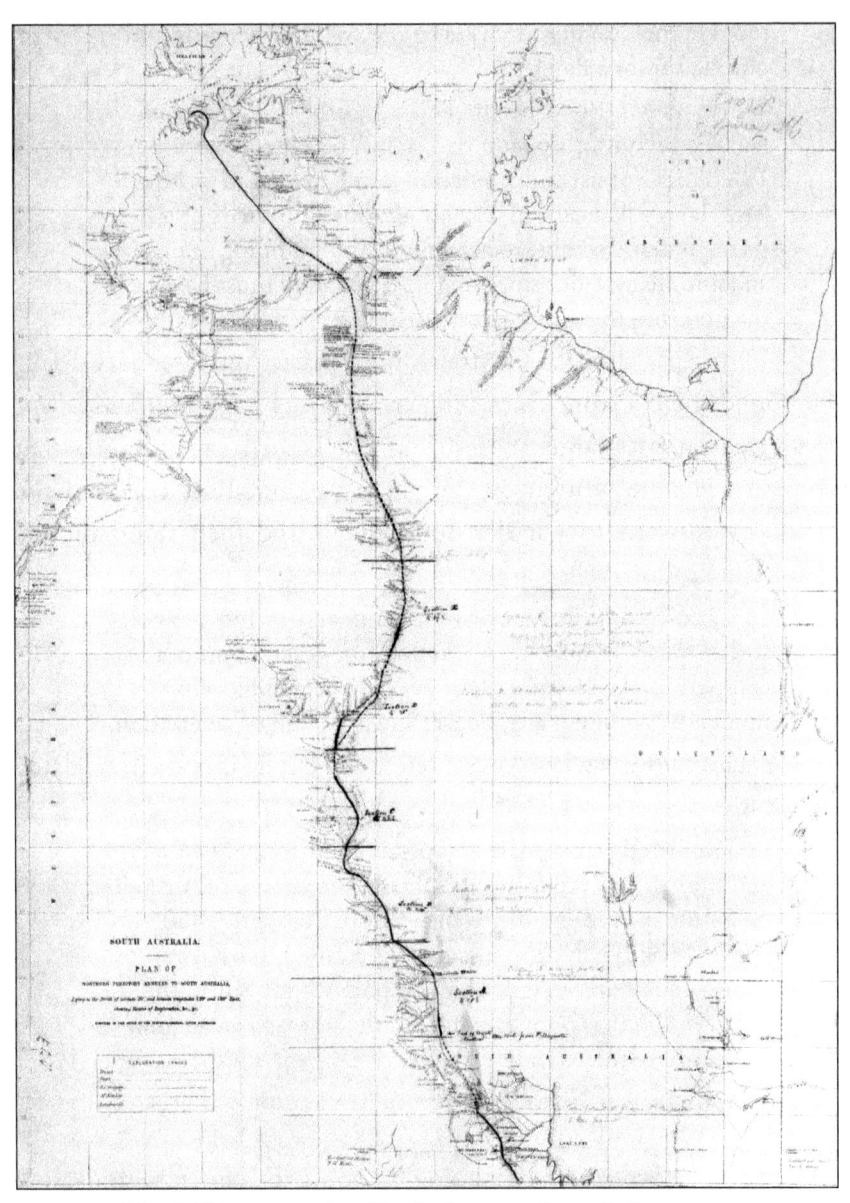

Map 2: This map, produced by the Surveyor General's department c. 1871, shows exploration tracks taken by Stuart, Sturt, McKinlay, Gregory and Leichhardt. It was used by an O.T.L. manager, possibly Todd, who annotated it in pencil and red ink. The work sections, the route of the telegraph lines, and details of natural features are marked. Details of each section A–E are reproduced in Chapter 5. (SLSA, map C54).

group to cross the continent from south to north through the centre, after Stuart[*].

Dr Millner sent Ross back to Adelaide immediately on the *Omeo* to recover his health. He had played a significant role in the O.T.L. after all. He worried, before he left, that the men working on the O.T.L. in the centre of the country, 'not hearing of Mr. Ross for so long a time, [would] be very anxious respecting his safety'[†]. Fortunately, a telegram on the soon to be complete line would save such worry[‡].

---

[*] Symes, 1976a.
[†] *Express and Telegraph*, 6 October 1871.
[‡] In later years, John Ross was employed by Thomas Elder to explore between The Peake and Western Australia, but lack of water prevented him from finding anything useful. He went on to manage properties in Victoria and Queensland but died in Adelaide, in poverty, at the age of 85 in 1903.

Gallery
O.T.L. workers

Figure 5 (above): Overland Telegraph Line managers and officials of the construction parties: L–R John A.G. Little, Robert C. Patterson, Charles Todd, and Alexander J. Mitchell, 1872 (Sweet, SLSA, B-4639).

Figure 6 (left): A page from the *Illustrated London News* of 23 February 1873 reproduced some of the early O.T.L. photographs (LANT, ph1089-0001-3).

Figure 7: Some of the leaders of the survey parties for the Overland Telegraph Line: William McMinn, Richard Randall Knuckey, Richard Austin Horn, Alfred Thomas Woods, Charles Nash, Charles Musgrave*, E.R.C. Bromley, and William Mills† 1871 (SLSA, B-10451).

* Charles William Musgrave left the Territory in February 1875 on the *Gothenburg*'s fatal last voyage and was one of her 88 victims (See *Darwin: Origin of a City*, Pugh 2019). In 1873, Musgrave, along with McMinn, Horn and Bromley, had returned to Port Darwin on the *Atalante*, employed by the Alexandra Gold Mining Company (Express, 8 May 1873).
† Alfred T Woods was a first-class surveyor with Goyder. He and Musgrave worked on the central portion of the line with Gilbert McMinn, Richard Knuckey, and Richard Austin Horn. Horn was a survey hand on Alexander Mitchell's team in 1869.

Figure 8: Overland telegraph workers (probably Dalwood and Darwent's teams) at Southport. The masts of Captain Sweet's schooner, *Gulnare,* are in the river behind, 1870 (Sweet, SLSA, B-9763).

Chapter 4

The southern section

Port Augusta

The port city of Port Augusta lies at the northern end of the Spencer Gulf in South Australia. In 1802, Matthew Flinders mapped the gulf during his search for a waterway through to an inland sea, and fifty years later it was settled. The port was named after Lady Augusta Sophia Young, the wife of the South Australian governor. Infamously, she was also the daughter of a slave plantation owner from the West Indies.

In the nineteenth century, Port Augusta was primarily important for its proximity to the sheep stations of the Flinders Ranges area. Over 10,000 bales of wool passed through the port in 1860. In 1872, with a population of 450 people, a valuation of the Port Augusta developments showed they were worth £4,040:

> … The town then had a bi-weekly overland mail and a bi-weekly coast service, an aboriginal station, public pound, post-office, and branches of insurance companies and banks. There were two hotels and carrying firms, one consisting of 100 camels and 30 donkeys. The town was supplied with fresh water from springs 140 miles away, the charge being £1 for 1,000 gallons. There were three jetties, a Customs house, many substantial residences, and even a racecourse*.

In 1870, the telegraph linked the port directly to Adelaide in 1866, and it wasn't long before the townsfolk learned that their

---

* *Chronicle*, 21 July 1932

Figure 9: Tassie Street, Port Augusta, showing the loading of wool bales outside the premises of PR Warren's grocery store, c. 1870 (SLSA, B-9346).

line was to be extended nearly 3,000 kilometres northwards to Port Darwin. The first Port Augusta Telegraph Station was manned by James Phillips. He was, as the *Port Augusta and Flinders Advertiser* informs us, 'cribbed, cabined, and confined in a small office … For a very long time, Mr. Phillips did all the work of the office singlehanded, and legends are extant about his being often aroused at night and having to transmit telegraphic messages under difficulties"'.

Edward Meade Bagot contracted to build the 500-mile southern section of the O.T.L. at £41 per mile, and his teams were ready to travel and start constructing in September 1870. Two work parties left the 'Survey Paddock' in Adelaide:

> … under the charge of Messrs. B. H. Babbage and W. H. Abbott, each of whom is to lay out and have the superintendence of 250 miles of the line, extending from Port Augusta to the principal depot at The Peake.

---

* *Port Augusta and Flinders Advertiser*, 12 August 1882.

Figure 10: The Port Augusta Telegraph Office, c. 1870 (SLSA, B-47759).

Mr. Blood*, who has been appointed to the charge of the depot, with Mr. Abbott, left Adelaide for Kapunda by train this morning. Mr. Babbage remains for some time longer, and then proceeds for Port Augusta by sea†.

William Abbott undertook to manage the first 250 miles of line from Stirling North, just outside Port Augusta, and Babbage the second section. His men had few problems, and those were mainly to do with the supply of poles. He was permitted to erect the line with 10 poles per mile on a temporary basis (every 160 metres) and used metal poles when timber was unavailable.

Benjamin Herschel Babbage was the better known of the two leaders, as he was an experienced explorer. In 1856, Babbage was employed by the South Australian government to undertake geological

---

* John Henry Smyth Blood was born in County Clare and grew up in Kapunda. He worked on the construction team establishing the Overland Telegraph and later became the Postmaster and Telegraph Officer stationed at The Peake. He married Mary Enock and they had five children. He died at Auburn, S.A., aged 49.

† *Brisbane Courier*, 14 October 1870.

and mineralogical surveys of the state. He discovered Emerald Springs in 1858 and explored the Lake Eyre area (a peninsula on the lake was named after him in 1863). However, his explorations were so desperately slow, people began questioning his abilities[*]. Numerous letters appeared in the newspapers expressing frustration at his lack of movement. Eventually the government tired of him and he was replaced by Peter Warburton, in 1858.

Babbage spent the next few years dabbling in business, politics and building his winery, The Rosary, but when Bagot employed him in 1870, he successfully superintended the construction of the line from Port Augusta to Mount Margaret.

Charles Todd travelled with Babbage up the Spencer Gulf to Port Augusta on the steamer *Kangaroo*. The *Register* followed Todd's every move:

> ... Horses are waiting at Port Augusta for Mr. Todd, who will ride part of the way, and drive the other. After inaugurating the work at the mount, he will proceed as far as The Peake should circumstances require it[†].
>
> ... Information has been received that the three advance parties for the construction of the central portion of the overland telegraph line reached Beltana about a week ago. Mr. C. Todd has left Port Augusta for Mount Margaret, travelling in an express wagon. Mr. B. H. Babbage, who has charge of the northern portion of the line covered by Mr Bagot's contract, accompanied him. The more southerly section is under Mr. W. H. Abbott's care, and the sub-inspectors are Messrs. Le Wante and Ray Boucaut.
>
> Mr. Ross, who arranged to be back from his exploratory trip into the interior about-the middle of this month, has received instructions to meet Mr. Todd at Mount Hamilton, on the way between Port Augusta and Mount Margaret[‡].

---

[*]   Symes, 1969.
[†]   *Register*, 5 October 1870.
[‡]   *Register*, 12 October 1870.

The Peake

The work parties were fed a diet of mutton, damper, and tea. A Mr Jarvis purchased 2,000 sheep* from Beltana Station and employed a team of five shepherds to look after them, one of whom, Thomas Frederick Smith, wrote a diary of his travels.

Smith was then about 30 years old. As well as a shepherd, he was a butcher, and he kept meticulous records of the animals he butchered, how much meat was used fresh, and how much was salted for later use. He and the other shepherds took the flock to the new depot at The Peake, managed by J.H.S. Blood, as a larder for the construction teams. Their journey was not without its difficulties: getting the wagons through soft, boggy plains was a major problem after rain. For instance, their wagon was bogged three times on 11 September:

> … got her out, loaded up and made another start. Just as we got to our halting place, down she goes again …†

Smith and his mates also had trouble with their horses. Nearing The Peake on 12 September 1870:

> … Lost our horses, some of them going back 40 miles in quite a different direction they came. They had broken their hobbles … 18 of them are away and no tidings of their whereabouts … found five only after traversing the country for miles … did not find our horses until sunset. They had travelled south 60 miles; one of them got clear away to Port Augusta …

Bagot's contract meant erecting the cable through 500 miles of South Australian bush, but of the three sections, the southern was considered the easiest. The country was mostly flat, relatively well known, and much of it had already been surveyed. The line passed:

> … to the west of Thompson's Station, close by Loudon's Head Station, west of Mount Eyre, across the Hookina and Morilina Creeks, slightly to the west of the eating-house at Ediowie, and

---

* *Evening Journal*, 16 September 1870.
† Smith's diary, 1870–71. Lead solder can still be seen attached to the rusting detritus of these cans at many sites along the O.T.L.

Figure 13: The Peake c. 1880 (SLSA, Peake B-11363).

Figure 11: An Afghan cameleer at The Peake c. 1880 (SLSA, B-414).

so on along the course of the projected railway to Survey Point A. If the nature of the country permits, it is intended to take a short cut thence to the south and west of Termination Hill, via Mirrabuckinnah and Porter's Hill, to the Horseshoe of Chamber's Creek, thence northwards to Mount Margaret. This station is about 400 miles distant from Port Augusta, and the chief depot for the central party will be some 45 miles beyond that at the Peak [sic]*.

---

* *Evening Journal*, 16 September 1870.

Figure 12: The Peake c. 1872 (SLSA, B-11364).

The Peake, which became the first of several depots, is on the western side of Lake Eyre, about 1,000 kilometres from Adelaide*. A second depot was later established by Harley Bacon on the banks of the Hugh River, south of Alice Springs. These were the destinations of the camel, horse†, and bullock teams that hauled the hundreds of tons of wire, food, tools, insulators, and everything else that was

---
* The Peake is 95 km south of the modern town of Oodnadatta.
† The horses were terrified of the camels: 'They are a great nuisance. They frighten the horses in every direction,' wrote Smith.

needed through the settled pastoral country of South Australia. The Peake was already occupied—it was an outstation of Philip Levi's Mount Margaret Station—and it became a huge temporary village for the O.T.L. parties moving north. Here they paused in their travel long enough to rest, repair equipment, and re-shoe their horses and bullocks[*]. 'The place is all bustle and confusion', wrote Smith, 'the men are working away shifting flour into casks, some into cases. The perishable food was put into square tins and soldered'[†] before leaving Adelaide.

Todd already knew that there were about 480 kilometres (300 miles) of treeless plains north of Chambers Creek where timber for telegraph poles would not be available. He therefore ordered 1,500 iron poles[‡] for Abbott and Babbage to install, initially at 10 to the mile. Where timber was available to cut or cart to the line, they placed wooden poles alternately with the metal poles. The wire was suspended from them by 2 January 1872 and the first telegrams were sent from the MacDonnell Ranges on 3 January. The linesmen continued to add in the missing poles—so that the full complement of 20 poles per mile was installed, and their section of the line was fully complete by March 1872. Todd rode its length, declaring that it 'would stand for a number of years with very little attention'[§].

Once the line was operational there were several problems with lightning hitting the iron poles, especially between The Peake and Charlotte Waters.

> … interruptions caused by lightning have occurred where iron poles have been used … The lightning in each instance smashed several insulators, leaving the wire in contact

---

[*] Cattle used to pull drays were shod with pairs of shoes on each side of their cloven feet called 'cues'. Cattle cannot stand on three legs like horses when being shod, so slings were needed to hold them up, or they were shod lying on the ground.
[†] Smith's diary, 1870–71.
[‡] By 1873, there were 2,500 iron poles in the southern section.
[§] Todd, 1873.

with the iron pole, thus making 'earth' and stopping the communication*.

A 'piece of ordinary line wire' was therefore placed on every alternate pole as a lightning conductor. The wire was stapled down the length of the pole, and it ended in a coil beneath the base, so was difficult to remove and:

> ... they have proved an effective protection from lightning, for although the line for many hundreds of miles passes over treeless plains, and is exposed to thunderstorms of great severity and extent, we have scarcely had a pole destroyed by lightning ...

North of The Peake, across the modern border into the Northern Territory, and north through the MacDonnell Ranges, Todd was less sure of the route the line would take.

Alfred Woods had an opinion:

> ... we have but one object—to put up from 120 to 150 miles of telegraph line in the straightest possible direction to Newcastle Waters, in the shortest possible time, and bring our parties safely back ...†

---

* Todd also arranged for lightning conductors to be installed on the northern poles, where tropical storms are common.
† Woods, 1871.

Twenty to the Mile

Chapter 5

The central section

Charles Todd led the O.T.L. construction in the central section of the line with government-employed surveyors and construction teams. He divided the line into five subsections that he called A to E*. They stretched through some of the most unknown parts of Australia and had not been visited by white men since John McDouall Stuart, 10 years earlier. The logistics of supplying the teams with food and other resources—as well as iron poles where they were needed—were huge. However, Todd did his job well, and all parts of his section were finished in early January 1872, right on time.

Section A: Charlotte Waters

Section A was the most southerly section, extending 193 kilometres (120 miles) from the north end of Bagot's line at latitude 26° 5', as far as the Goyder River. It is desolate country, often completely treeless, though usually grassed but with patches of stony plains 'utterly bare of vegetation'. It changes near the Northern Territory's modern border, to sand dunes that are covered with acacia trees,

---

* The locations of the subsections and leaders were as follows:
Section A: 27°00' to 25°30' S; Richard Randall Knuckey.
Section B: 25°30' to 24°00' S; Gilbert Rotherdale McMinn.
Section C: 24°00' to 22°30' S; William Whitfield Mills.
Section D: 22°30' to 21°00' S; Alfred Thomas Woods.
Section E: 21°00' to 19°30' S; William Harvey.

Figure 14: Richard Randall Knuckey, 1875 (SLSA, B-7232).

and there is water available—large waterholes exist in the Stevenson and Goyder Rivers.

Section A was built under the direction of Richard 'Dick' Randall Knuckey, an experienced surveyor who had been with Goyder in the surveying of Palmerston in 1869. In his 'central section A', he had the pleasure of naming both Charlotte Waters where a telegraph repeating station was built, and Dalhousie Springs. The construction was begun on 1 January 1871 when Knuckey and his team left the overlanding caravan that consisted of all five of the government groups. The latter groups, 'E' and 'F', were still many months away from their starting points.

Knuckey needed to use 50-kilogram 'Oppenheimer' metal poles across the treeless country. Oppenheimer poles are telescopic galvanised steel poles that were short enough to be carried by camels and were extended on site. They were a German invention manufactured near Manchester in England, so they were not cheap. Fortunately, they were not needed everywhere—parts of the route were well-treed, and many good poles could be cut from the bush. For example, the Finke River region in the section's far north had usable timber as far as the MacDonnell Ranges. Todd was pleased::

> … I did not see a single bad pole on the line. Twenty to the mile are planted throughout. The line has been laid out with judgment, crossing the creeks at the best places and at right angles, and carefully avoids lowlands subject to inundation*.

Knuckey returned to Adelaide with Todd after the line was operational from Central Mount Stuart. In 1873, he was back, this

---

* Todd, 1873.

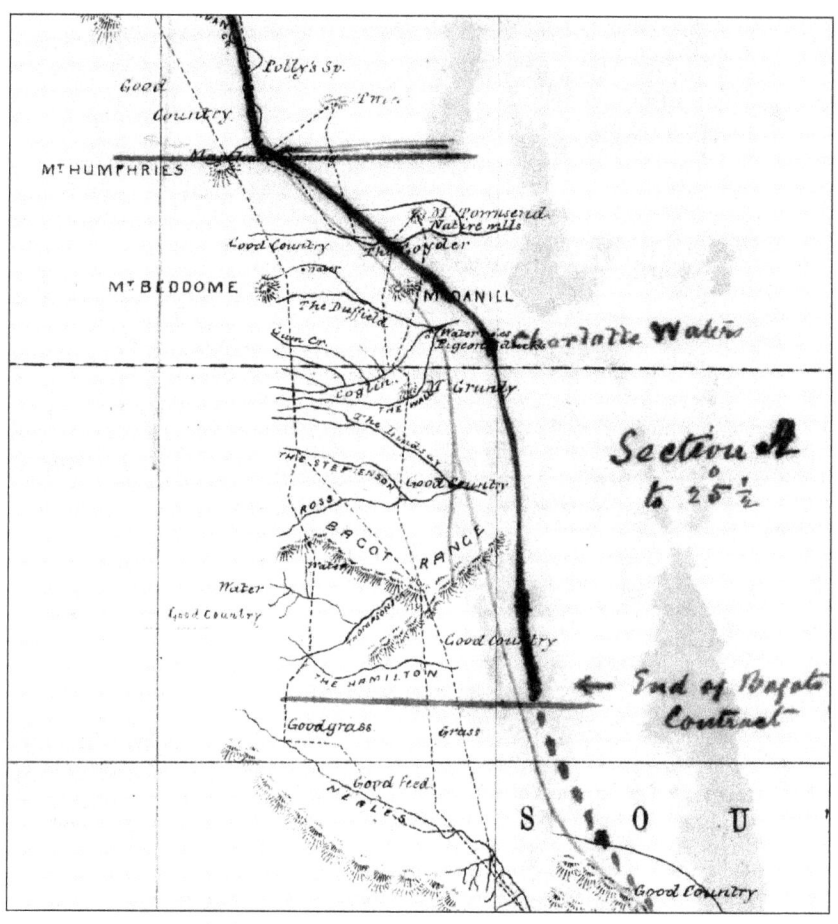

Map 3: Detail of Map 2. Section A, from the end of Bagot's contract. Also shows Stuart's exploration routes, c. 1871 (SLSA, C54).

time leading a team of 60 men on a repair mission (listed in the Appendix). They travelled via the Roper River and moved down the line, replacing the wooden poles with Oppenheimer poles that would last for many years.

Knuckey's services remained in high demand and continued his career in subsequent years surveying for new lines that stretched west to Eucla, and he was an overseer of telegraph extensions for many years. When he died, his eulogy was one that any 71-year-old would have been proud to hear:

... No man had a wider experience in Central Australia than he, and there were few parts of Australia where his name was not a household word. It is said of him that he had hundreds of friends, and that he never made an enemy...*

Section B: Finke

Figure 15: Gilbert Rotherdale McMinn, 1868 (SLSA, B-16791-7).

Gilbert Rotherdale McMinn was another highly experienced surveyor in the Northern Territory†. He took charge of Section B and joined Section A on the Finke River near its junction with the Hugh River and ran through the ranges as far as the Alice River, where it met Section C. McMinn discovered Simpson's Gap through the MacDonnell Ranges, which was a better route for the telegraph than Stuart's path, far to its east. Its final

---

* *Adelaide Advertiser*, 16 June 1914.
† Gilbert Rotherdale McMinn (1841–1924) arrived in Adelaide as a nine-year-old in 1850. After school, he was trained as a surveyor. In 1864, he joined the First Northern Territory Expedition as a labourer, on a salary of five shillings a day. Despite his qualifications, he went to Escape Cliffs for adventure and to join his brother, William, while hoping to win a position as a surveyor. When he did, his salary jumped to 16 shillings 6 pence per day. McMinn then worked at Escape Cliffs under James Manton until the expedition was recalled. In 1866, he returned north with George Goyder as a first-class surveyor and assisted with laying out the new town of Palmerston. He remained there in 1870 and became surveyor-in-charge of Section B of the central section of the Overland Telegraph Line, from Marchant Springs to the Alice River. He also had a role in the building of the Alice Springs Telegraph Station. In June 1873, Gilbert McMinn became the Senior Surveyor and Supervisor of Works in the Northern Territory at a salary of £350 per annum. He also acted as government resident for fourteen months before the arrival of Government Resident Parsons. In 1886 he was appointed resident magistrate and customs officer at Borroloola. He died at the age of 83, in 1925 (from Pugh, 2019).

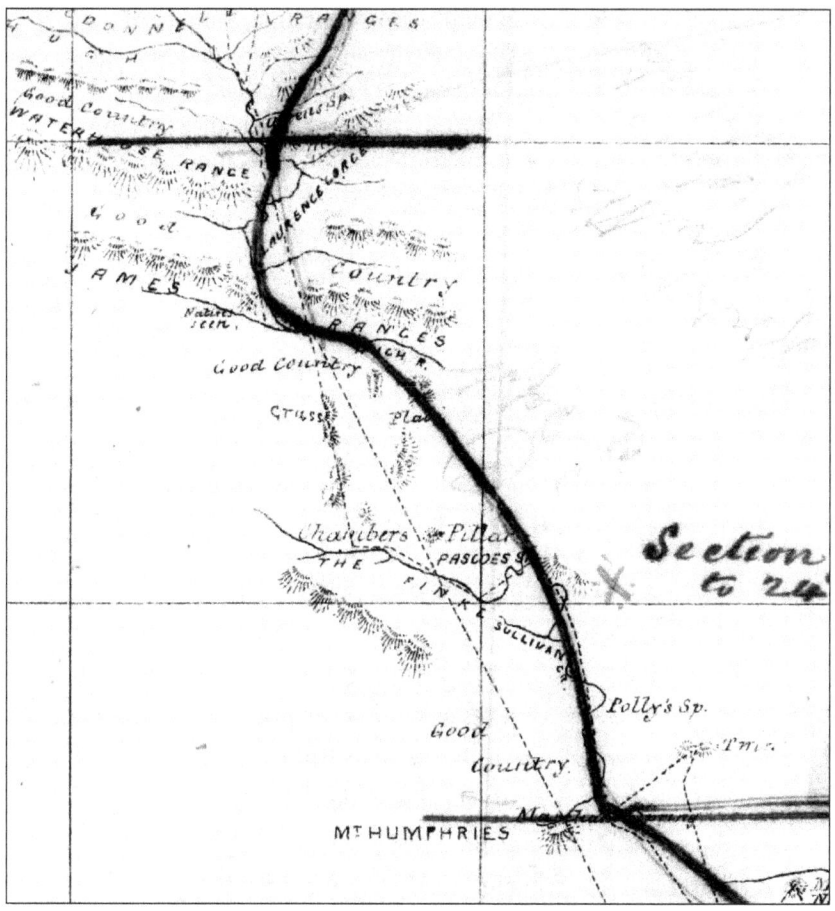

Map 4: Detail of Map 2. Section B, Finke and Hugh Rivers, Chambers Pillar. The Finke Depot is marked with a cross. Also shows Stuart's exploration routes, c. 1871 (SLSA, C54).

length was '142 miles nine chains' (228.5 kilometres).

Both the Finke and the Hugh Rivers were crossed several times as they meandered northwards. In January 1872, there were problems at Marchant's Crossing of the Finke when a flood washed away several poles. They were replaced with masts, installed some distance from the river's banks. They were 52 and 59 feet tall (16 and 18 metres) to keep them above the flood level.

Water was never much of a problem for McMinn's team:

> ... Water is found in many places in the Finke, Hugh, and the smaller creeks running into them—at Marchant's Springs, Mount Musgrave, Polly's Springs (Horseshoe Bend on the Finke), at St. Patrick's Camp, Whinham Springs (near Mount Burrell), first crossing of Hugh, Kragen's Creek, junction of Minnie Creek and Hugh, Stuart's Camp (in the James Range), McCure's Springs, and Owen's Spring*.

Section B was started in February 1871 and was finished by 16 November, and the men were reassigned to work on other sections. All the poles were cut from the surrounding bush. They were 'sound good gum saplings', although Todd admitted they were vulnerable to termite attack. He reported:

> ... some poles which had been in the ground for nineteen months were recently taken out by Mr. McMinn, who found that the white ants had commenced at the foot of the pole where they had eaten out a hole about the size of his finger.

Todd agreed with McMinn's recommendation that iron poles should be used alternately with wood on the sandhills. Luckily, there did not seem to be any termites attacking the poles on the flat country, and as Todd remarked, 'as timber is plentiful in the Finke and Hugh, there may be no occasion to use iron poles.'

Gilbert McMinn stayed in the centre and built the original telegraph station that still sits beside the Alice Spring.

Section C: Alice Springs

Section C was constructed by William Mills, an experienced surveyor who had arrived in Port Darwin with Goyder on the *Moonta* on 5 February 1869†. He was recruited by Charles Todd in 1870 to build

---

* Todd, 1873.

† William Whitfield Mills was a second-class surveyor on the Second Northern Territory Expedition in 1869. On board the *Moonta* he was punished by Goyder for swearing, and demoted for six days. He remained in the NT for most of the 1870s, surveying in Palmerston, The Shackle and Yam Creek, and working sometimes in the mines. As a surveyor he named nothing after himself, although Mills Streets in both Millner (Darwin) and in Alice Springs are named after him. In subsequent

Section C, which took from 22 March to 29 December 1871. Mills is remembered as the man who discovered and named Temple Bar Gap, (now called Honeymoon Gap) in the MacDonnell Ranges through which the O.T.L. could pass easily. He also discovered Heavitree Gap and then a string of waterholes in the Todd River, in country belonging to the Arrernte people. On 11 March 1871, he renamed a waterhole that had been called Atherreyurre for thousands of years, after his boss's wife, Alice Todd. Irony lies in the fact that Alice Spring is not a spring at all, but a waterhole in the Todd River.

Figure 16: William Whitfield Mills, 1868 (SLSA,B-16791-14).

Mills was joined in the final weeks of construction by Gilbert McMinn and his team, which released him to move forward to Section E to help William Harvey.

Section C was 211 kilometres (131 miles) long, and it extended from:

> … Lawrence's Gorge on the north side of the Waterhouse Range, from whence the line crosses a well-grassed mulga plain, following up the Hugh, and then the Jay, both of which are splendidly timbered, to the foot of the MacDonnell Ranges where it crosses a low gap, and turns abruptly to the eastward, keeping between rugged parallel ridges for several miles to Fenn's Gap, where a practicable crossing was found leading generally north-east to the Alice Springs, where a station has been built, and finally emerges from the range about 12 miles north. Leaving the MacDonnell Ranges the line crosses the mulga plains to the Reynolds Ranges, keeping to the west of the

years, Mills ran a camel transport business to The Peake and Charlotte Waters and provided camels for Sir Thomas Elder's exploration party. He died in Western Australia, aged 72 in 1916 (Mills, 1993).

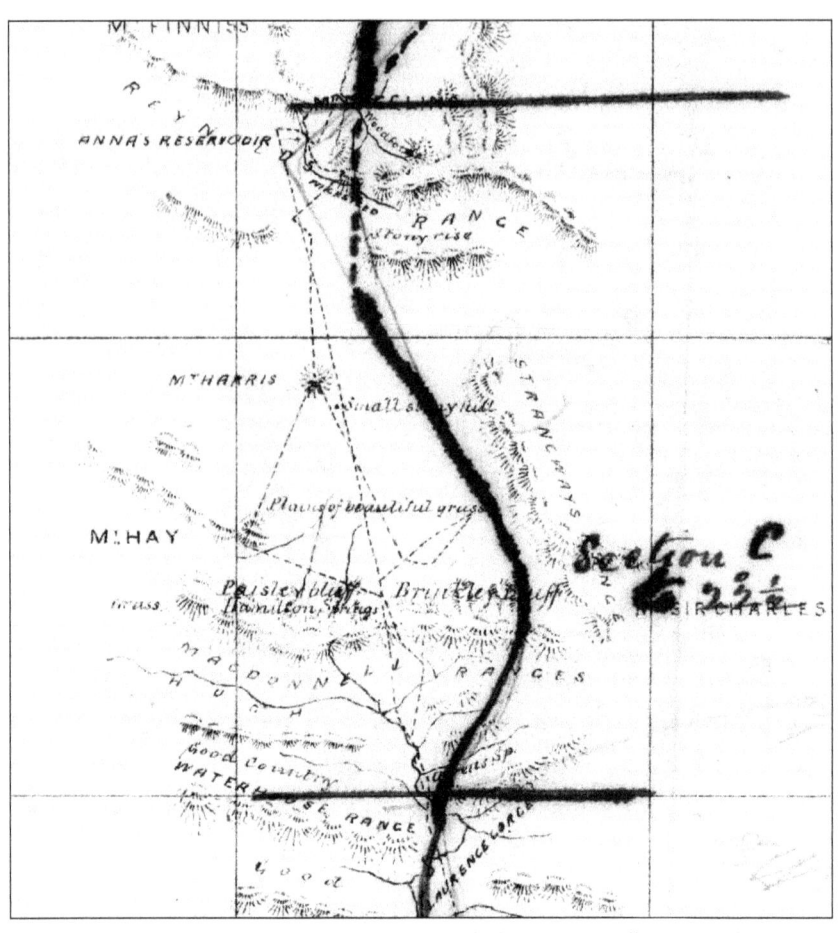

Map 5: Detail of Map 2. Section C, through the MacDonnell Ranges. Also shows Stuart's exploration routes, c. 1871 (SLSA, C54).

Strangways Range, and crossing a low gap in the intervening Hann's Range. The plains are well-grassed, but the mulga is very dense in places, and water is scarce, but can be obtained by sinking on the flat. A native well was opened one mile to the west of the line near the Burt, 25 miles from the MacDonnell Ranges, which yields a permanent supply at a depth of only ten feet. The next water is found 35 miles further on[*].

The lack of water between the MacDonnell and Reynolds Ranges, a distance of 113 kilometres (70 miles), created difficulties. Wells were

---

[*] Todd, 1873.

dug with varying success, and water was also carried from a spring Mills discovered in the Strangways Range, about 15 kilometres (9 miles) northeast of the line. Todd was pleased with the final result:

> ... With few exceptions, however, the line is equal to what we have in the settled districts. From the Waterhouse to the north side of the MacDonnell Ranges the poles are all good full-sized gum poles. Between the MacDonnell and Reynolds Ranges they are not so good but are quite sound; and in the mulga there are more white ants, the soil being a light red sandy loam, splendidly grassed.

The Alice Springs Telegraph Station became the most famous of the O.T.L. Stations, perhaps mostly because of its central nature and the fact that the town of Stuart (now called Alice Springs*) grew up not far from it.

The first stationmaster assigned to the station was 21-year-old Johannes [John] Ferdinand Mueller. He was already experienced but the Alice Springs position had been awarded to an older man, Carl Wilhelm Kraegen. Arrangements changed during the long journey north, when Kraegen failed to arrive

The new telegraphers appointed to the central section's stations mustered at The Peake depot in November 1871. Led by equipment installer Ben Clarke, and escorted by the surveyor Ray Boucaut, they were to be dropped off at their new postings as their 'caravan' moved north. The group consisted of Johannes (John) Mueller (Barrow Creek), Carl Kraegen (Alice Springs), Richard Watson (Tennant Creek), Joe Johnston (Charlotte Waters), and two others: Ernest Ebenezer Flint and Ted Harris.

Joe Johnston was the first to be delivered to his posting. He was an assistant for Christopher Giles at Charlotte Waters. Clarke installed the station's batteries and checked that the equipment was working well. He then needed to wait for the arrival of several other wagons that carried the heavy batteries he needed for the stations up the line.

---

* For an excellent and accessible history of Alice Springs, see Traynor (2016), *Alice Springs: from singing wire to iconic outback town*, Wakefield Press.

Mueller, Watson and Kraegen were impatient. They were given sketch maps of the route showing water sources and permitted to move ahead by themselves. Harris and Flint remained at Charlotte Waters with Clarke, and so did Boucaut, whose job was to 'escort' the telegraphers.

Mueller, Watson and Kraegen took two pack horses and left Charlotte Waters on 4 December. They had trouble almost immediately. Within two days, one of the pack horses was knocked-up and had to be left, and they ran out of water. Mueller and Watson dug for it at the junction of Alice Creek and the Hugh River. They used a knife because they had no shovel, but unfortunately:

> … the heat on the white sand bed of the creek was most intense and we had knocked ourselves up completely and feeling the want of liquid most severely … We now had to lie down to rest[*].

Forty-year-old Kraegen looked after the horses while his colleagues were digging, so he was in the best position for the next option—moving ahead alone to find water, and return with full waterbags.

Two days later, Kraegen had not returned. Mueller and Watson were in dire straits and in 'fearful suspense and agony'. In desperation, they shot a horse and drank its rapidly congealing blood, then gave a final push along the road until finally, late in the afternoon of 10 December, they found a small waterhole in the Hugh River. They drank water until they were sick, then drank more.

Wisely, they decided their best course of action was to return south on their one remaining horse. A few days later they met Benjamin Clarke and a line inspector named Thomas Young, and later Boucaut, Flint and Harris.

It was Thomas Young who discovered Kraegen's body—lying face down at the base of a telegraph pole—about 10 kilometres from where he had left his companions, and a few hundred metres from a hidden waterhole on the Hugh River. He was buried nearby, and a low railing was built around his grave to mark the site. Ironically, within hours, the skies opened, and it began raining.

---

[*] Mueller, 8 December 1871.

The rain was so heavy that the travellers spent Christmas Day sheltering from it at McClure's Springs, eating 'a good plum pudding'. On 28 December, they finally rode into Gilbert McMinn's camp beside the spring named Alice.

With the death of Kraegen*, Clarke needed to do some rearranging. He decided that Mueller would remain at Alice Springs, Watson would take Barrow Creek with Ernest Flint, and he would manage Tennant Creek himself until a replacement could be found. Mueller was only 21 years old but had been a junior operator for a number of years already in Adelaide and Mount Barker. He also had the appropriate adventurous spirit, so Todd agreed by telegram that he should stay at Alice Springs. Mueller, however, was initially unimpressed with his new posting, although he liked the 'nice hole near camp for bathing'†.

Gilbert McMinn and his team had started building the house, but only the foundation was finished when Mueller arrived. Mueller pitched in, building a chicken house on his first day in the valley.

Alice Springs Telegraph Station became operable on 30 December 1871 with a message sent by Benjamin Clarke. In the evening, after contacting Charlotte Waters, they celebrated with fireworks—the local Arrernte people must have been astonished!

The first staff appointed to aid Mueller were the linesmen John Loudon, Tom Hanley‡, a man named Coles, and a cook named Robinson, who had been a part of McMinn's team.

Mueller remained at the Alice Springs station as the stationmaster and postmaster until 1879, then transferred to Bordertown in South Australia, and spent some time in the Adelaide Telegraph Office. He was

---

* Kraegen's gravesite was discovered by his grandson in 1962 and a headstone was erected. In 1964, a memorial was constructed which incorporated the headstone (see monumentaustralia.org.au/display/115338-carl-kraegen).

† Mueller, 1871.

‡ Tom Hanley retired 39 years later at the age of 65. By then he was a line inspector and constantly travelled with two colleagues between Oodnadatta and Attack Creek, maintaining and repairing the line as he went—each trip would take a year by buggy and 10 horse wagons (Traynor, 2016).

back in central Australia in 1887 as part of the gold rush to Arltunga, where he tried his hand at mining, then in 1895 he took over the position of Gold Warden from Mounted Constable (MC) William South. The town of Arltunga was by then a lively community east of Alice Springs, sweating with gold fever. Unfortunately for Mueller, he was caught with his hands in the till in 1906. He was dismissed and escorted to Port Augusta by MC Fred McLeod. In court, Mr Justice Homburg found him guilty of embezzling £42 worth of gold and sentenced him to six months in Port Augusta Gaol*. Afterwards, he returned to the gold fields as a prospector, and later became a bookkeeper for Bond Springs Station. On New Year's Day in 1922, after celebrating the end of another year, Mueller fell off a sulky near Wigley Waterhole, and died, aged 72. He is buried in the Stuart Town Memorial Cemetery in Alice Springs†.

Section D: Barrow Creek

Alfred Thomas Woods not only led the construction of Section D, but he also worked as the superintendent of all five of the central sections. He was a first-class surveyor on Goyder's survey expedition in 1869 and had surveyed much of the southern area of the new colony with Alexander Mitchell‡.

Section D was 200 kilometres (124 miles) long. The pole collectors had difficulty in collecting enough poles, but 500 were found in Woodfords Creek and it was 'stripped of all its serviceable trees for a distance of 15 miles'.

Figure 17: Alfred Thomas Woods, 1864 (SLSA, B-3857).

---

* *Observer*, 1 December 1906.
† Traynor, 2016.
‡ Pugh, 2018b.

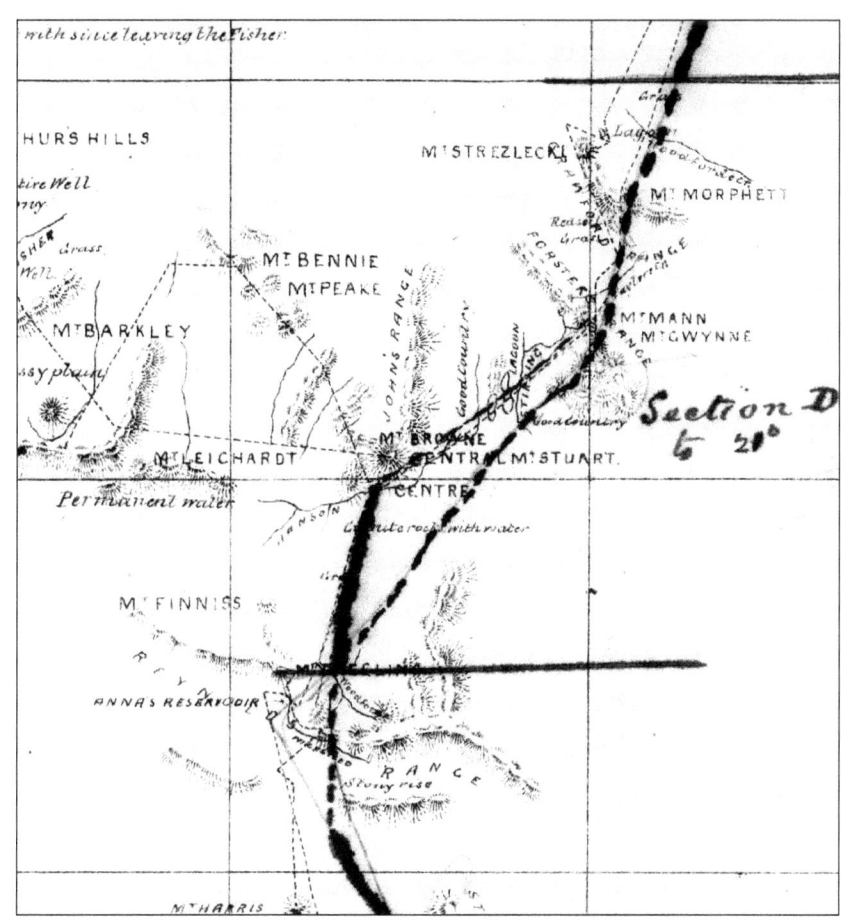

Map 6: Detail of Map 2. Section D, Central Mount Stuart. Also shows Stuart's exploration routes, c. 1871 (SLSA, C54).

Section D travelled north through Barrow Creek, where a semi-permanent spring was discovered and a repeater station was built, and then a further 35 kilometres (22 miles) to meet with Section E.

Similar to the buildings constructed in Alice Springs and Charlotte Waters, the Barrow Creek Telegraph Station was a simple stone-walled construction built by Alfred Woods, Stephen Jarvis*, and Samuel Grau

---

*   Jarvis was a former manager of Mount Margaret Station near Lake Eyre, was a sub-overseer under Alfred Woods, and an accomplished stone mason. The Barrow Creek Telegraph Station still stands today, 285 km north of Alice Springs.

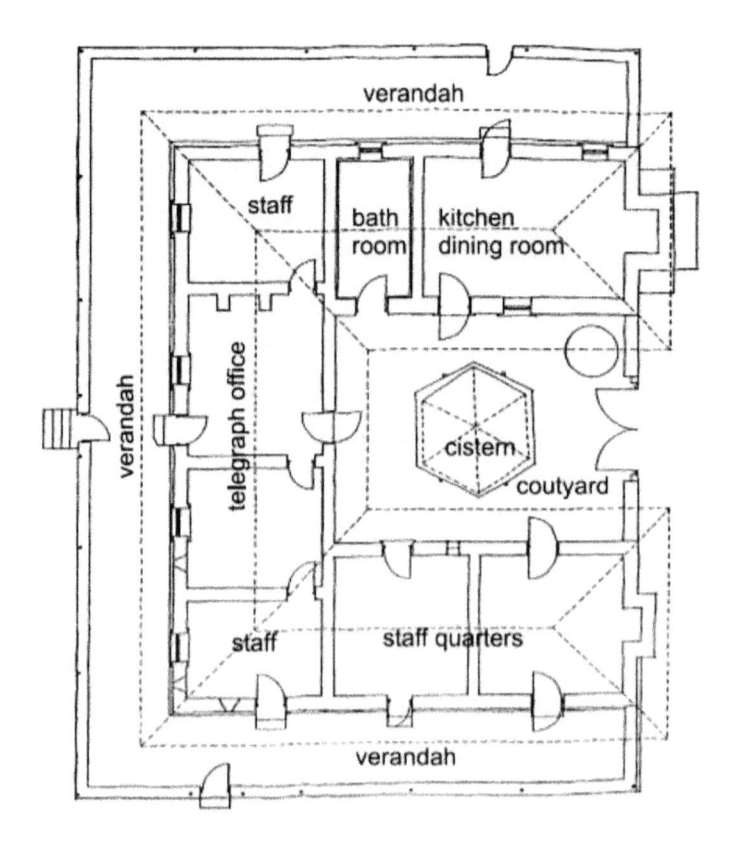

Figure 18: Floor plan of Barrow Creek Telegraph Station. Alice Springs and Charlotte Waters stations were of the same design (nt.gov.au).

Hübbe* in 1872. It was sited near the surface water that John Ross had discovered during his exploration, but it proved not to be a permanent source, and the well yielded brackish water. As a result, water had to be carted 24 kilometres (15 miles) from Taylor's Creek, until Ned Ryan's well-sinking party provided a deeper well in 1879.

The *Evening Journal* described the station:

... Barrow Creek is the prettiest station on the Overland Line, but it is a perfect hotbed of hostility. The building, like that

---

* Samuel Hübbe also helped build the Hermannsburg Mission buildings. Later he explored the Nullarbor Plain for a stock route. In 1899, he joined the South Australian Bushmen's Corps and went to serve as a captain in South Africa. He was killed by the Boers near Mafeking in August 1900.

at Charlotte Waters and Alice Springs, is of stone, and forms three sides of a square, with high walls and a strong iron gate across the back. In front of the house there are four windows, well protected with iron bars; there are also loopholes all-round the house, but no other openings to the outside. All the doors open into the yard, the house is roofed with iron, and when the iron gates are closed it is a perfect fortress, which could be successfully held by three or four resolute men against very great odds. There are six men all told at each of the interior stations, and sometimes the work is warm enough for them*.

Alfred Woods was impressed with some of the country, and his report to Todd must have been eagerly read by cattlemen of the day:

> ... Adjacent to this part of the line is some very good stock country, not only open and attractive in appearance, but probably the most healthy country for stock north of the MacDonnell Ranges—perhaps on account of the prevalence of saltbush, which is deficient or altogether absent elsewhere. There is much good grazing country throughout the length of Section D. The grasses are not rank; they are varied and nutritious, our stock thriving well. By judicious burning, green grass can be secured throughout the year, many of the grasses being perennial. There is a large admixture of spinifex, but after burning, other grasses spring up with it. With regard to water, in ordinary seasons there is probably an ample supply all the year round and can generally be got by sinking in the sand in the creeks, which have an uneven clay bottom covered with sand...†

Section E: Tennant Creek

Section E, the most northern part of the central section was constructed by William Harvey, who had surveyed the town of Southport and its surrounds‡ in 1869, when working for Goyder.

---

* *Evening Journal*, 23 February 1874.
† In Todd, 1873.
‡ Harvey was disciplined by Goyder after he destroyed some canoes belonging to Larrakia people in revenge for the death of J.W.O. Bennett who was speared by Wulna men at Fred's Pass in May 1869.

One advantage Harvey enjoyed was that he already knew the country in Section E, as he had accompanied John Ross on his route-finding expedition. It was 173 kilometres (107 miles, 76 chains) long, but it was the last of the central section to be constructed, because, although the equipment had left Adelaide in August 1870, it took him nearly 10 months to arrive at the starting point. Harvey's first pole was erected on 1 June 1871, and the team worked through to 1 November. Todd then sent him instructions to keep going past the end of his section because the northern section looked like it was going to be delayed, and every mile counted. The extra line into the northern section ended up being 132 kilometres (82 miles) long. They were helped by William Mills's team, and this extra piece brought them near to Frew's Ironstone Ponds, where the line was finally joined on 22 August 1872.

Figure 19: William Harvey, 1868 (SLSA, B-16791-6).

Harvey reported the country he passed as 'rather poor'. Near Mount Samuel he had difficulty with his theodolite because the hill is 'crowned with immense ironstone rocks, highly magnetic, every fragment being polarized—rendering the compass needle of the theodolite useless'*. The line ran past Attack Creek, where Stuart had turned back on his 1860 exploration, and Tennant Creek, where they built a repeater station.

Harvey's men, like some of the teams further south, had difficulty in finding enough poles, and they often had to cart them long distances. Todd reported that:

> … many of the poles on the northern end of Section E, and from there to the end of Mr. Harvey's work, are small and very

---

* Todd, 1873.

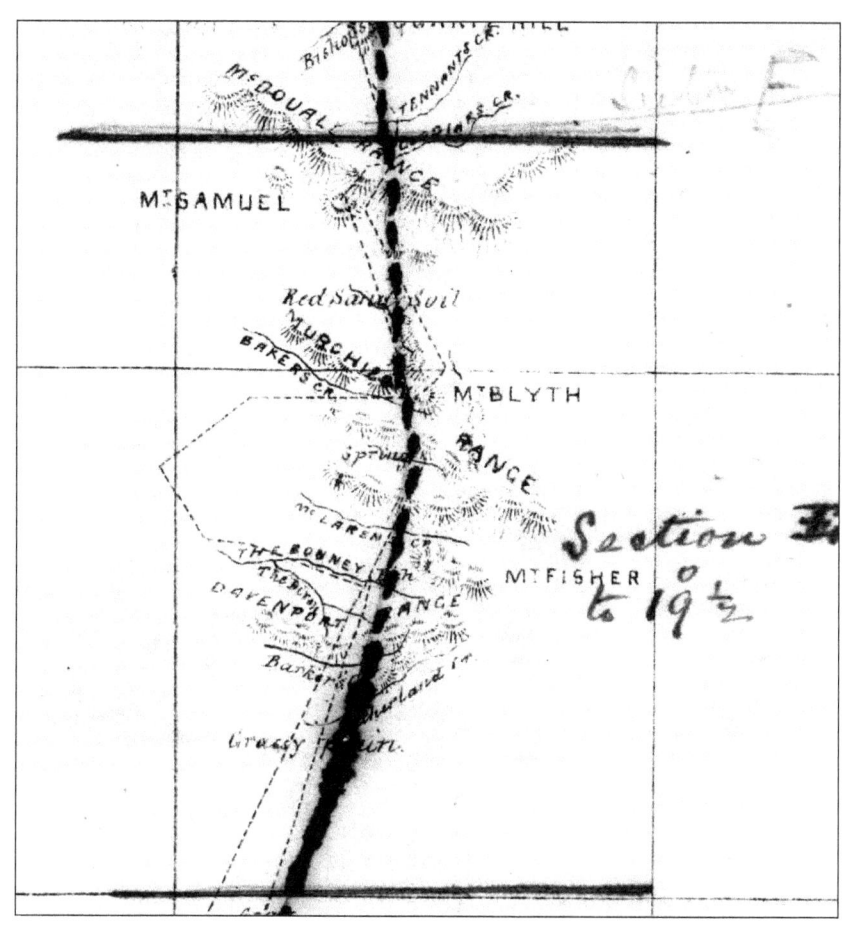

Map 7: Detail of Map 2. Section E, Davenport and Murchison Ranges, and Tennant Creek (Attack Creek is north of the section). Also shows Stuart's exploration routes, c. 1871 (SLSA, C54).

crooked; they were, however, the best he could procure. The bulk of the poles are full-sized and good; the others, although unsightly and small, are sufficiently substantial, and will probably last as long as the rest. When this section is repoled, I would advise iron throughout, indeed, iron poles for the north end of the section have already been provided.

Figure 20: A large group of men assist the arrival of the telegraph cable on 7 November 1871. It was then laid under the sea to Banjoewangie (Banyuwangi) where it arrived on 18 November 1871. The cable ship *Hibernia* sits at anchor (Sweet, SLSA, PRG742-5-84).

Figure 21: The Telegraph Fleet in Darwin Harbour, November 1871: *Hibernia*, *Investigator* and *Edinburgh*. (Sweet, SLSA, B-9743).

Chapter 6
The northern section

The undersea cable

Three British ships arrived in Port Darwin with the undersea cable on 26 October 1871. The *Hibernia* and *Edinburgh* were loaded with giant reels of insulated telegraph cable, and the passenger ship, *Investigator*, carried the engineers and electricians ready and waiting to lay the cable. The B.A.T. were on time and would be ready as agreed. South Australian government officials began to worry. If penalties were levied because they had failed, they would be hugely embarrassed.

On 7 November, several horses and dozens of strong men hauled the cable onto the beach below The Residency and Captain Sweet, fortunately again in port with his camera, was there to photograph the moment (see Figure 20).

The engineers then installed a small, prefabricated hut above the high tide mark, and the cable was connected to wires leading up to a temporary telegraph station, constructed of bush timber on the plateau above.

Adelaide heard the news of the safe arrival of the *Investigator* in the usual circuitous way before the telegraph was installed:

> ... A letter received by Mr. J. Darwent from Messrs. J. Feet & Co., dated Batavia, October 19, says, 'The steamer *Investigator*, carrying part of the cable which is to be laid down between Java and Port Darwin, is now here, and will leave in a day or two for the latter port'. Telegrams forwarded from Sourabaya to Galle reported the safe arrival of the *Bengal* at the Northern Territory

Figure 22: The temporary Palmerston Telegraph Station in 1871. The telegraph wires can be seen attached to the tree (Sweet, SLSA, B-9744).

on October 25 with Mr. Finniss, Mr. Squire, and other officers connected with the British-Australian Company and South Australian Government telegraph staff on board, all well …*

The *Edinburgh* and the *Hibernia* sailed to Java, laying the cable across the sea floor as they went. When each roll ran out, it was spliced to the next. Within two weeks they had arrived in the Javanese port of Banjoewangie (now Banyuwangi). On 20 November 1871, Captain Robert Halpin of the *Investigator,* sent the first telegram to Palmerston. Australia was at last connected to the rest of the world, albeit only to a little grass-roofed, bush-log cabin, in the most remote settlement on the continent. The first international message was more memorable than the messages sent by Todd and Millner ten months later:

'Advance Australia,' Halpin wrote, proudly.†

The B.A.T. were ready—Todd had less than two months to complete his contract.

---
* *Observer*, 2 December 1871.
† The full text was: 'I have the honour to announce to you in the name of the Telegraph Construction and Maintenance Company that we yesterday completed a perfect submarine cable, connecting your Colonies with Java, the mother country, and the Western world. May it long speak words of peace, and reiterate "Advance Australia".'

Figure 23: The cable shed on the beach below The Residency, 1879 (Foelsche, LANT, ph1060-0019).

The first pole

The men who won the £47,000 contract to install the northern section of the line, Joseph Darwent and William Trevett Dalwood, departed Adelaide on 20 August 1870 on the S.S. *Omeo*. With them was Dalwood's wife and a construction team led by W.A. Paqualin. There were six officers (including Joseph Darwent Jnr—Joseph's nephew—and Charles Tymn), 80 men, 78 horses and 10 bullocks. Darwent and Dalwood were to be paid varying amounts per mile, according to the distance from Palmerston. From Port Darwin to Southport (61 km, 39 miles) the price was £39 per mile and the subsequent 250 miles from Southport, £60 per mile, then £89 per mile to the end of the northern section. The government supplied the wire, insulators, and other essential equipment.

Over a thousand well-wishers, family members, politicians and the curious, caught the two o'clock train from Adelaide to watch the *Omeo* depart. It was an exciting time:

> ... the S.S. *Omeo* left the McLaren wharf about half-past
> 3 o'clock ... with the men, stores, horses, and cattle fitted out
> by Messrs. Darwent & Dalwood for the prosecution of their
> part of the great telegraph undertaking ... The passengers are
> as follows: Messrs. W. A. Paqualin (in charge), Joseph Darwent
> jun. [sic], Stephen King jun., Charles Tym Dalwood, Wm.
> [William] McMinn, Burton, Stapleton, and Howley. The four
> last named gentlemen are sent to act for the Government.
> Seventy-five laborers engaged by Messrs. Darwent & Dalwood
> went in the steerage.

The ship was heavily loaded. Port Darwin and the fledgling town of Palmerston had few resources to back them up if anything was forgotten:

> ... Amongst the various stores on board are over 1,000
> bundles of telegraph wire and a quantity of insulators and
> pins belonging to the Government ... The vessel presented
> a lively aspect, every space above and between decks being
> made to accommodate some portion of the equipment of the
> expedition. Eighty splendid draught horses are well provided
> for on board, together with a dozen head of cattle. The hands
> appear to be men well fitted for their task. Many of them have
> been in the Northern Territory before, and nearly all have
> had experience in survey or telegraph-construction work, or
> income employment of a similar kind[*].

Mr Darwent gave a rousing speech, promising them extra riches for fast work. He was pleased, he said:

> ... to see how well they had come forward to the muster.
> They would remember that a great deal depended on them
> as to the success of the work, and he felt sure they would
> individually assist in forwarding the undertaking. Everything
> had been done to ensure their comfort during the voyage, and
> a great amount of time and care had been taken with regard
> to furnishing them with proper stores after landing on the
> Northern coast. He further pointed out that the sooner the
> work was completed the better it would be for them all; for
> although they were each engaged for 15 months, still if the
> work was finished before that time, they would still receive full

---

[*] *Advertiser*, 24 August 1870.

Figure 24: Harriet Douglas (with tamping tool in hand) 'planted' the first telegraph pole in Darwin on 15 September 1870, on the corner of Smith Street and the Esplanade. Dan Daly is to her left and William Dalwood to her right. The man in the dark jacket is William Bloomfield Douglas. On his right is Mrs Ellen Douglas. Their daughter Nellie is on the left, and Willie is seated in front. Robert Burton is second on left with a shotgun, 1870 (Sweet, SLSA, B-4638).

pay, and if they completed the work within the twelve months, they would receive a bonus of £1,000 between them.

Charles Todd, who was not at that time accompanying them, was also called upon to speak. He observed:

> … that the work they were going to perform was of national importance, and he was pleased to see the expedition so well equipped. He should leave the vessel side with a feeling of confidence in the men who were going and the manner they had been provided for.

Then amid cheers and high spirits, the *Omeo* slipped from the wharf and was on her way.

Twenty days later, on 9 September, the *Omeo* dropped anchor in Port Darwin. The stores and equipment were immediately unloaded under the supervision of the foreman, Mr W.A. Paqualin, using a lighter because no jetty then existed.

The *Omeo*'s arrival and purpose were a surprise to Government Resident Douglas. He learned that plans had changed, and that the South Australian government had won the contract from the British Australian Telegraph Company to construct an overland telegraph line from Port Darwin, 2,839 kilometres (1,764 miles) south to Port Augusta. It meant the orders that arrived on the *Bengal* were no longer relevant, and McLachlan had been sent on a survey trip to the Roper for nought. It also meant more work for him, as the government was managing the building of the line instead of the B.A.T.

On 13 September, the *Gulnare* sailed back into Port Darwin. Captain Sweet had gone to Timor to purchase fresh meat and vegetables 'for the government staff'. His arrival was good timing, as Sweet had a camera—and the planting of the first telegraph pole in Palmerston was an occasion to be celebrated.

On 15 September 1870, six days after the arrival of the construction party in Port Darwin and 12 months before the deadline written into the contract, a 'gathering of the whole community' in Palmerston formed around a freshly dug posthole on the corner of Smith Street and the Esplanade.

Miss Harriet Douglas, eldest daughter of Government Resident Douglas, was chosen to 'plant' the pole, and was given a special tamping tool made of local timber, to compress the earth around it. Mrs Dalwood then broke a bottle of wine over the pole and drove in the first insulator pin*. The pole was then raised, Harriet tamped the earth, and then gave her first public speech, admitting to a 'certain degree of nervousness':

> ... I declared the pole 'well and truly fixed' after I had rammed the earth well round it, and, wishing success to the contractor

---

* Alfred Giles, 1925.

and his expedition, the first section of the overland telegraph was begun'.*

Captain Sweet organised the crowd, and they posed for what has become an iconic early Darwin image. In it, Harriet Douglas holds the tamping tool. Beside her is Daniel Daly, a surveyor and Harriet's future husband. Harriet's father, Government Resident Douglas, poses with Mrs Ellen Douglas and their four other children. Closest to the pole in white tails and a fancy white hat, stands William Dalwood. They are surrounded by officials of the British Australian Telegraph Company (probably including John Squire, the cable superintendent, and future husband of Nellie Douglas), and other residents of Adelaide's northern colony, Robert Burton† stands on the left holding a shotgun. Other people who are likely to be in the crowd include Ned Tuckwell, W. A. Paqualin, Joseph Darwent, Stephen King, Charles Tymn, William McMinn, James Stapleton, and Andrew Howley‡.

This was the first pole in the northern end of the Overland Telegraph Line, and it would soon be joined by 36,000 others, at '20 to the mile', in a line that loosely followed John McDouall Stuart's track south to Port Augusta, 2,839 kilometres (1,764 miles) away.

But it would not be without trouble.

William McMinn

Dalwood and Darwent's teams began work in the dry season of 1870 under the superintendence of Government Surveyor William McMinn. They initially moved quickly because at first it was easy going, even if the heat of the 'build-up' season was increasingly

---

* Daly, 1887.
† Robert Burton was sent to the Litchfield area to search for gold by Goyder in 1869. His party was promised that 'all gold found [would] be sold at market price ½ reward to Burton, other ½ to party besides a bonus' (Deane, 1868–9). They found very little.
‡ George McLachlan and his team of surveyors were away on their survey expedition to Roper River, and Sub-Inspector Foelsche, who also owned a camera, does not appear to have been there either.

oppressive. The telegraph poles had to be cut to precise minimum measurements, as ordered by Todd. They were to be harvested from the surrounding bush, if there was timber available, and placed at a rate of 20 per mile.

Good progress was made from October to December. By the first rains of the wet season, they had erected poles and strung the telegraph wires for more than 300 kilometres (190 miles). But then the wet season hit—and hit hard. The resulting muddy roads, quagmire bogs, and difficult working conditions slowed the teams considerably. By March 1872, they were still only half done and, with conditions worsening, the men complained bitterly of rancid food and disease-spreading mosquitoes. They stopped work on 7 March 1871. The sensible thing then might have been to rest the men, wait a month or six weeks, and start again when the rains were finished. But rather than deal with the issues, Surveyor William McMinn, the government's superintendent of the project, declared the contract with Darwent and Dalwood null and void—and without any real explanation, he sailed for Adelaide on the *Gulnare* on 3 June*. It was an awkward journey—McMinn's fellow passengers included Joseph Darwent, Charles Tymn and about 30 telegraph line workers that he had sacked.

McMinn's odd behaviour and mishandling of the contractors meant that nothing was done in the northern section for nearly five months—and the dry season was wasted†. The newspapers were immediately suspicious:

Figure 25: William McMinn, 1875 (SLSA, B-7233-3).

---

* Donovan, 1981.
† Gill, 1998.

... the *Gulnare*, which arrived on Saturday last, brought back the greater part of the construction party, together with Mr. McMinn (the Government Overseer), who, for reasons which, to him no doubt, appear satisfactory, had determined the contract, and proceeded hither to justify his action ... on the face of it, his own statement that the work could have been completed within a few weeks of the specified time appears suggestive of undue precipitancy on his part. The fact, too, that he was the next lowest tenderer causes his action in the matter to be regarded by some with a jealous eye ...[*]

McMinn reported his actions to Charles Todd:

... Sir—I have the honour to report that in consequence of the inability of Messrs. Darwent and Dalwood to proceed with their contract for the construction of the Overland Telegraph from Port Darwin beyond the 3rd of May on account of inefficient means, and with no prospect of the arrival of adequate reinforcements in order to fulfil the contract by the stipulated period, I declared the contract void on that date, and immediately took possession of the works, and the plant, stock, etc, belonging to the contractors, in pursuance of the clauses contained in specifications authorizing such action ...[†]

And there were indeed clauses in the contract that allowed McMinn to act that way, but he was severely criticised in the South Australian Assembly. The Government was furious. Minister Glyde called McMinn a bad appointment from the start—he was a failed tenderer for the project, and therefore a rival. He had no business being the superintendent of the successful tenderers[‡].

... The Government were very indiscreet in sending a man like Mr. McMinn to the Northern Territory to cancel the contract as they did. It was unwise to put so much power in the hands of a person like that, as it was empowering him to ruin a contractor ...[§]

---

[*] *Kapunda Herald*, 14 July 1871.
[†] *Adelaide Observer*, 15 July 1871
[‡] *Evening Journal*, 2 August 1871.
[§] *South Australian Register*, 7 September 1971.

McMinn was dismissed*. Darwent and Dalwood laid a complaint with the government and, after a lengthy inquiry, were compensated with £11,000.

McMinn's mishandling of the contractors delayed the project for an extended period. With more than 495 kilometres (308 miles) of the northern section yet to be started, the work was stalled for nearly five months. At last, Robert Patterson and his teams arrived—just in time for the next wet season.

Captain Sweet and the *Gulnare* were assigned to the Overland Telegraph and were expected to transfer stores and equipment to a landing and depot set up on the Roper River, as far upstream as was possible. However, Government Resident Douglas had other ideas. He became more and more possessive of 'his' equipment and staff. It was he who dispatched the *Gulnare* to Adelaide with William McMinn on board, plus Darwent and Dalwood's staff. This was against clear orders, and it would, as Minister Arthur Blyth furiously pointed out, delay the transportation of wire and equipment to the Roper River.

In fact, the delay stretched to five months and caused great anxiety. The B.A.T. threatened to revert to its plan of running a line through to Normanton, and the Minister was cognisant of the penalties that the government was required to pay if the line was not up and running by January 1872.

Robert Patterson

From June 1871, Todd needed a party of government employees to finish the missing 495 kilometres (308 miles) section of the line to replace the failed contractors. Robert Charles Patterson, a railway engineer, was given the leadership role, and by mid-July, he had a shortlist of 80 applicants to join his team. More than 600 men had

---

* William McMinn salvaged his career by working as an architect. He designed and built houses, hotels, the original wing of the Adelaide Children's Hospital, and in partnership with Edward John Woods in 1877–8, the first building of the

applied, although many were not suitable*. Within a week he had made his choice† and the men and their equipment were loaded onto the S.S. *Omeo* and left Adelaide for Port Darwin without delay. Their equipment included 'nine wagons, six watercarts, and over 2,000 packages of stores'‡.

Patterson's team arrived in Port Darwin on 24 September, just before the 1871–72 monsoon. They were met by John Archibald Graham Little, who was appointed telegraph station master on 1 August 1871. The telegraph line was a year away from completion, but Little's role was to employ telegraph operators for the repeater stations being built along its length and get them there in time for the joining of the line. He also had to organise a site and arrange construction of the telegraph office in Palmerston. Little employed 'six persons at each station, viz., the Stationmaster, Assistant-Operator, and four men'§. They also needed stock, and each held about 20 horses, a team of bullocks, and cattle for food. Each station needed to be well provisioned, and self-sufficient for months.

There is no doubt that Patterson did an extraordinary job. He had a lot of help, of course, and this included the entire Northern Territory Police Force:

> ... It became clear to Patterson, after he had commenced work, that unless he received additional labourers quickly, he would have to withdraw to the Roper River Depot for the duration of the approaching wet season ... Among the reinforcements were the men of the police force. In October 1871, 'the whole force with horses [was] transferred to Mr. Patterson, Commander of the N.T. Overland Telegraph Expedition'. The police remained under Patterson's command, acting as guards, bullock drivers, couriers, police, and storekeepers, until February 1872 when they returned to

---

University of Adelaide. He died aged 40, in North Adelaide in February 1884. (ADB, 1974).

* *Kapunda Herald*, 21 July 1871.
† For lists of the men in each party, see Appendix 1.
‡ *The Argus*, 31 July 1871.
§ Todd, 1873.

normal duties to deal with an influx of prospectors ... There is no similar instance of a police force being transferred to command of another organisation*.

Patterson was nevertheless somewhat of an annoyance to Charles Todd, and he complained about him numerous times in letters to his wife, Alice. For him, progress was still too slow, and with the deadline looming, he travelled north to sort things out—which apparently annoyed Patterson, and started the rumour that Todd had 'superseded his control of the project'. Todd was clearly worried that Patterson was not the right man to complete the job. In private letters to his wife, Alice, he wrote:

> ... Patterson ... is naturally despondent, disgusted with the line, and never thought it would be completed—My plan ... was to keep him away from the working parties as much as possible, as he only frightened them about the climate, & urged the withdrawal of the party before the work was satisfactorily completed—But, when I say this, I believe he means well, & would do nothing dishonourable. He does not seem to realise the extent to which his own feelings influence his activities & the spirits of his party. I shall do all I can for him†.

> ... Much that you [Alice] say, from report, about Patterson is quite true. He was not fitted for this sort of work and is too easily disheartened. He spends too much time in reading, instead of moving amongst his men, & is always writing to his wife & others—but at the same time I thought it better to avoid, if possible, the extreme measure of suspending him & after some correspondence managed to settle matters amicably & hope soon to have things on a more satisfactory footing. He is gentlemanly & now he knows that my intentions towards him are not hostile he will work with me—I hope, zealously‡.

Patterson's underserved reputation of disorganisation and poor decision-making hung around for months—despite Todd

---

* Wilson, 2000.
† Todd, family letters, 1872, PRG 630/2/2 page 5.
‡ Todd, family letters, 1872, PRG 630/2/25 page 43.

insisting that he came 'more as a visitor to their camps' than as a manager. Later, his reputation was restored when Burton, King, Ringwood, Rutt and others met him at the Prince Alfred Hotel in Adelaide and 'bore testimony to the able and zealous services rendered by Mr. Patterson and endorsed the remarks relative to no disorganisation in Mr. Patterson's expedition having taken place'[*]. In the euphoria the opening of the line created, Patterson was lauded for his leadership[†].

Patterson's party was helped on 22 June 1872 when they were suddenly gifted more time: the undersea cable laid by the B.A.T. broke somewhere between Darwin and Banyuwangi and the pressure was off until it was fixed. At the time, Todd, Dr Renner, and Robert Patterson were at Daly Waters Telegraph Station with Mr Tucker, the first stationmaster, and Todd was communicating directly with London when the cable broke[‡].

For the South Australians, the break under the sea was pure luck, because their line was completed seven months behind schedule, but no late fee was ever asked for. The undersea line was not operational until two months after the landline was ready.

Todd rode the full length of the northern section. To his relief, he found that Darwent and Dalwood's team had completed the 362 kilometres (225 miles) section from Port Darwin to the King River well. He had been worried about it as it had lain 'disabled' through the wet season. Nevertheless, Todd ordered the line to be:

> … thoroughly overhauled, every bad pole taken out, and between Port Darwin and the Katherine, iron pins have been substituted for the ironbark pins, which, although soaked in boiling petroleum, were found to attract the white ants and the boring beetle …

---

[*] *Advertiser*, 5 December 1872.
[†] Patterson had a long career in engineering and built railways in South Australia and Tasmania, and even entered politics in 1903. He died of a cerebral haemorrhage in 1907, during a board meeting, (Obituary: *Hobart Mercury*, 22 June 1907).
[‡] John Lewis, 1922.

They replaced 150 poles because they were damaged by termites, bushfires, or dry rot, but the line was strong, well-built, and 'constructed in a proper manner'.

Todd knew that the ubiquitous termites ('white-ants') of the Top End would always be a major problem, so he planned ahead, and ordered 6,500 metal poles before they were needed:

> … my principal reason for ordering the iron poles now was that they could be more expeditiously and economically carted now while we have a large number of acclimatized teams, both horses and bullocks, in the Territory than we could do at any future period. Besides which I think it desirable to have the iron poles on the ground to take the place of the wooden ones as they decay to the extent it is intended to use them. My present idea is that we should gradually introduce iron poles, planting them alternately with wood where suitable timber is plentiful and near at hand, and consecutively where timber is inferior and difficult to get*.

By 1873, the line already contained 2,500 iron poles in the southern region because of the treeless plains it crossed. Todd planned that all the wooden poles would eventually be replaced. They would 'introduce the remainder gradually, spreading the expense over a series of years.' Eventually all 36,000 poles were metal Oppenheimer poles.

Rum Jungle

The road Todd rode on, south from Darwin, closely followed the telegraph line. By 1872, it was well used—and as it soon entered the gold fields, there were always plenty of men using it. About 70 kilometres from Darwin, the line and the road crossed the headwaters of the Finnis's River, which had been surveyed and mapped by Goyder's men in 1869. The extended area around it was still relatively unknown, but a permanent spring gave a plentiful supply of water to travelling teamsters to spell their horses and bullocks. Thick riparian

---

* Todd, 1873.

jungle clung to the banks, green grass grew on the flats, and it was a pleasant place to camp.

In December 1872, two teams employed by the telegraph company stopped there and let their horses stray from their camp. Unfortunately, as they were 'no bushmen', they were unable to find them again. Then, while waiting for help, they noticed in their load two 'quarter-casks' of rum, containing 40 gallons each. That was the end of their search for their horses—at least until the boss sought them out and collected the horses himself.

The place became known as 'Rum Jungle' and within two years the 'Rum Jungle Hotel' was opened a few hundred metres from the camp. It was big business—in a single order, publican David Lithgow, imported 52 cases of rum*. The hotel still survives as a part of the township of Batchelor, a living memorial to the men of the O.T.L.

The end of the *Gulnare*

Meanwhile, Minister Blyth's furious response to Douglas's misuse of the *Gulnare* was to put the ship under the command of Robert Patterson. Douglas's authority was limited to supervision of the inhabitants of Palmerston town. Greatly offended, he grew morose and drank more heavily.

Up to October 1871, the gallant little *Gulnare*, under Captain Sweet, had made five journeys to Port Darwin from Adelaide since her first arrival in April 1870. Behind schedule because of the delay in the northern section, it was decided that the easiest way to get the telegraph line, insulators, and the rest of the equipment to the men on the line was to establish a depot on, or near, Roper Bar on the Roper River. The route from the line to the river was already planned:

…An expedition, under Mr. S. King, jun., left Palmerston
on the 18th June, and returned on the 18th August. Mr. King,
travelling from the line of telegraph, struck the Roper at

---

* Barrie, 1982.

Leichhardt's Bar, at the head of the navigation. He found the route easy and reports most favorably of the country he passed through. Previous to this Mr. McLachlan had travelled up the river to the same point and found a most passable route[*].

At last, McLachlan's work of September 1870 became useful. It was known that much of the river was navigable by ships up to a rocky 'bar', and the *Gulnare* was as suited to the work as a sailing vessel could be.

> ... a member of one of the Northern Territory expeditions, who knows the river, says there are 18 feet of water on the entrance bar at high tide, and after that, five or six fathoms for 50 miles as the crow flies, or say 100 miles, calculating bendings of the stream. The deep water leads nearly to the head of the navigation. From this spot the distance to the nearest point of the projected telegraph-line is 80 miles [130 km], the distance from that point to Port Darwin being nearly 300 miles [483 km][†].

Avoiding 220 miles (354 km) of overlanding stock and equipment was a no-brainer. The depot on the Roper became a busy place for many months.

But it was not without its own problems. In October 1871, Captain Sweet was dispatched to the Roper River with a heavy load of telegraph equipment. Unfortunately, the *Gulnare* struck a reef in the Vernon Islands within a day of leaving and sat there, unmoving. The Vernons are not far from Port Darwin but there she sat, stranded on the reef, for eight days[‡]. In calm seas, Captain Sweet managed to transfer the equipment to the barque, *Bengal*, and then limp back to Port Darwin. When Douglas saw the damaged *Gulnare*, he was delighted—he could now replace her with something more suited to his position, he thought[§]. Her condition was so poor she

---

[*] *Express and Telegraph*, 6 Oct 1871.
[†] *Express and Telegraph*, 21 July 1871.
[‡] *Observer*, 2 December 1871.
[§] This was to be the *Flying Cloud*, under Captain Henry Marsh, but it took many months to arrive. When it did, much criticism was directed at Douglas after he made several journeys that were more recreational than official.

was condemned immediately, stripped of anything useful, and then moored as a hulk off Fort Point in Darwin Harbour*.

The Roper River on the *Bengal*

Patterson chartered the *Bengal*, under Captain Hummel, to take *Gulnare*'s place. *Bengal* was to sail up the Roper River to meet Patterson and surveyor Harrison Packard† and their party of 40 men—including a cook majestically named Augustus Caesar. The site chosen for the depot, near Roper Bar, was described by Ludwig Leichhardt in 1845. This group would travel overland to the depot during December. They could have learned from mistakes made in 1866 by John McKinlay‡, but inexperience hid the difficulties they would face due to the wet season, and two men lost their lives because of it. The plan was that the overlanders would build a landing on the banks of the Roper River in preparation for the delivery of wires and insulators, men, animals, and supplies, by ship. They would then be carted 130 kilometres (81 miles) to the O.T.L. by dray.

Captain Sweet joined Captain Hummel on the *Bengal* for the voyage. On the deck, they amassed a huge pile of telegraph equipment,

---

* Ironically, this was not the last Douglas saw of the *Gulnare*. A few months later, in an alcohol induced paranoia, Douglas climbed to the roof of The Residency and threatened to shoot the police because he thought they were after him as a debtor. Dr Millner took him into care and locked him in the *Gulnare* and moored the ship off the beach. Douglas was forced to dry out—for a while, at least (Pugh 2019).

† Harrison Packard was a surveyor who had worked at Escape Cliffs with Finniss, arriving in 1864 with his wife Mary and daughter Edith, as part of the second party of reinforcements. Mary gave birth to Adam Manton Finniss Packard, the only white child born at Escape Cliffs, in December 1866. Packard returned north as a member of Goyder's 1869 survey party and Mary and the children returned on the *Kohinoor* in June 1870. The couple had another two daughters: Eleanor in 1870 and Harriet Emily in February 1871. Unfortunately, Packard died in 1874 from gangrene in an ulcerated throat. He was 38 years old and had served the government for 18 years. Mary, then widowed, returned to Adelaide with the children (Pugh, 2019).

‡ Pugh, 2018a.

plus the cutters *Larrakeeyah* and *Dolphin*. There was so much gear on deck, when moving forward the crew had to swing around it, holding the tie-down ropes.

Bengal sailed from Port Darwin on 21 November and arrived off the coast near the Roper River in the Gulf of Carpentaria on 11 December.

In the lee of Maria Island, the *Larrakeeyah* was lowered over the side, ballasted, and equipped with stores. John Little and a Mr. Murray* then set off with a crew for the Norman River. Little needed to get to the telegraph station in Normanton to send telegrams ordering the stores and telegraph equipment to be sent on the *Omeo* from Adelaide as soon as he could.

Cadet William Crowder—diarist

Many of Patterson's team were young men like William Crowder and Rob Tapscott, who were two teenagers employed as cadets and excited for the adventure. Crowder, who turned eighteen on the Roper River, kept a diary† of his year in the north. The two friends were sent to Melbourne on the *Aldinga* to meet up with the *Omeo*, and Crowder was looking forward to a 'fine chance to see a little bush life'. However, he discovered himself to be a poor sailor and remembered little of the trip on the *Aldinga*. 'I felt as if someone had rigged a force pump down my throat and was trying to get my liver out', he wrote.

Crowder recovered and spent several days in Melbourne with Tapscott attending Shakespeare (*The Merchant of Venice* and *Othello*) and the Victorian Museum, plus a tour of a soap factory. They even squeezed in an opera, *Il Travatore*.

On board the *Omeo*, the boys found they were to be separated in the Northern Territory, with Tapscott going to Port Darwin

---

* This was possibly Robert Murray, subsequently a long-term stationmaster at Katherine Telegraph Station.
† Crowder, 1871–2.

with Patterson, and Crowder to the Roper River with Walter Rutt. Crowder was transferred to the *Antipodes* in Newcastle under Captain Kirkpatrick, to look after a herd of 100 bullocks on the ship's deck. He suffered from seasickness most of the way.

Surveying the river

In December 1871, using the *Dolphin*, Captain Sweet and members of both the *Gulnare* and *Bengal's* crew began the survey of the Roper River. They marked the deeper channels and drew an accurate chart. The *Bengal* was a large ship, and care needed to be taken getting her through the river mouth. The wet season had arrived with a fury, and it rained 'tremendously and blew very stiff'*.

Some members of the *Gulnare's* crew had already surveyed parts of the Roper River the year before, and a few of them had stayed out in the *Gulnare's* cutter overnight. At 1.30 a.m. on the night of 17 December 1870, 37-year-old Second Mate William Read, a tall South Australian, was sleeping with a leg hanging over the side of the boat. Suddenly, he was pulled into the water by his leg, shrieking in terror. He was briefly seen splashing on the surface, but then went under, and was never seen again†.

Large crocodiles inhabit the Roper River, and the O.T.L. workers who arrived during 1871 were forewarned by Read's death the year

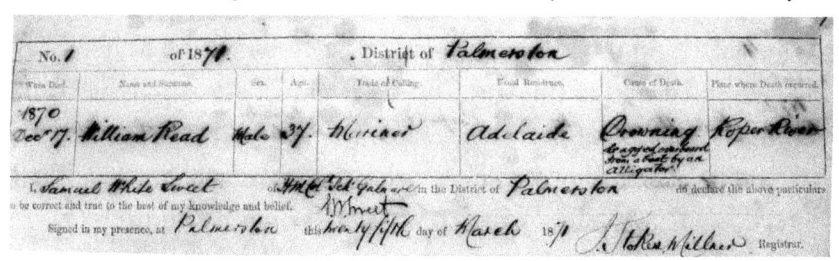

Figure 26: The first death registered in the Palmerston Book of Deaths, William Read was killed by a crocodile in the Roper River on 17 December 1870 (LANT).

---

* Crowder, 1871–2.
† *Advertiser*, 4 March 1871.

before. William Read is number one in the Register of Deaths for the District of Palmerston, which the government began in 1871.

By 18 December 1871, buoys were installed by the cutters and long boats to mark the channel into the river. Earlier, on 13 December, the *Dolphin* had sailed 100 kilometres (62 miles) up-river with supplies for Patterson, Packard, and the party of overlanders. As they had not yet arrived, the supplies were buried under marked trees to await them.

The *Dolphin* returned at dawn on 24 December, the crew reporting that they had seen about 70 friendly natives and lots of 'alligators.' Captain Hummel of the *Bengal* had waited till then for the spring tides to arrive and so, with the *Dolphin* leading, he weighed anchor and sailed into the river. That night the ship was moored in 6½ fathoms opposite Paninnyilatya Creek. The men quickly gave it their own name, *Mosquito Creek*, for good reason:

> … Christmas Eve. Had to rig my mosquito curtain and turned into it at 6.30 pm, as the mosquitos commenced to get bad. At about 9 p.m. they were awfull [sic], like so many kettles wistleing [sic] around me, so much so that I could not get to sleep until 12 pm. All the crew had no curtains, and did not get a wink of sleep all night … they were so thick and plagued them so much they were driven up to the tops of the masts, but they were nearly as bad up there…*

Captain Sweet continued his survey to mark the channels in the *Dolphin* the next day, which was Christmas. Crowder went with him to take field notes but was pleased when they were beaten back by a rain squall and in time for Christmas dinner of roasted ducks the cook had hunted that morning.

Progress was slow. Each day the channels were recorded and marked, and members of the crew went fishing or hunting. Huge catfish that were 'so large and strong they could hardly be pulled up' and 'Ducks, Geese, Turkeys, Cockatoos &c' loaded the dining table, but at night the mosquitoes nearly carried them away, and the men

---

* Crowder, 1871–2.

needed to sleep inside because of the rain. Crowder wrote that 'it was so close that I had to sit up and let the perspiration drip off me' before he could sleep.

The days passed by. The river swelled due to the wet season deluge and rowing the small boats up stream against the current was hard work. On 31 December, Captain Sweet went on shore close to the anchorage and planted pumpkin, radishes, and onions in the soil of the riverbank, with the intention, as sailors of the nineteenth century often did, of starting a wild garden that might be of use later on.

Finally, on 3 January, Crowder's eighteenth birthday, they were hailed from a punt that had come from Roper Bar. It was made, Crowder wrote, 'from the body of a waggon [sic] with a low sail to it, lined with canvas and 5 vinegar kegs lashed to each side, a mast with a fly as a lug sail & paddle to steer with'. On board were Robert Patterson, E. Bayfield, Tom Dyke, Robert Burton, and a store master named Stratton. Patterson said that 40 men were waiting for them at the bar in a 'state of starvation'. Unfortunately, E. Bowman had already died of 'apoplexy'*, and J. Harcus was lost in the bush, presumed dead. Food was immediately dispatched to the camp, but the *Bengal*, with the majority of their supplies, was still weeks away— she was finally moored at the new jetty on 3 February.

John Little's trip to Normanton took longer than expected— over a month—because they were delayed by a cyclone in the Gulf, but he and the *Larrakeeyah* finally appeared on 14 January. Little had telegraphed his orders via the Queensland network—and the *Omeo* had been dispatched on 30 December with the stock and stores Patterson needed.

Little was able to tell the men in the river the most recent news: the wife of the governor, Lady Edith Fergusson, had died; the Hart

---

* 'Bowman, one of Mr. Hack's bullock drivers, had died suddenly with symptoms of apoplexy, hastened by sunstroke' on 4 November 1870 (Rutt, 1870). Patterson auctioned his belongings the next day, 'for the benefit of his relatives'.

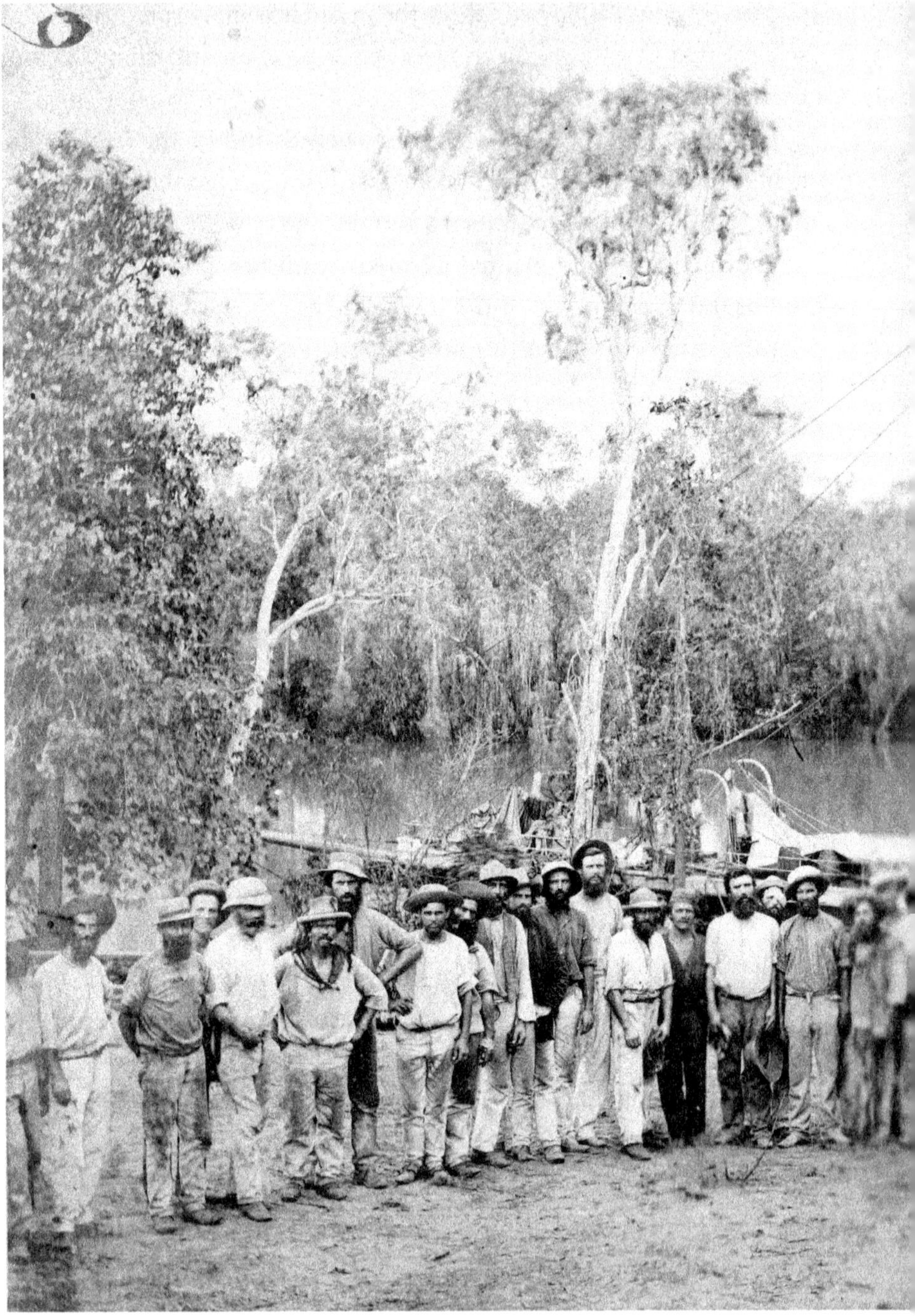

Figure 27: Patterson's party at the Roper River Depot jetty, 11 March 1872 (Sweet, SLSA, B-9762).

ministry of South Australia had been 'turned out'; and 'another war in Europe was rumoured'*. They also heard that the government had bought a steam tug in Port Adelaide called the *Young Australian*, and that she was *en route* for Port Darwin and would soon join them in the river.

Little's arrival and the long wait for the *Omeo* played on people's nerves. When Little was overheard denigrating the men, the whole ship's company knew very quickly:

> ... The steward told me that he had heard Messrs Patterson & Little talking about our rations, pass uncalled remarks about us. Mr. Little remarking that we did not earn nor were we worth the food we eat and could not be trusted. Now I know he is prejudiced against us, and it shows that he is no gentleman, and also his ignorance in settling [sic] his spite in that matter, in trying to turn Mr. Patterson to the same mind, but I know it is only done to help him crawl, and if ever there was a crawler he is one, and he is a great hypocrite, for after he said that he came out smiling and borrowed my compass ...†

The men at Roper Bar completed the jetty in time for the arrival of the *Young Australian* on 4 February, with Charles Todd on board. He stayed in the camp for several days, made several rousing speeches and gave them all enough rum to make them 'tight'. Crowder proudly wrote that he was among the group invited into the cabin for the evening by Patterson. They drank champagne—unwisely, as it turned out, because the evening 'finished up with a drunken row'‡.

The *Young Australian*

The *Young Australian*, under Captain Lowrie, was a 'paddle steamer tug' used to tow ships up the river to the depot. Her first tow was the *Omeo* on 8 February 1872, and then the S.S. *Tararua* four weeks later. Captain Sweet had his camera with him and, on 11 March, took

---

* Crowder, 1871–2.
† Crowder, 1871–2.
‡ Crowder, 1871–2.

Figure 28: The Roper River Depot camp, 11 March 1872 (Sweet, SLSA, B-4635).

Figure 29: The Roper River Depot, 11 March 1872: *Tararua* with the tug *Young Australian* along side, and *Omeo*. The man in the boat may be William Crowder, as he claimed to be in all of Sweet's photographs that day (Sweet, SLSA, B-4635).

Figure 30: The Roper River, S.S. *Tararua*, 1871 (Sweet, SLSA, B-4643).

photographs of the camp, the jetty and the ships moored in the river. Crowder claimed that he was in all the photographs.

The *Young Australian* was stationed in the Roper River for the duration of the O.T.L. operation. There was, of course, no coal available to power her, so Captain Lowrie organised timber gathering parties, and stored timber in piles along the river. The poor communication with the outside world meant the *Young Australian* needed to wait for days and weeks at the mouth of the Roper River if cargo ships were expected, because no one knew when they would arrive.

Lowrie and his tug later stayed after the O.T.L. was complete, because the depot remained an important staging post for metal poles, as the wooden poles on the line were replaced. Unfortunately, she was damaged on several occasions by large ships she was towing, and repairs could only be done using materials they carried and local timber. The tug's stern suffered a collision in December 1872, and the damage was never satisfactorily fixed. This may have contributed to

Figure 31: Wreck of the *Young Australian*, 1873 (Foelsche, SLSA, B-10132)

the manoeuvring difficulties she had towing the *Flying Cloud* on the day she ran aground. Her stern dropped, water poured in through the damaged area and, despite numerous efforts, Lowrie was unable to re-float her. She was declared wrecked and abandoned. Her remains are still in the river, some 20 kilometres from Roper Bar, near Tomato Island (Munbililla) where Captain Sweet planted his tomatoes.

The *Young Australian* was replaced by the *Enterprise*, which became Captain Lowrie's new command, but she did not arrive until 12 May 1873. By then the captain, who had stayed in the river as a customs officer, suffered from scurvy. Nevertheless, he and the *Enterprise* remained in the north until December 1873, when enough new poles for the section between Tennant Creek and Katherine were in stock at the depot. Lowrie then took his ship back to Adelaide, under steam*.

---

* *Engineers Australia*, 2021.

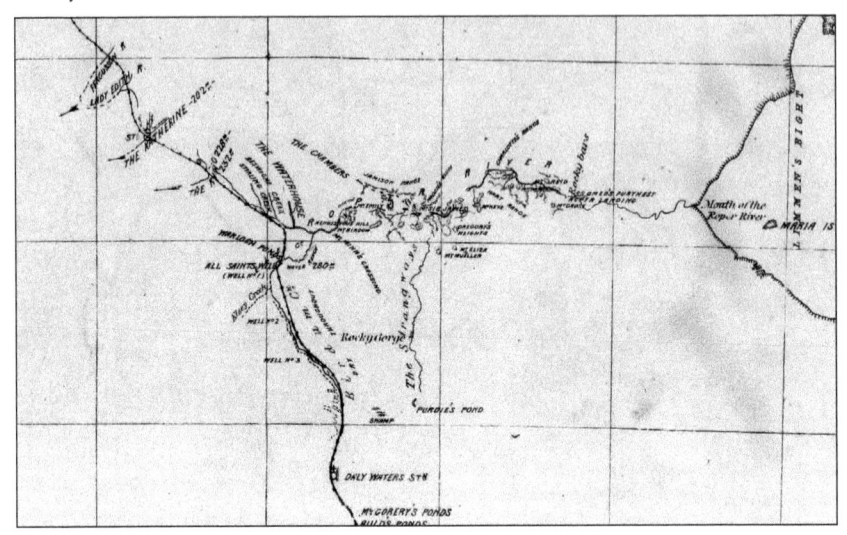

Map 8: Richard Knuckey's hand-drawn map showing the cart track from the Roper River to the line, dated 3 March 1871 (SLSA, C34).

From the Roper to the Line

By March 1871, the Roper River Depot was stocked with telegraph line equipment, but it was of no use until it was transported to the line. The wet season was slowly drawing to an end, but much of the 130-kilometre (81-miles) track westwards was still a quagmire that would mercilessly bog any horses or drays that ventured along it. Finally, Stephen King, who had mapped the track the previous dry season, Alfred Giles, and telegrapher Charles Henry Johnston, led a party of 10 men and 50 packhorses west from Roper Bar. Johnston recorded that they:

> … Left Roper Landing for Rutt's Party, in company with R. Price (& Crowder) with 9 horsemen & 50 packs of provisions—Arrived at the Bar (8 miles)—Giles & King follow tomorrow[*].

William Crowder also noted:

> … Road very bad for miles up to stirrups in muck had to get off in mud several times to put on pack bags … one bay mare died. Camped at 4 P.M. …[†]

---

[*] Johnston, 1872–75.
[†] Crowder, 1872.

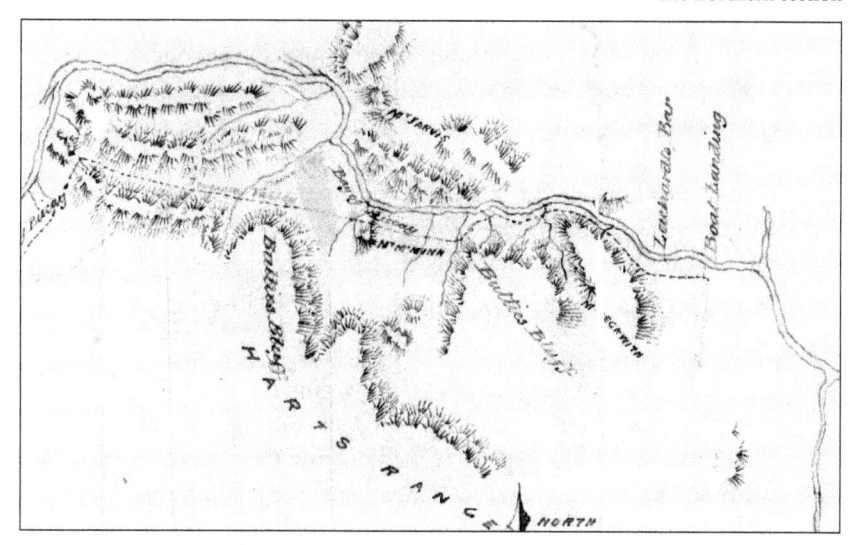

Map 9: Detail of Richard Knuckey's hand-drawn map showing Roper River Depot area, dated 3 March 1871 (SLSA, C34).

King and Giles went ahead but found the track only became worse, so the party settled into a camp at the base of Mount McMinn and waited for better weather. Crowder and his mate, William Easther[*], spent a few days exploring, climbing the mountain, hunting kangaroos, and just waiting. Despite occasional rain, on 23 March the road was 'drying up fine' so they packed up the horses and set off again but after two days of horses getting bogged and 'knocked up', they camped only about 5 miles from their last camp. It was a torrid time:

> … Monday 25th Got along 8 miles right, then came to the worst bog of any we have had—Got 12 horses thru' by unpacking and great trouble—Fine creek—compelled to keep remainder of the horses this side—Would not be able to cross—1 hopelessly bogged—Sun very powerful—burnt neck and hands all blistered—Country not fit for whites to work— Last night wild dogs howled dismally close to camp.

In the end, they were forced to leave the hopelessly bogged horse behind.

On 27 March, they were attacked by Aborigines:

---

[*] William Easther was one of the 88 people drowned in the *Gothenburg* disaster in 1875. At least five other O.T.L. men were also on board: J. McCarthy, W. Floyd, R. Martin, D. Harris, and S. Lizzer (Pugh, 2019).

> ... all except Messrs Giles, Johnston and myself were out looking up horses, we were startled by one of our dogs rushing across the camp and barking and on looking round we saw 15 or 20 niggers with spears crawling up behind some bushes behind us, about 30^{yds} from us, we all three seized our arms, and jumped up and fired on them just as they were aiming their spears & they immediately scampered off*.

Johnston had stayed in camp that day because he was ill with 'the Ague'. He also wrote of the attack:

> ... about 15 or 20 niggers crawled in within 10 yds of the camp with their spears and all arms when the dogs rushed at them, they ran a few steps & turned putting their spears in the wummeras and were about to throw when we fired on them and they ran like fun with a few shots in their rears to hurry them along—all our men were moving the horses leaving Giles, Crowder (a cadet) and I in the camp—the blacks must have watched and thought there was only 1 or 2 hands in camp—they meant mischief†.

All the diaries of the O.T.L. men mention difficulties with the horses. Some of the pack horses would wander away while the men were extricating others from the bogs, and they would have to spend hours looking for them. One day, the horse carrying Crowder's swag went missing, and a whole day was spent searching for it.

King's party was travelling so slowly that they were soon overtaken by Robert Patterson and a small party that had left Roper Bar days after them, although they had also had trouble getting their horses through the bogs. One of the horses broke its leg and was shot on 1 April and another one was 'knocked up' and left behind.

Finally, on 3 April, the travellers reached Red Lily Lagoon and camped near the O.T.L., close to Ralph Milner's sheep camp. The men from the Roper were pleased to be eating fresh mutton after their awful journey.

Ralph Milner had brought 2,000 sheep north from South

---

* Crowder, 1872.
† Johnston, 1871.

Australia to feed the work crews constructing the O.T.L.*. Travelling with his brother John, they followed the O.T.L. north from South Australia. They endured many difficulties, including a delay by drought and then stranding by floods. Poisonous plants killed many of their flock, but worse, John Milner was clubbed to death by an Aborigine in a jealous rage over a woman named Fannie. Ralph Milner must have been relieved to sell his remaining sheep to the Overland Telegraph workers†.

Crowder was assigned to work with Stephen King, and for the next few weeks he helped him with surveys towards Daly Waters. Surveyor Alexander Ringwood joined them in mid-May, and they worked southwards towards Newcastle Waters, camping at the sites John McDouall Stuart had used 10 years earlier. Crowder cut his own initials into trees that already had J.M-D.S. carved into them‡.

The section of line Patterson was required to complete extended from the King River to the northern end of Harvey's line (latitude 18° 26½'), near Frew's Ironstone Ponds where Stuart had camped in 1862. The ponds were described by John Lewis as a 'pretty spot':

… the pond is only a hundred yards round and twenty feet

---

* Rose, 1964.

† Ralph Milner then travelled on to Port Darwin with a mob of horses, thinking that he could breed them for the horse trade with the army in India. He was too late—Dillon Cox had already become a favourite of the government resident and Milner was refused a lease of his own. He left the Territory in January 1873 on the 327-ton *Springbok*, which then disappeared. By April, the ship was presumed lost with all hands (*Advertiser*, 14 June 1873), but then a telegram arrived in Adelaide from Dan Daly in Bowen, Queensland. The recently married husband of Harriet Douglas wrote: 'arrived after great perils. I brought her to Cape York, suspended Captain Harrison as imbecile. Passengers, who have recovered from scurvy and dysentery, navigated the ship here …'. The *Springbok* was 119 days at sea with only 69 days of provisions, and a drunk and insane skipper. Daly, who had never mastered a ship before but knew about navigation from his training as a surveyor, took over and brought her safely in (*Observer*, 10 May 1873). Ralph Milner thus survived to return later to the Territory to try his hand at mining.

‡ Stephen King had been here before, of course, with Stuart. It is likely that it was King who carved Stuart's initials into that same tree, as that was one of his roles on Stuart's expedition.

deep and is covered with wild fowl. On the banks are gum and bloodwood trees, ironbark, and a little hedgewood*.

About half of Patterson's men had headed south from Port Darwin with Walter Rutt, Patterson's second in command, and engineer and overseer Robert Burton, to restart the building of the stalled line, while Patterson led the rest to meet the ships at the Roper River. For them, the worst of the wet season (and the major rivers) had already been passed and the men were refreshed in a more comfortable dry camp, then about 70 kilometres (43 miles) south of modern Katherine. Charles Johnston arrived at Rutt's camp on 10 April, after a 'dreadful night with the ague'†. He had camped with Patterson and his men, and they had taken the watch overnight while he was ill, to 'watch for niggers this being a bad place for them'.

Johnston was a young man who always had one eye on the future. He noted in his diary various conversations he had with other telegraphers about the potential for employment in the stations:

> … Have just had a long yarn with Howley at the Catherine. [Katherine River] He speaks well of that station. There is plenty of game duck & kangaroo. It is the farthest Stn North & is 200 miles from Pt Darwin—Stapleton is to be located there—he has asked me to be his assistant—I said I would like it very well if Mr Todd did not offer me a Stn and I spoke of salary—he said he could get me £140 per annum. If Mr Todd does not give me a Stn that would be very good. In 3 years, I could save I should think £300 and be out of debt and then perhaps a station … I remember Mr Stapleton—I find I met him at Penola years since in Terry Woods time. There is no communication with Pt Darwin from the Catherine. Mr Stapleton will not be able to start for 2 weeks for want of horses—it is 45 miles from here‡.

Johnston was pleased to learn on 26 April, when he was in Katherine, that he was indeed to be Stapleton's assistant when the O.T.L. opened:

---

* John Lewis, 1922.
† Malaria. Johnston says he was taking quinine three times a day.
‡ Johnston, 1872–5.

... he thinks salary £160 ... This is the best place I have been in the Territory—The Catherine is a fine stream—rocky banks, high rocky hills around and plenty of grass on the valleys.

In the meantime, for the following few months, Johnston travelled the section of the line between Daly Waters and Tennant Creek, making any necessary repairs and replacing dodgy poles, and copying, sending, and receiving official dispatches. The latter was not always the most pleasant of duties:

> ... Monday 29th July 1872, Wire men off working again—I with waggons [sic] make line and stop for dinner with wire men, then having tried to speak, proceeded on 3½ miles to camp for night—Wire not up to camp in evening so went out 3/4 mile to end of wire and spoke with my fly for a break wind and with candles commenced taking memos & msgs for Express at 8 P.M., strong wind very cold & miserable, finished 2 AM copied business and started for Harvey's camp N Tomkinson to deliver to Boucaut which was done at 5 AM Tuesday Eyes very sore and weak with night wind and work—Wire party came on today—yesterday 5½ miles wired to 2½ miles back—Wire wagons arrived 12 noon & party in evening—wired 5 miles today Wednesday 2 miles wired shoeing horses—busy telegraphing all P.M.*

On the Line

King, Ringwood, and the others joined Burton and his camp for a night on 22 May. Crowder says he yarned with Burton and came away with the impression that the line would not be finished soon 'for the strange way they are going licks me altogether'. The route took:

> ... a general S.E. course, crossing the Elsie Creek at 281 miles, and thence follows the Birdum to the Daly Waters (where a station has been built), 368 miles from Port Darwin. The line then takes a more southerly course, passing to the east of King's and Frew's Ironstone Ponds, across Stuart's Plain to the north end of the Ashburton Range. Passing between the

---

* Johnston, 1872–5.

range and the Newcastle Waters the line enters the range at the Watson, crossing Powell's Creek, where it passes over to the east side of the range*.

While the explorers scouted ahead and determined the easiest route, the construction party felled and collected timber poles they could source locally. Cypress pine seemed to be the best, as it is resistant to termite attacks, but there were also good stands of 'blood wood, gum, and ironbark' around Daly Waters. The lancewood forests on the Stuart Plain further south slowed them, as it took a lot of effort to clear the line and there were few good poles within it. Then, south of Newcastle Waters, most of the trees were stunted or hollowed out, so the poles were harder to find.

There was good news though. The surveyors found two reliable sources of water, one between the Elsey and Daly Waters that would 'make the whole of this piece of line easily accessible for repairing purposes at all seasons.' The other was a handy 30 kilometres south of Powell's Creek. They called it Renner Springs, after Dr Frederick Emil Renner, who had followed some birds there when looking for water.

Dr Frederick Renner

There were two doctors employed to care for all the workers on the line.

Dr Renner's practice stretched 2,200 kilometres, from Port Adelaide to the Roper River. Further north the 'government chemist and medical officer' was Dr Edward Cecil Rix.

By chance, Renner was near Frew's Ironstone Ponds when he was needed by strangers on the line. King's survey party were at the ponds in the afternoon of 29 May 1872 and were surprised at the sudden arrival of three strangers. Crowder recorded that:

... 2 men & a black boy with 1 pack & some lose [sic] horses come into camp from south ... the first man ... Anderson†,

---

* Todd, 1873.

† Chawner was a travelling hawker selling goods to the O.T.L. workers. Anderson and an Aboriginal boy about 12 years old from Macumba they called 'Jim Crow', had

was so excited that he could hardly speak … he had had no water since yesterday … he wanted to get a doctor for his mate, Chawner, who had met with a gun accident, on Monday last [two days earlier]. It seems he was on horseback and was reaching a gun from a tree, he caught ahold of it by its muzzle, and dragged it against a twig which caught the hammer & the contents buckshot was sent through his left hand*.

Figure 32: Dr F. E. Renner 1875, (SLSA, B-7938)

Chawner's hand was a mess, so he and Anderson were escorted to Daly Waters where Dr Renner was currently camped†. They described how they had been 'stuck up' by Aborigines. The exploring party, now joined by Robert Burton and Alfred Woods, were just starting for Newcastle Waters, and were glad to have a forewarning of the hostile reception they might receive. On 1 June 1872, as they crossed the Ashburton Ranges:

> … we saw 6 natives following us, & they did so until we got in some lancewood scrub when they tried to stick us up. The first fellow darted behind a bush & had his spear shipped at me, but I saw him in time & jumped off & had first shot. I am confident I hit him & he dropped his spear & boomerang & bounded along like an adder … I think 2 or 3 of them got it. One was in 10 y^{rds} of King with his boomerang but Ringwood saw him in time.‡

---

    joined Chawner to travel north. Chawner thought there was a road all the way to Darwin and would not take the advice of the surveyors not to travel in such a small party (Lewis, 1922).

*   Crowder, 1871–2.

†   Dr Renner was particularly busy in June 1872. There was another accidental shooting (Fred Moles at Attack Creek), and Stretton and King both suffered severely from fevers. It took him days of travelling between his patients to see them all.

‡   Crowder, 1871–2.

Exploring the Ashburton Ranges

The next week, Stephen King was so ill with a fever he stayed in camp. King was:

> ... struck down by ague[*] and fever at Powell's Creek. It was unfortunate, as it was arranged that he was to carry the first message over the gap between the lines—a telegram to Her late Majesty, Queen Victoria. That illness laid him up for over a year[†].

Crowder went south with Knuckey, Ringwood and a wiring party, towards Tennant Creek looking for route through the Ashburton Ranges.

They came across Chawner's cart just as it was being ransacked by local Aborigines. Charles Johnston describes chasing them away as starting 'one nigger off as if the devil kicked him'[‡].

Burton had the hawker's stock collected and kept it at 'government expense'. It was sold to the men on Chawner's behalf. Johnston bought a coat, which was handy, because the June nights were getting very cold. Crowder bought 'boots 15/-, towel 2/- and puggery 3/- (altogether £1)' from the wagon.

About this time the first Australian trans-continental message was sent. In Stephen King's absence, Charles Todd telegraphed a message to Richard Knuckey, who was near the Elsey River, from Port Darwin in late May 1872. Knuckey wrote it down and sent Ray Parkin Boucaut, with it on horseback to Tennant Creek. It was then transmitted south. The message arrived in Adelaide on 20 June 1872, a month after Todd had sent it.

The system worked well. A horse express, like the famed 'Pony Express' of the United States of America, was a good idea. The government therefore employed John Lewis, who happened to be

---

[*] Stephen King nearly died of malaria when at Fred's Pass during the Second Northern Territory Expedition in 1865 (Pugh, 2018a). His 'ague' this time, may have been a return of the disease..
[†] *The Mail*, 10 January 1914.
[‡] Johnston, 1872–5.

travelling the line with a mob of horses *en route* to establish a pastoral empire in the north*. He was joined by Ray Boucaut.

The horse express

The horse express then travelled up and down the gap in the line every few days during July and August 1872. It was hard work—in the first week of July, Boucaut rode 262 miles in 131 hours—of which 101 hours were spent in the saddle. When the riders reached either end of the line, James Stapleton, Andrew Howley, or one of the other telegraphers, would send the messages forward and write out the replies. The 18-year-old cadet, William Crowder, wrote out his own telegram—contacting his family at last, saying that all was well.

One day, Lewis carried a telegram for Charles Bagot, telling him his brother had bought Mount Margaret Station and he needed to return quickly. The linesmen also heard there was talk in Adelaide about a transcontinental railway. Information is very valuable, and Lewis's horse express was big business. The *Adelaide Advertiser* reported:

> On Monday, July 9 … 38 messages were received at the Telegraph Office for transmission to England per horse express from Tennant's Creek, thence to Port Darwin.
>
> The particulars are as follows: Adelaide, 6; New South Wales, 5; Queensland, 2; Victoria, 24; Tasmania. 1; total, 38. The value of the messages amounts to £423 11s. 9d. distributed as follows: Due to South Australia, £45; to British-Australian Company, £372 7s.; and to other colonies, £6 4s. 9d†.

Once the explorers plotted the line through the Ashburton Range, they turned back to re-join Robert Burton, who was completing about 2½ miles of poles each day. On 21 June they had a stockpile of 120 poles—about 6 miles worth, and the 'sinkers &

---

* John Lewis was already in Barrow Creek with his brother, four stockmen, 40 horses and a buggy. His plan was to take horses from Adelaide, lease Cobourg Peninsula and harvest the huge herds of feral buffalo there, descendants of stock left by the British at Victoria Settlement in Port Essington, three decades earlier (Pugh, 2020).

† *Adelaide Advertiser*, 10 July 1872.

clearers' (hole diggers and axemen) were busy indeed. Every couple of days they shifted camp as the line progressed. The ground became easier to dig. They planted 5½ miles of poles on 23 June and reached near that length every day for a while, across some easy country.

John Lewis was back on June 29 with 'half' the news. The cable had stopped working during transmission, but they heard that 'England and America were at logerheads [sic] & England had given them 24 hours to think of terms'*. Also if America was not satisfied with England's arrangements on the 'Alabama question', they would be at war. Unfortunately for those interested in this news, the undersea cable north of Port Darwin had broken, and the information stopped flowing.

On his next return, Lewis had news from the Roper River. The *Lucy* had arrived there with 'a lot of grog, potatoes & onions &c which Mr Todd had purchased, and it is now at Daly Waters, Messrs Todd, Patterson, & Rutt's party at Daly Waters, everyone spreeing there …'.

Lewis had been in contact with Mitchell, who was constructing the line northwards towards Frew's Ironstone Ponds for Harvey. Harvey turned up in Burton's camp on 1 July, and he and King planned the final route for the lines to join. They were getting close.

Lewis passed through again on 11 July, carrying £600 worth of business messages for 'different parts of Europe'. Todd and Patterson were both at the depot near the Fergusson River and the telegraph line northward was open and operational to Darwin. Unfortunately, since the undersea cable had broken on June 22, the messages would now have to be transferred by sea to Banyuwangi or Singapore.

The stress starts to show

The diaries written in the last few weeks before the connection show increased stress between the men. Todd's orders of '20 posts per mile'

---

* Crowder, 1871–2.

overruled Patterson's plans of short-cutting at '10 to a mile' to get the line up and working, with the intermediaries going in later. Todd's rule was written into the contract, and he was the boss—so Patterson had to agree. At 20 to the mile, the posts were 80 metres apart. The axemen were particularly busy in forested areas as, apart from cutting poles, a clear strip of land on each side of the line was needed for it to run through.

Each post hole had to be hand dug. The poles, with their bases scorched by fire and tops ringed by a hooped iron 'ferrule', were then erected, and the insulators installed. The wiring parties would then follow, stringing the wire to each pole in the line. A 520-metre roll of No 8 galvanised wire, weighing 51 kilograms, and specially shipped from Manchester in England, would stretch between 6 and 7 poles only, and the ends of each roll were soldered to the next one using the 'Britannia method'. Each wiring party averaged about 32 kilometres a week.

The teams were pushed hard. Some of the men were 'awfully whild'[sic], wrote Crowder, about the extra work, but Patterson promised them they would all be back at the Roper, on their way home, by 1 November. The men were tired, many of the horses were 'knocked up and dying' and 'Mr Burton is that disgusted with the gaffers that he does not care if the line is finished or not'*. Burton's poles were of 'not much account' on 19 July, as his men worked faster, and more sloppily, with only a few miles to go.

On 24 July, Ray Boucaut arrived with news that the southern wire had reached Attack Creek, three ships had arrived in Port Darwin with 300 diggers on board from Adelaide (the gold rush was gaining momentum), and Mr Todd was at Tennant Creek and had run out of tea. Could Mr Knuckey send some down to him from Attack Creek?

News then arrived every few days, from both the north and south, as the horse express gathered it at each end of the line: Lady Daly, the wife of ex-Governor Daly, died in Adelaide; America had withdrawn from their Alabama confrontation with England; there was a great

---

* Crowder, 1871–2.

row in Rutt's camp on the south line … 'rum the cause, Wiltshire, and others off the pay sheets; Bishop Shield had also died' …[*]

Surveyor Alexander Ringwood arrived in Rutt's camp on 10 August, and divided luxuries among the men: an onion, 3 apples, two or three oranges and a feed of potatoes each. Mr Hack arrived with more luxuries, including grog, which led to 'a lot of men drunk and fighting'.

Mitchell, on the southern line, had finished his poles by 12 August, but Rutt needed nine more days to string the wire. King's and Mitchell's parties were ordered by telegraph to go and help him put in some intermediate poles.

The lines connect

The overland lines finally met in the thick of a lancewood forest on 22 August 1872, some 7 months behind schedule. Crowder was then near Newcastle Waters, but he arrived at Frew's Ironstone Ponds the next day and heard that:

> … the wire was joined at 12 o'clock on plain by ours and
> Rutt's [sic] wiring parties & communication through[†].

Crowder was told that Patterson had left already for Rutt's camp. He had 'wanted to be at the joining of this great line [so] he had cut it down there [at Frew's Ponds] & another joint made, but ours & Rutt's wirers are the real joiners'[‡]. Patterson pulled rank and made sure that he was the man to make the final splice of the wire, by cutting it at Frew's Ironstone Ponds and re-joining it at the correct time. Rutt's wirers, in Crowder's view, were robbed of the glory.

But it was no easy task—once the tension of the wire was released, it was almost impossible to get the two ends back together.

---

[*] Crowder, 1871–2.
[†] Crowder, 1871–2.
[‡] Crowder, 1871–2.

'Half the party seized hold of me and the wire', Patterson wrote:

> ... and the other half the other end and stretched with all might and main to bring the two ends together. All our force could not do this. I then attached some binding wire to one end. The moment I brought it to the other end the current passed through my body from all the batteries on the line. I had to yell and let go. Next time I proceeded more cautiously and used my handkerchief to seize the wire. In about five minutes I had the joint made complete, and Adelaide was in communication with Port Darwin ...*

John Lewis, the express rider, was present, and he recorded his recollections in his memoir *Fought and Won*:

> ... On August 22, I went with Patterson and Mitchell to a point a few miles east of Frew's Ironstone Ponds, where the two ends of the wire were to be joined, connecting Adelaide with Port Darwin. We met with Harvey, who told us that the wires would not be joined until twelve o'clock; so we returned to the camp, then made for the last join, and arrived there at about twelve o'clock. At ten minutes past twelve† on August 22, 1872, the wires were really joined. Twenty-one shots were fired from our revolvers, and a bottle of supposed brandy was broken over the last post. (I think it was tea). Among those present were Messrs. Patterson, Rutt, Mitchell, Howley, Ricks, Hands, Bayfield, Hack and myself. It had long been a desire of mine to see the wire connected between south and north, and I was glad that I had seen this accomplished.‡

The very first *message* sent was probably something like 'stand by', but the first telegram listed by the newspapers the following day was penned by Dr James Stokes Millner, who was acting Government Resident in Palmerston due to Douglas's absence on the Roper River. Dr. Millner's historic telegram was tapped out by John Little and addressed to His Excellency Sir James Fergusson, Governor of South Australia. It read:

---

* Patterson, 1872.
† Some sources, including the plaque installed on the Stuart Highway memorial in 1954, state the time of the first message as 3:15 pm.
‡ John Lewis, 1922.

> In the absence of the Government Resident, I have the honor to congratulate your Excellency on the completion and opening of the Overland Telegraph line. I trust this great undertaking will increase the trade, and develop the varied resources of the colony, and prove the pioneer of still greater works, uniting more firmly the various Australian colonies to each other and them to the mother country. God save the Queen!

Then came congratulations from the government's Chief Secretary in Adelaide:

> In the name of the Government of South Australia, I beg to thank you all for the untiring exertions and energy displayed in prosecuting the important work this day satisfactorily concluded.

And to Charles Todd, waiting beside the line at Central-Mount Stuart:

> We opened the line at 1 p.m. this day as it was completed and the public from the previous notifications fully expected it to-day. I took that opportunity of sending a message in the name of the Government of this country thanking the officers and men of the Construction party for-the praiseworthy efforts and untiring diligence they have displayed in bringing to a successful conclusion this great work, under your able superintendence. Accept my congratulations that your troubles are now over. Anything you wish to say respecting the construction and opening of the line, I will take care to get published in tomorrow's papers

Todd had considered what he wanted published in the papers already, so he sent his reply immediately:

> Many thanks for your kind congratulations on the completion of the Adelaide and Port Darwin Telegraph, which, as an important link in the electric chain of communication connecting the Australian colonies with the mother country and the whole of the civilized and commercial world will, I trust, rebound to the credit of South Australia, and amply repay her for the great outlay she has incurred in its construction by advancing her material interests and prosperity, notwithstanding the delays and mishaps which have occurred on the northern portion of the work. We have

this day or within two years from the date it was commenced, completed a line of 2,000 miles long through the very centre of Australia a few years ago a terra incognita and supposed to be a desert, and I have the satisfaction of seeing the successful completion of a scheme I officially advanced 14 years ago[*].

Congratulatory messages from the mayor, senior public servants, consuls of a dozen or more foreign kings and queens (Norway, Holland, etc), and empires such as Brazil, then dominated the line the whole afternoon—each of them printed for the public in the newspapers of 23 August.

In the bush, maintenance crews were needed on the line, and teams were established to remain behind and continue their work. It didn't take long—'the line was down for three days at Charlotte Waters in late August'[†].

W.J. Cunningham, the acting Superintendent of Telegraphs in Adelaide, offered members of the press the chance to observe 'the wonderful steadiness and precision with which the Adelaide and Port Darwin telegraph line works':

> Shortly after 3 o'clock we repaired ... to the operating-room where one of Morse's self-registering instruments was placed in direct communication with Port Darwin. The length of the wire is computed at nearly 2,200 miles so that, to complete the circuit of the magnetic current, a distance of something like 4,400 miles—more than half the diameter of the globe—had to be traversed. Nevertheless, the batteries worked as freely, as powerfully and as instantaneously as if they were simply telegraphing to Port Adelaide.
>
> For upwards of half an hour, a lively conversation was maintained with the Port Darwin operator and with most of the leading men of that sparsely inhabited community who, to the number of nearly half a dozen, speedily flocked to the scene of action.
>
> And the first topic of conversation? The weather.
>
> ... but the conversation speedily diverged into such friendly chit-

---

[*] *The Express and Telegraph*, 23 August 1872.
[†] Todd, 1873.

chat as might pass between two persons meeting in the street. We need scarcely add that it was 'not intended for publication'.

… Among other questions, the Port Darwin operator was asked what o'clock it was, and whether he received the time signal dispatched daily at 1 o'clock from the Adelaide Office to all the South Australian Stations. He replied that the signal duly reached him and that the then time was twenty-one minutes past 3. The transmission of the whole of this question and answer occupied from first to last exactly twelve seconds*.

Twelve seconds as opposed to weeks of hard travel! It was an astonishing triumph of technology—so Adelaide partied.

Back to the Roper

A telegram came through on 2 September and the news spread fast: the *Omeo* would be at the Roper River Depot on 27 September. Anyone going home needed to be there by then. Luckily, travel between the line and the Roper was now easy because the road was dry and the creeks were low. Crowder travelled with Ringwood and Mitchell. They led a bullock team across the plains and arrived at the Roper River Depot without any major difficulties on 14 September. At one point they met some drovers led by D'Arcy Uhr. They had brought 144 cattle from Queensland belonging to the Northern Territory's first pastoralist, Matthew Dillon Cox, and they were on their way to Port Darwin.

After few days at the depot, they travelled downstream on the *Young Australian* to Maria Island to await the *Omeo*. They spent the next fortnight resting, cutting wood, collecting oysters, reading, and fishing.

While waiting, Captain Douglas arrived on the *Claymore*, with surveyors McLachlan and Packard. He spoke to the men of the gold found at Yam Creek, and convinced some of them to travel overland

---

* *Observer*, 24 August 1872.

with Dillon Cox's cattle and try their luck on the gold fields*. He ordered George Deane to take the government horses back to Palmerston and allowed the aspiring miners to join Deane and ride the horses to Yam Creek. One of them was William Brock who then discovered gold at Brock's Creek and enjoyed more than 20 years of success in his mine, until he was killed when his buggy tipped over while crossing a creek in 1896†.

The *Omeo* dropped anchor off Maria Island on 9 October 1872, and the men boarded and set sail for Port Adelaide two days later. Then, after a month at sea, Charles Todd met them on the wharf in Port Adelaide to give them rousing speeches of welcome and thanks, and train tickets to the city.

Like many others, William Crowder, the diary writer, had been away for 16 months. Crowder arrived home just before his nineteenth birthday‡.

The O.T.L. was in full operation.

Some of Crowder's contemporaries had remained behind in the Territory to work in maintenance parties, or man the repeater stations. James Stapleton and Charles Johnston were two who enjoyed full employment and postings to the telegraph stations. Unfortunately, as we shall see, both their careers were violently cut short.

---

* Douglas was tempted by the gold. It was not long before he had resigned as government resident, and joined the rush (Pugh, 2019).

† Brock's Creek developed into a thriving town. By 1886, Brock's Creek had the largest Chinese population in the Northern Territory—at one time it was reported to have reached 400. The township had its own railway siding and was officially gazetted as a town on 5 May 1898. There is little to be seen there today, apart from the old cemetery and a modern gold mine. William Brock is buried in the Brock's Creek Cemetery (*NTTG*, 19 September 1896).

‡ William Crowder never worked for the Telegraph Department after that. He had a career as a commercial traveller and married Isabella Brown in Strathalbyn during July 1878. They had at least three children—a daughter Margaret in 1881, a son in 1884 and another daughter in 1889. Unfortunately, Crowder's life was not long. He died in 1891 at the age of 37.

Gallery
Adelaide

Figure 33: Telegraph lines in Grenfell Street, Adelaide. The growth in the use of the electric telegraph was unstoppable, 1883 (Sweet, SLSA, PRG-742-5-17).

Gallery

Figure 34: King William Street, Adelaide, looking south, 1885 (Sweet, SLSA, PRG-742-5-30).

Figure 35: King William Street, Adelaide. Telegraph lines were strung down both sides of the street, 1905 (Ernest Gall, SLSA, PRG631-2-464).

Figure 36: 1872: Telegraph Office Operators' room in the Adelaide Telegraph Office, 1872 (SLSA, B-8026).

Figure 37: 1902: Telegraph Office Operators' room in the Adelaide Telegraph Office. More operators were needed as telegraph traffic increased, 1902 (SLSA, PRG-280-1-1-44).

Gallery

Figure 38: The Port Adelaide Telegraph Office, 1900 (SLSA, B-22765).

Palmerston

Figure 39: The B.A.T. Offices in Palmerston, c. 1885 (W. Barnes, LANT, ph0238-0388).

Figure 40: Staff from the Palmerston Overland Telegraph office in 1886. Written on back: 'Back row L-R. 1 Albert McDonlad, 2 Tom Morris, 3 Temporary officer, 4 Fred Killian, 5 Florence Bleezer, 6 (…) Burgoyne, 7 Dudley Kelsey, 8 Jim Shanahan, 9 Fred Price, 10 A.P. Ward, 11 George Reid, 12 Mr Lawrie, 13 Percy Bryant. Front row L-R, 1 Mr Cleland, 2 Cecil Marsh, 3 John G. Little, 4 Ted John, 5 ?', 1886 (LANT, ph1134-0001).

Figure 41: Telegraph lines along the Esplanade in Palmerston pass the government offices and court house to the Telegraph and Post Office (marked with a flag), 1915 (LANT, ph0781-0033).

Figure 42: By 1920 the number of telegraph lines had increased in Palmerston. Mitchell Street and the Club Hotel (Bill Littlejohn Collection, LANT, ph0386-0140).

Chapter 7
Life on the O.T.L.

Adelaide

Life in Adelaide probably changed little at first. When the Overland Telegraph Line was connected in August 1872 there was still no quick communication with the world. However interesting it was to hear the news from Darwin or Alice Springs, the South Australians were still waiting for a full international connection. In the days before the undersea cable was repaired, the excitement grew, and everyone listened out for news and information from Europe. Finally, the newspapers breathlessly announced:

> … We are rejoiced to be able to announce that definite intelligence has at last arrived respecting the submarine cable between Port Darwin and Java … the Telegraph Department authorises us to state that the through line between Adelaide and London will be available for public traffic this morning at 9 o'clock. South Australia is to be congratulated upon being at length able to utilize to the full the wire running through the centre of the Continent, and the whole of the colonies upon being actually as well as nominally in telegraphic communication with Great Britain[*].

That evening the city put on a 'jollification'. Bells, music, and fireworks from the top of the post office tower, and a dozen rockets from Montefiore Hill, announced to the entire population that something important was about to happen. They:

---
[*] *Adelaide Register*, 21 October 1872.

> ... set the Albert Bells a-ringing, and for hours the ear of the public was assailed with their discordant notes. When the ringers had rung themselves faint, Schrader's Band took up the running ... and drew together an excited audience, chiefly consisting of juvenile ragamuffins.

Then, at last:

> ... the cable from Port Darwin to Java has found its voice and is speaking with a rigour which warrants the belief that it is anxious to make up for lost time ... on the Tuesday it broke silence, and it has been talking volubly ever since ... the first message, directed to Melbourne, was flashed through; and after this the telegrams came thick and fast. The Governor, the German Consul, the Mayor of Adelaide, and other notabilities did themselves the honour of sending complimentary messages to the crowned heads and a few uncrowned heads in Europe. Next day came the replies, breathing the extravagant gratification of the senders at being privileged to shake hands with South Australia. Among the crowd, Governor Kennedy (of Hongkong) and the Governor of the Straits Settlement sent their congratulations, sagely hoping that the completion of the line would have a tendency to cement the union between their Provinces and, this. His Excellency (who, by-the-way, is, with his usual ill-luck, absent from Adelaide) has despatched cumbrous replies, reciprocating the kindly wishes of his imperial, gubernatorial, and official correspondents for the future of the colony[*].

From then on, the newspapers were full of European news, proudly announcing that it was just a day or two old. The news item, plus hundreds of congratulatory telegrams between VIPs, were passed along the single galvanised steel telegraph wire across the continent of Australia, under the seas of the world within insulated cables,

Opposite page:
This telegram, from 23 October 1873, show the range of news transmitted—from horse-race winners to the name of the new mayor of London. It didn't matter—the people were hungry for any news.[†]

---

[*] *Kapunda Herald*, 25 October 1872.
[†] *The Evening Journal*, 23 October 1872.

ADELAIDE TO LONDON TELEGRAPH. TELEGRAPHIC DESPATCHES. Bombay, October 21, 16.25, September 29 to October 22, 1872. GREAT BRITAIN.

The Church of England Congress at Leeds has closed after a highly successful meeting. The Bishop of Salisbury has advocated a comprehensive spirit of indulgence towards Church differences and demonstrated the impolicy of ecclesiastical litigation. The Bishop of Salisbury at the distribution of prizes at Manchester expressed the opinion that the Oxford local examinations was the best movement that had ever been instituted in England for the encouragement of popular education. The number of candidates examined was 3,500. An important Conference of Nonconformists has been held at Birmingham. The resolutions passed were in favour of the disestablishment of the Church of England. Sir John Wauchope, Sir Stirling Maxwell, Sir Alexander Grant Ramsay of Kidalton, and Principal Tulloch, D.D., have been gazetted the Board of Education for Scotland. Sir Charles Wentworth Dilke in a speech at Glasgow has denounced class legislation. The Czarewitch Stakes were won by Salvanas, Silver second. The Enfield Cup was taken by Roy. The Middle Park race resulted in a dead heat between The Kaiser and Surrin, and the stakes were divided. Ontargis came third. Baron Hatherley, the Lord High Chancellor, has resigned his office in the British Cabinet, and Sir Roundell Palmer has been appointed his successor. Sir Roundell Palmer has been gazetted as Baron Selbourne. Mr. Justice Willes has committed suicide. The act is attributed to an attack of gout on the brain. The Hon. George Denman, Q.C., has been appointed to the vacant Judgeship. Sir William Maynard Gomm has been appointed Lord High Constable of the Tower of London. Alderman Sir Sydney Headley Waterlow is the newly elected Mayor of London. For the Tiverton Section the candidates are Massey in the liberal interest, and Waldrun Conservative. The Conservatives will contest Richmond, vacant by Sir R. Palmer's creation as a Peer. The Right Hon. Sir W. R. Seymour Vesey-Fitzgerald contests Horsham in the Conservative interest, Aldridge withdrawing. Robert Cunliffe has been elected member for the Flint Boroughs. The reported outbreak of the rinderpest in Lincolnshire has been contradicted. The foot and mouth disease is rapidly spreading in Yorkshire and Warwickshire. The Scotsman states that the harvest in Scotland has been the most disastrous since 1816. The bakers' strike has collapsed. Four thousand Liverpool dockyard labourers have struck work, and a lock-out is threatened. five thousand colliers in Staffordshire and a large number in Wales, in order to avert a lock-out, have resolved upon submitting their demands to arbitration. The great slacking of orders in the iron and coal districts has induced the iron and coal masters at Cardiff to resolve upon meeting the claims of their workmen by entering into a combination to close their works within four weeks. The colliery proprietors at Oldham have raised the price of coal 5s. per ton. The coalmasters of Glasgow have reduced their rate to 31s. per ton for shipment. The Darley Wane Coal Mine at Barnsley has been on fire and has in consequence been closed. The revenue of Great Britain for the quarter ending September 30 amounts to £15,812,000. The National Debt has been reduced by a million and a quarter. The exports from Great Britain for September reached £23,125,000. A special Cabinet Council has been held to discuss the proposed Anglo-French Treaty. The signature of the parties to the treaty is imminent. The American Consul at Zanzibar has received a letter from Dr. Livingstone, dated Unyanyembe, July 2, extolling the energy of Mr. Stanley and his kindness towards him. Sir George Pollock has been interred in Westminster Abbey.

and through numerous nations between London and Adelaide. Some items were relevant and interesting, others mundane, but as only one message could be passed at a time, the telegraphists were suddenly extremely busy. In the first week, 152 cables were sent to Palmerston, and 148 received in Adelaide (at a rate of 42 per day)[*].

The O.T.L. cost nearly four times the expected amount, at £470,720, but Adelaide was now Australia's centre for telegraphic communication. The country was jubilant:

> ... no one will ever know the full measure of the difficulties and privations that the men engaged upon the construction of the Trans-Continental Telegraph line have had to put up with. The very rapidity with which the work has been completed is calculated to create an erroneous impression as to the obstacles that have had to be surmounted and the risks that have had to be run. The men who have stretched the electric wire across the continent have had to do duty as explorers as well as telegraph constructors and are conscious that had they not been of resolute spirit they would have succumbed to the pressure of the hardships and discouragement to which they have been exposed. Especially is this true of the parties who for nearly two years have had to 'rough it' within the tropics bearing up under delays and disappointments, the inclemencies of the season, and the apprehension of falling victims to the attacks of fever and scurvy, to all who have assisted in the enterprise but to the last in particular, South Australia owes a debt of gratitude which she will never be able to repay[†].

People were used to telegraphed news travelling between South Australia and the eastern states, of course, so the novelty was short lived. Up-to-date international news and information rapidly became the norm. People were only reminded of its importance when there were breaks in the line and it was 'down' for a time. In January 1873, Todd reported that between 21 October 1872 and the end of the year, there were 835 messages from Australia, and 1,008 to Australia

---

[*] Pike, 1971.
[†] *Sydney Morning Herald*, 16 November 1872.

(an average of about 26 each day). South Australia held receipts worth £2,271, which, Todd estimated, meant an income of around £12,000 a year, plus £300 per month for local traffic[*]. Telegrams were not cheap. In 1873, a 20-word telegram between Adelaide and Darwin cost £1, but the same message to London cost nearly 10 times that.

When the voltage on the line was weak, messages were transferred, or boosted, by the repeater stations as they arrived, and the line was open 24 hours a day. The telegraph stationmaster and his assistant took it in turns to work the Morse key. Other men had ancillary duties—there were cooks, animal caretakers, and linesmen. The remote stations were staffed by a workforce that was reasonably mobile. John Kelsey, for instance, worked at a number of stations in the Top End, although some men stayed in their positions for many years. The Alice Springs Telegraph Station was particularly remarkable for the longevity of its stationmasters. Between 1872 and 1932, only eight men held the position:

1872–79	Johannes Mueller
1879–87	Ernest Ebenezer Flint
1887–92	Joseph Skinner
1892–99	Francis J. Gillen
1899–1908	Thomas Bradshaw
1908–16	John McKay
1916–24	Frederick Price
1924–32	Ernest Allchurch[†]

Adelaide, of course, had many more telegraph lines, and therefore many more telegraph officers. Photographs of the streets of the city show them festooned with cables, and each one of the cables meant an operator sitting at his Morse key, receiving, or sending telegrams.

---

[*] Todd, 1 Jan 1873.
[†] Ernest Allchurch was Thomas Bradshaw's brother-in-law. He had already worked in Alice Springs for nine years from 1902.

Batteries and handsets

The telegraph system relied on electricity. The role of each telegraph station was to boost the power in the galvanised steel cable, and the electricity was provided by large banks of chemical batteries. Known as Meidinger Cells, they were made of glass, stood about 25 centimetres tall and produced electricity from the chemical interaction between copper sulphate crystals and a solution of magnesium sulphate on zinc and lead electrodes. Each cell produced about one and a half volts of power, and to run the telegraph line at 120 volts, large numbers of batteries were needed at each station. At Daly Waters, Fred Goss:

> … built racks for the batteries, which aggregated 350 Meidinger cells. A section of these batteries was renewed each week in such

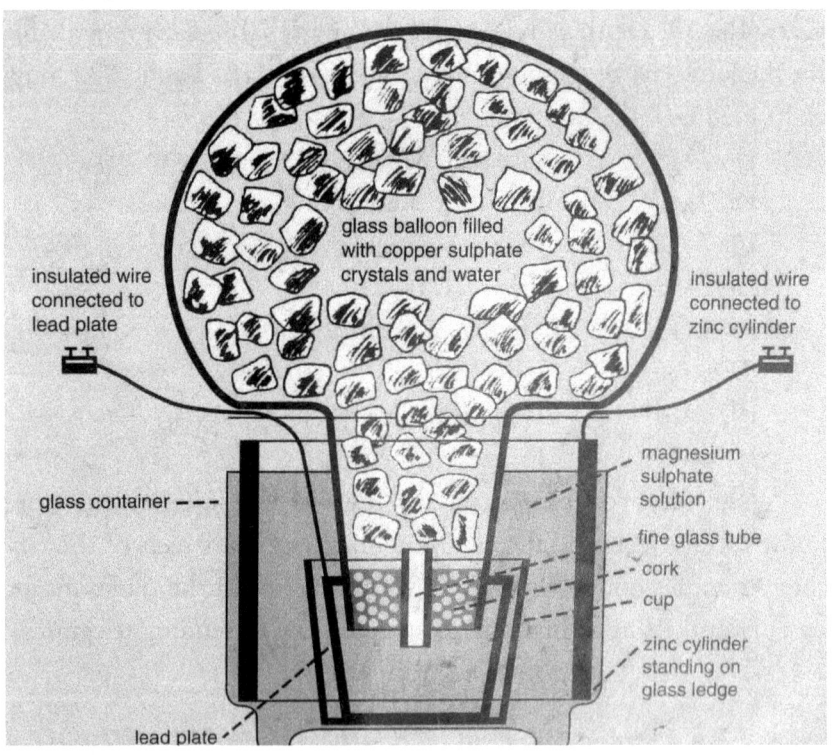

Figure 43: A Meidinger Cell: electric current is produced by reactions between copper sulphate and magnesium sulphate. From the Alice Springs Telegraph Station display board, 2021.

a manner that at the end of four months, the whole had been renewed, thus maintaining them at a level strength …*

There were only 150 batteries in Port Augusta. They could be replaced more easily in the port town:

> … In the battery room are two sets of sixty cells each, for the Port Darwin, and Western Australian lines, and one set of thirty cells, for the line to Quorn and Hawker.†

Maintenance of the batteries was a key role of the station staff, and it took up much of their time. Oddly, batteries are rarely mentioned by writers from the time, despite the fact that they must have been very difficult to transport, continually needed servicing, and required huge amounts of replacement chemicals. Doris Bradshaw, who almost never went into the battery room as a child, asked Leslie Spicer, an old operator, how 500 batteries were maintained in Alice Springs:

> … The batteries consisted of wet cells, each with a glass jar containing a solution of water and magnesia and a lead and zinc plate. Fitting neck-down into the top of each jar was a bottle containing copper sulphate, commonly known as bluestone. A small glass tube in the cork of the bottle allowed drops of copper sulphate to fall on the lead plate, which gradually became coated with copper. Insulated wires from the zinc and copper enabled the hundreds of cells to be linked together, thus generating a constant supply of power. Every few months the batteries were recharged with the addition of new copper …‡

Morse code

The early nineteenth century saw huge leaps in the understanding of electricity. Electro-magnetism was first discovered by Hans Christian Ørsted in 1820, and the electromagnet was invented by William Sturgeon in 1824. This led to lots of experiments and playing with electricity that finally produced an electric telegraph in 1837. It was

---

* Goss, 1956.
† *Port Augusta Dispatch*, 12 August 1882.
‡ Bradshaw, 1965.

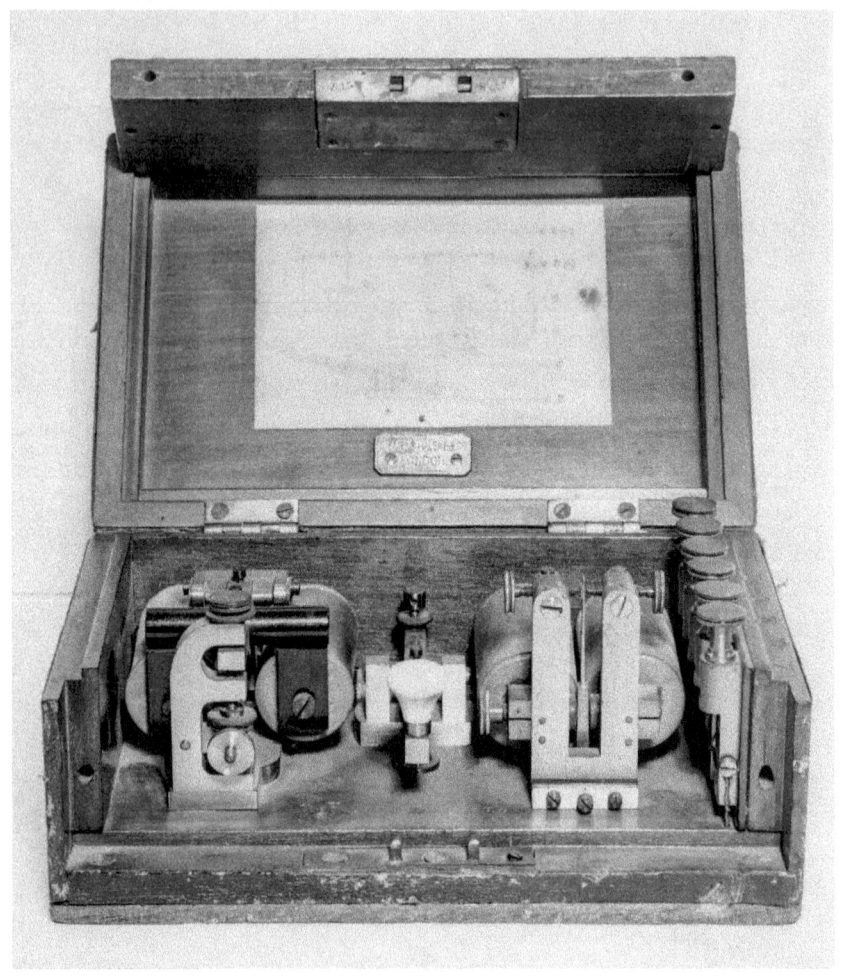

Figure 44: The Morse key used by Sir Charles Todd when the Overland Telegraph Line was joined in 1872 (SLSA, B-78443).

used on the London to Birmingham Railway with a code that relied on various word lengths, and one version even printed the letters.

An American artist named Samuel Morse, who was friends with a physicist, Joseph Henry, and an engineer, Alfred Vail, developed a code system that could be sent electrically using only electric pulses and the silence between them and print a physical representation of them on paper tape. Morse's code sent only numerals, and the receiver would have to look up a code book that listed words by number. It was Alfred Vail who invented a code that represented all 26 letters, using a variety of short and long sounds and silences. This became known as American Morse code, and it was used successfully on American railway networks.

The receivers were more clever than that, however. They learned a more efficient method by learning to read the code from the audible clicks made by the machines. They then wrote the messages out by hand, and the paper tape was no longer needed.

In 1848, a German telegrapher named Friedrich Gerde designed an even more efficient code, limiting the system to just two sounds, a 'dot' and a 'dash', and it was this system, which became known as International Morse Code in 1865, that the operators on the Overland Telegraph Line became so adept at using.

The code was later easily transferred to radio, and ever since has been a series of dots and dashes. A skilled operator can read more than 40 words per minute.

The Kelsey brothers and The Shackle

The large Kelsey family arrived in Port Darwin on the *Birch Grove* in July 1873. John George Kelsey had joined the gold rush and brought his wife and children to settle in the gold fields. Instead, he found employment in Palmerston. Among other occupations, he became a gaoler at the Fannie Bay Gaol and later was a clerk for the Palmerston District Council.

Two of Kelsey's sons were destined to have long careers on the O.T.L. and one of them, Dudley Evan Kelsey, who was a lad of eight when they first arrived in Palmerston, wrote a memoir on the 25 years he lived in the Territory and his career on the Line[*].

In 1880, when he was about 15, Dudley followed his elder brother John ('Jack') into the Telegraph Department as a messenger boy. Two years later, he took a job as Jack's assistant at The Shackle

---

[*] *The Shackle*, published by Ira Nesdale in 1975.

Telegraph Office. It was Dudley's first appointment out of Darwin, and when he arrived:

> ... the population [of Yam Creek] consisted of seven government officials (3 police, a goldfield's warden, the Medical Officer, Dr. Wood, my brother, myself). Others were Mrs Ryan [proprietress of the hotel], Miss Freeman [her sister], and a few Chinese gardeners*.

The Shackle was a part of a small mining town†. It was named after the 'shackle' installed on the line that allowed Morse operators to link a hand-instrument into the network. The tiny town had, at various times, a police station, a hotel, a miners' hospital, and the gold warden's office and other facilities. Without its establishment, local miners would have to travel many miles to send or receive telegrams. Eventually stations were built at Southport (in November 1873), Stapleton, Adelaide River, and Pine Creek, because the O.T.L. repeater stations, at an average of 250 km apart, were too distant for practical use for many on the gold fields.

Dudley Kelsey described the origin of The Shackle Telegraph Station in a letter to *The Advertiser* in 1927:

> ... Yam Creek is a mile north of Sandy Creek, and as both these places were unsuitable for a station, a site was chosen a mile south of Sandy Creek on a small open space surrounded by hills, and in a picturesque locality. A telegraph operator was stationed here, and lived in a tent, erected under the telegraph

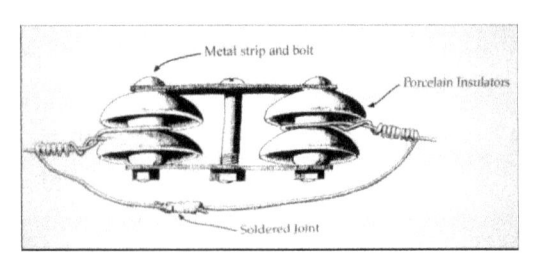

Figure 45: A telegraph 'shackle' (NT Heritage, 2014).

---

* Kelsey always used the name 'Darwin' in his memoir rather than 'Palmerston', as it was then officially known.
† The April 1881 census counted 96 Europeans, including three women, and 807 Chinese men and two Malayans living in the region of The Shackle (Donovan, 1981).

Figure 46: The Shackle Telegraph Station. Two telegraph poles can be seen on the left, 1879 (Foelsche, LANT, ph0001-0029).

line, at a 'shackle,' and the wires were brought down from the shackle into this primitive office, where a considerable amount of business was transacted. The people of the district (and eventually everyone in the Northern Territory) always alluded to the place as 'The Shackle', and although when the new station was built, it was named Yam Creek, everyone called this place 'The Shackle,' and does so to the present day*.

In 1885, Dudley Kelsey was transferred to the telegraph station at Southport, under Joseph [Joe] McLean William Johnston, J.P.†, who was also an assistant Customs Officer and coroner. Southport was a strategically important transport hub during the construction of the O.T.L., the railway, and the gold mines. Its telegraph station was connected to the O.T.L., but with the coming of the railway, it was already a shadow of its former self. It was finally abandoned as the

---

* *Adelaide Advertiser*, 24 Feb 1927.
† Aka 'Johnstone' … Joe was the brother of Charles Johnston, who appears later in this story. The Johnston brothers were John Little's brothers-in-law.

rails bypassed Southport entirely in 1889. Similarly, Yam Creek was superseded by the new town of Burrundie as the Palmerston–Pine Creek Railway was built:

> ... A new township has recently been surveyed at a bend of the McKinley River, named Burrundie. Some of the allotments were offered for sale at the Land Office, Palmerston, on Thursday, 11th December 1884. The new township will be the Government headquarters at the Reefs, and the Warden's Office, and Police Station have been removed from The Shackle, Yam Creek. The Post Office and Telegraph Office will also be removed to Burrundie. The new township has also been selected as the site for the Goldfields Hospital, which is now built, and will in all probability be open by January 1886[*].

When Dudley Kelsey arrived in Southport, the town boasted a single hotel run by Sam Brown, and three stores in the centre of town that were branches of Palmerston businesses: Adcock's (adjacent to the jetty), Jolly's (next to Adcock's) and J.P. Allen's (across the road). Two Chinese stores also remained open along Kersley Street: Sun Mow Loong's (on lot 222) and Quong Wing Lee's, next door. A saddler named George Bright worked in Cherry Street, near a blacksmith named George Gawthorn, and a wheelwright named E. Marker. On Barrow Street, the telegraph and the police stations were still manned—the latter by Constable Robert Stott[†]—and the Southport Chinatown consisted of about 100 homes on the southwest side of the town, next to the Blackmore River[‡].

Kelsey complained that Southport was 'rather quiet', except when the steam launches from Port Darwin and the inland coaches arrived. The Southport office was not a repeater station, so not even passing telegrams broke the monotony.

---

[*] Solomon, 1885.

[†] Robert Stott served at Southport, Burrundie, Katherine, Borroloola, was sergeant of the Mounted Police in Alice Springs, and then Commissioner of Police, Centralian Police Force. He was killed after being hit by a train in 1928, aged 70 (Kimber R. G., 1990).

[‡] Duminski, 2005.

The town was livelier in the wet season, as teamsters would camp there until the roads dried out. Kelsey writes of picnics, fishing trips, sporting events such as cricket games against teams from Palmerston and playing the accordion for the occasional dances at the hotel*.

Dudley was relieved from the social whirlwind of Southport in 1886 when the young assistant telegrapher who had replaced him at The Shackle, Waldemar Holtze†, shot and killed the Chinese cook in the neck when 'skylarking' about‡. Holtze was the 17-year-old son of Maurice Holtze, the government gardener and had been appointed just a few weeks earlier. The death was a tragedy—but luckily for Waldemar, the inquest brought in a verdict of accidental death, and he subsequently enjoyed a 60-year career on the O.T.L. He was stationed at Powell's Creek (7 years) and Daly Waters (30 years), and from 1930, was postmaster at Tennant Creek. He retired to a homesite on a 5-acre lease, 5 km from Powell's Creek Telegraph Station and lived there in an iron shack. He was, however, back on the job for a few years during World War 2§. He died in Darwin in 1963 at the age of 94, leaving numerous Aboriginal descendants¶.

Jack Kelsey needed to run the station without an assistant for a while after the shooting, and this meant it was unattended when he was away repairing or checking the line. This caused outrage:

> … during his absence telegraph communication between the country districts and Palmerston has been impossible. Men have ridden thirty miles from the Union to The Shackle, spent days waiting for the operator to return, and then had to ride another thirty miles back to their camp without being able to send important telegrams. Such a state of things is a disgrace to the community, and we very much doubt whether the Government is not equitably responsible for any losses arising

---

* *Northern Territory Times and Gazette*, 24 April 1886. Kelsey, 1934.
† Waldemar aka Wladimir, Vladimir or 'Wallaby' Holtze (c. 1869–1963).
‡ *North Australian*, 21 May 1886.
§ *The Argus*, 2 February 1953.
¶ Bisa, 2016.

from their neglect in not having any officer in charge of a telegraph station[*].

In time, Dudley arrived to help out and remained there for nearly two years. When his brother got married in 1888, Dudley transferred to the Daly Waters Telegraph Station. Jack Kelsey, however, stayed at The Shackle until it closed down. Its only value in the end was said to be the tin on its roof, and that was removed and recycled.

Jack was highly regarded. In 1887, the local community gathered around him and presented him with:

> ... a purse of 50 sovereigns ... as a mark of respect and regard. It is not often that a prophet is appreciated in his own country, but the above is an exception to the rule. We can remember no instance of a testimonial being presented to an officer in the Government service where the recipient has more thoroughly deserved the compliment[†].

Joe Johnston was sent to Pine Creek when Southport closed, and Dudley Kelsey moved there with him for a while, as his assistant, but managed to get a transfer back to Burrundie so he could marry the sister of the hotel owner, Miss Freeman[‡]. He was therefore again working with his brother, and he must have felt at home—the station building was the old Southport station, dismantled and hauled there by bullock wagon.

The new couple set up home in one of the railway cottages. Their son, Frank, was born in Burrundie and in 1891, the family transferred to Darwin for several years, and then Katherine for several more. The family finally left the Territory in 1901 and returned to South Australia[§]. Dudley then worked for 17 years as a telegraph officer in the Adelaide office. He then retired to a vineyard at Watervale and

---

[*] *North Australian*, 3 April 1886.
[†] *Northern Territory Times and Gazette*, 12 February 1887.
[‡] Sister of Mrs Ryan, who eventually built the Victoria Hotel in Smith Street, Palmerston.
[§] John Little's inspection report of 1901, says that Kelsey, his wife, and their son, were returning to Adelaide because of ill-health (*NTTG*, 30 August 1901). He was replaced in Katherine by George Stanley Rattray (ex-Port Darwin and Powell's Creek) who was married to Blanche. Rattray died in 1908, age 30.

died in 1953, aged 88. His memoir was retrieved from the files of the South Australian archives and published by Ira Nesdale in 1975*.

Jack Kelsey was an employee of the Telegraph Company for 33 years. His last position was telegrapher in Pine Creek in 1889, just as Alfred Pybus and a wiring party installed the second telegraph line on the poles†. Eventually, in 1906, ill health caused him to seek medical help in Adelaide but, unfortunately, he never made it:

> ... On the day the steamer left, Mr. Kelsey looked so wretchedly ill and weak that many of his friends—who had gone on board to bid him good-bye—were impressed with the belief that he would never live to reach Adelaide, and as is known, this fear proved to be only too correct ... After leaving Thursday Island ... At midnight on the 15th the doctor was called, and the patient passed away at 5 o'clock on the morning of the 16th, being quite conscious almost until the time of death‡.

The ship paused off the coast of Fife Island in the Torres Straits for Jack's funeral. The entire ship's company accompanied his body ashore and buried him. His grave, which could be seen from the sea, was marked with a wooden cross and a white azalea, and 'creeping plants'. The words on the cross simply said:

SACRED TO THE MEMORY OF J. E. KELSEY, WHO DIED ON BOARD THE S.S. EASTERN, OFF CAPE WEYMOUTH, 16TH MARCH 1906, R.I.P.

Travellers on the Line

Maintenance crews were needed to continually monitor and repair the line. In the first five years of operation, there were 118 days when the telegraph did not operate because the line had been interrupted 51 times, somewhere along its length. The telegraph operators easily identified the stretch of line where the breaks occurred when messages

---

* Kelsey: *The Shackle*, published in 1975 by I. Nesdale.
† *North Australian*, 10 August 1889.
‡ *Northern Territory Times and Gazette*, 20 April 1906.

to and from neighbouring stations failed. After a break, the station on either side of it would send out a repair party to fix it, and most breaks were repaired within two or three days. The reasons for the interruptions were most often short circuits between the insulators and the poles ... 'Insulators off, line touching pole' ... 'Line touching lightning rod' ... In the northern section, particularly in the wet season of 1877, many insulators and poles were struck by lightning.

> **Overland Telegraph of South Australia.**
>
> Port Darwin Station,
> May 4th, 1883.
>
> OFFERS will be received up to noon on MONDAY, MAY 14th for the following work on the Overland Telegraph :—
>
> Clearing undergrowth from Port Darwin to Roper Creek, 252 miles.
> Cutting and erecting any new wooden poles required between Port Darwin and Roper Creek.
>
> Specifications and full particulars can be obtained at any Telegraph Station.
> The lowest or any tender not necessarily accepted.
>
> J. A. G. LITTLE,
> Senior and Inspecting Officer.

Figure 47: Maintenance of the line was on-going. John Little regularly advertised for maintenance crews (*NTTG* 19 May 1883).

For example, between Yam Creek and Southport on 8 December: 'Lightning broke five insulators and line touching pole'*.

Floods washing poles away, and fires burning them were also problems. So too were Aborigines who discovered that the insulators could be fashioned into useful spear points: 'Natives broke insulators, wire touching iron poles' Todd wrote in his report, but interference from Aborigines was rare—it was recorded just six times between 1875 and 1878. Lightning, floods, and fire were the major causes of disruptions[†].

The O.T.L. Station staff were required to pass all messages on that came from either direction, so the line was usually busy. The staff sometimes did not understand what they were resending, as many messages were encrypted. Many operators found everyday life in the stations monotonous, and much preferred the regular line inspections they were asked to do. Each station along the line was responsible for about 200 miles of it and needed to regularly inspect it to either repair it or mark it for the contracted maintenance team.

---

* Todd, in Ferres, 1878.
† Ferres, 1878.

Figure 47: A horse team in operation in 1885 (NLA, nla.obj-420571715).

Figure 48: A camel train arrives in Alice Springs, c. 1890 (SLSA, B-1434).

Figure 49: Camel team in Alice Springs, 1907 (SLSA B-21913)

As well, the isolated telegraph stations as far as Powell's Creek relied on horse teams reaching them from Port Darwin for their annual re-supply of food, equipment, and the mailbags. The more southern stations used camel trains from Beltana (and eventually Oodnadatta) for their supplies. The teams would take up to four months to complete their journey, leaving after the end of the wet season, and their arrival in the stations was the 'greatest event of the year.' The mailbags would contain letters, packets, and papers from home and friends and books that would be read and re-read. Stations ran their own cattle and sheep, and meat was the basis of their diet. However, sugar, flour, rice, and salt were brought by the travelling teams, and if the stations ran out, they just had to go without.

In 1873, Charles Todd advertised for cartage operators to tender for a three-year contract for:

> ... cartage in the Northern Territory: Southport to Telegraph Station, River Katherine, six tons (more or less) per annum. Southport to Telegraph Station, Daly Waters, fourteen tons (more or less) per annum. For a term of three years, commencing from April 1st, 1883. subject to the following conditions:
>
> 1st. Tenders to state price per ton of two thousand two hundred and forty pounds (2240 lbs) dead weight. Each and every package will be weighed by an officer of the Telegraph Department in the presence of the contractor or his representative. No weight by measurement allowed.
>
> 2nd. The distance by telegraph line from Southport to the river Katherine telegraph station is one hundred and sixty-five (165) miles, and from Southport to Daly Waters telegraph station three hundred and thirty-one (331) miles. These distances are to be accepted as correct[*].

There were 16 stringent conditions set by Todd, covering everything from the size of tarpaulins to a 'bond for the due fulfilment of the contract in a sum not exceeding twice the amount of the annual payment'. The contractors were also required to pay a £40 surety,

---

[*] *Northern Territory Times and Gazette*, 5 March 1873.

Figure 50: Bob Carew, a telegraph linesman, up a pole near Alice Springs. Two shackles are in the lines, where an operator could connect a Morse hand instrument. Climbing aids were bolted to the Oppenheimer pole, 1921 (Laver Collection, SLSA, PRG-1365/1/133).

which they could lose if a single parcel were mislaid or damaged. Nevertheless, there were cartage operators willing to take them on, and the slow system worked well.

With all these travellers, the road beside the line was remarkably busy. Hawkers, maintenance teams, O.T.L. staff, and cartage operators continually moved up and down its length. Then came the drovers: Alfred Giles, after his role in building the line, began a meat supply business. In a single drove that took more than a year, he brought 7,000 sheep and some horses from South Australia to the northern stations. Near Barrow Creek, he suffered the loss of nearly 2,000 of his flock overnight after they ate poisonous plants, but for a while at least, the stations he passed were well stocked.

Maintenance men undertaking their inspections in isolated stretches of the line were obviously vulnerable, but 'as a rule, the natives gave the linesmen no trouble', although it was 'necessary to be on guard constantly against treacherous, surprise attack'. Kelsey, writing fifty years later, recalled such an attack just once, when camping on the Fergusson River:

> ... I sat with my rifle across my knee through the silent hours but was overcome with tiredness and fell asleep and knew no more until hurriedly roused by [Joe] Barwis. I saw him on his knees with his rifle poised—then he fired. Several blacks disappeared in the long grass, fleeing towards the river. Barwis was awakened suddenly by a feeling that all was not right, and when he looked about, he saw the blacks crawling towards us through the night. We looked to see if his shot had taken effect, but couldn't find anything, but if Barwis hadn't awakened in time, we would have been massacred.*

Fortunately, very few attacks were made by Aborigines. They were well aware of the danger of the white men, and they mostly stayed well away.

Having said that, several times Aborigines crossed the white men's line. Their motives can only be guessed at—perhaps they were

---

* Kelsey: *The Shackle*, published in 1975 by I. Nesdale.

Figure 51: Skeletal remains of a Chinese man who died of thirst next to a telegraph pole, 1914 (SLSA, Searcy Collection, PRG-280-1-16-36).

seeking revenge, were resisting the arrival of strangers in their lands, had been offended by white men breaking traditional laws, or were responding to interference with their women. Or perhaps they just wanted food and equipment. Whatever their motives were, several of the O.T.L. workers were to pay a high price for being on Aboriginal lands.

There were other dangers. Some travellers, looking for work or adventure, were not prepared for the distances involved or the paucity of water, and many found themselves in trouble. One way to get help in emergencies was to cut the line. This would interrupt it and within a short time, station staff would turn up to make repairs. Few travellers carried the tools necessary, however, and some died without finding help. Fred Goss recalled that when he was at Daly Waters:

> ... Foot travellers headed the list of men in distress, generally trying to interrupt the line to bring relief. We had many such calls for assistance, but I knew of none that succeeded. In my own time one man, named Little Coffee, walking from Port Augusta to Darwin, attempted to cut the line, south of Daly Waters, but had apparently left it too late. It was seen where he had tried to climb a pole, and fell, striking his head on a stone, leaving blood and hair on it. He was dead when the party, who was going to The Katherine, found him.*

Remote area mounted policemen could also be relied upon by travellers to look for lost white men. However, it did not always end well.

---

* Goss, 1956.

Mounted Constable John Shirley

The Barrow Creek Telegraph Station lies within the lands of the Kaytetye people, and for young men, newly arrived from Adelaide, it must have seemed very foreign indeed. When Richard Watson and Ernest Ebenezer Flint first saw Barrow Creek, it was a camp that many of the O.T.L. had used as a base—including Charles Todd—during the construction time. Their first accommodation was a temporary hut with a grass thatched roof, but at least they had protection: a police officer, Mounted Constable John Charles Shirley, was then stationed there.

Watson was, nevertheless, still wary of the Aborigines and 'had no confidence' in them. He told the *Times* that:

> ... the blacks had behaved in a threatening manner on several occasions to people who were out looking for horses; and he therefore kept them at a distance from the station and was very careful about his firearms*.

Several events suggested that Watson was being wise. In August 1883, a teamster named J.E. Martin was speared and killed when travelling along the telegraph lines near Lawson Springs ('30 miles north of Powell's Creek'):

> ... The blacks attacked our camp at the Lawson Springs at about 10.30 on the night of the 29th ult. and killed my mate (J. E. Martin) to the best of my belief, as there was no visible signs of life. They tried to get both of us, only I woke up in time to save myself and my mate from being burned as well as killed. Please send me some assistance as soon as you can. My cook and wagons are right. J. Rees August 31.

> Mr. Jones, assistant at Powell's Creek, and two men left Powell's Creek yesterday afternoon ... Arrived at wagons 11.30 last night, loading all night. Went to Springs this morning with Rees and saw J. E. Martin; skull smashed in just above forehead on right hand side; face covered with blood ...†

Constable Shirley was sent to investigate with a party of seven: Alan M. Giles, George Phillips, John Rees, Arthur Phillips, James

---

* *Northern Territory Times and Gazette*, 27 February 1874.
† *Northern Territory Times and Gazette*, 1 September 1883.

Figure 52: Barrow Creek Telegraph Station, 1885 (LANT, ph1035-0055).

Hussey, and two 'blackboys' (Gumen and an un-named man).

About the same time, Harry Readford, the manager of Brunette Downs Station, and some stockmen were rumoured to have been attacked by a band of Aborigines and were either lost or speared to death. Shirley's rescue party of 8 men and 18 horses were also expected to find them.

Then Shirley and his police party were themselves attacked:

> ... At forty minutes past 3 on afternoon of Monday, October 1, about twenty-one miles east of North Newcastle, during temporary halt, party were suddenly attacked by large body of natives, including offenders against whom warrants are issued, whose tracks party had followed since September 22 last. Natives first threw a boomerang, which struck tracker's horse, and immediately advanced towards party, throwing spears and yelling. Party mounted quickly, and as natives would not halt for parley were compelled to use firearms in self-defence when the natives retired into dense hedgewood scrub, followed by party, when natives threw spears in the air, so that they fell amongst party, fortunately without inflicting injury. Being unable to move through scrub at more than a foot pace, natives escaped without any arrests having been made. Party had to push on for water.
>
> Rees and Blackboy Gumen recognised all the offenders amongst natives except Nambina, who may have been present, but was not seen. Cannot state effect of firing, but believe the offenders, second and fourth named in descriptive telegram, were severely wounded. Believe quite seventy natives were present. Their tracks have gone past here ... in southerly direction.*

---

* *The Express and Telegraph*, 5 October 1883.

Alan Giles was asked about rumours of the attack on Readford and his stockmen, and his answers were readily printed by the *Adelaide Observer*:

> ... yes, heard rumour of murder of Mr. Readford's party but think it must be some distance east of Attack Creek, as Mr. Shirley and myself, with the police party from Tennant's Creek, left Mr. Readford and party camped on Attack Creek, about ten miles east of line on September 5 last ...*

It turned out Readford was alive and well, but the rescue party was not so fortunate. They were last seen on 4 November and all but two of them perished of thirst about 25 kilometres from Attack Creek. Alan Giles survived, rescued by his Aboriginal colleague, Gumen, who came back for him with water while he lay dying.

The next February, Giles returned with Mounted Constable William Willshire to find the bodies. They recovered Shirley's, but Rees, Hussey, and the Phillips brothers were never seen again. Shirley had written some letters in his last hours:

> ... Travelling allowance is due to me for all the time I have been out, please pay it to my mother, also give her and my sisters and brothers my dying love; I am too weak to write anymore; I died in executing my duty. (Signed) J. C. Shirley.'

On another paper addressed to Mr. Michael, Barrow Creek, he says:

'Good-bye, old man, remember me to all on the line. J. C.'.†

Shirley was 27 years old. According to the Police Association of South Australia, he was the first policeman to die in the line of duty in the Northern Territory.

James Stapleton

A 38-year-old Canadian telegrapher with a pet monkey named Jacko was the first officer in charge of the Katherine Telegraph Station, in 1872. For James Stapleton, Katherine was a 'plum position', but

---

* *Observer*, 6 October 1883.
† *Chronicle*, 23 February 1884.

eventually he planned to return to Adelaide, where his wife was raising their four children alone. In the meantime, as he was a skilled officer with a great deal of experience, he was sent to Barrow Creek Telegraph Station to relieve Richard Watson.

Most of the remote telegraph repeater stations had a staff of six—a stationmaster, an assistant telegrapher, general hands, linesmen, and a cook. Usually, one or more of them organised the planting of vegetables to improve their diet. This did not work everywhere, and several officers were sent to Adelaide on sick leave from the telegraph stations. Perhaps any vegetables planted at Barrow Creek failed to survive, because on a diet of mutton and flour, Watson's time there was cut short when symptoms of vitamin C deficiency started to show. In November 1873, he returned to Adelaide to recover his health and James Stapleton was sent to replace him:

> … Mr. Stapleton has been removed to Barrow Creek in the place of Mr. Watson; and Mr. Johnston, from Powell's Creek, will succeed Mr. Stapleton*.

James Stapleton held a different view to his predecessor regarding the Aborigines. He was one of the earliest arrivals among the telegraph workers in the Northern Territory†, and had mostly positive experiences with Aborigines at all of his postings. When he arrived at Barrow Creek, he was happy to issue rations for the old people and employ others in return for flour—as all the stationmasters were permitted to do by Todd.

Figure 53: James Stapleton, c. 1855 (SLSA, B-19711-1).

---

* *Northern Territory Times and Gazette*, 7 Nov 1873.
† Stapleton and another, Andrew Howley, were early enough, in fact, for both of them to have creeks named after them by McMinn in the region that later became the gold fields.

Stapleton made a point of only giving flour to fit and healthy men if they worked for it. On the morning of 22 February 1874, he refused flour to a number of Kaytetye men who were demanding it without reason. This is often given as the cause for what happened next, though the truth is by no means certain*. At about 8 p.m. that night, the staff were smoking, and relaxing on the station veranda after a blistering hot day. Without warning, the Kaytetye men returned:

> … all the white men, with some friendly natives, were sitting outside the Telegraph building at the time of the outrage, and the blacks rushed upon the party suddenly—some coming from one side of the building and some from the other. The first spear which struck Mr. Stapleton went through his body, and after that there were three spears driven into his bowels. The man Frank† was speared through the heart and died at once. Mr. Flint was speared in the thigh; and the black boy was struck by three spears.
>
> No provocation had been given to the natives, beyond the circumstance that Mr. Stapleton had refused flour to several of them—telling them that unless they worked, they could not receive flour.‡

Most of the telegraph workers managed to take shelter in the station. Linesman Alex Murdock, blacksmith James Maddock and a Chinese cook named Si Jin were unscathed. An Aboriginal lad named Jemmy, from The Peake in South Australia, was wounded, but pulled to safety through a window of the station. Mounted Constable Sam Gason, a new arrival at Barrow Creek was there too. They quickly found their weapons and began to shoot. Some of the attackers were hit, Gason later thought mortally, and the warriors moved off. The

---

* Another reason was given by T. G. H. Strehlow, who heard from elders that because the tribe couldn't take out revenge on white criminals who had abducted and raped their women, they decided to punish the only whites in their vicinity (Kimber R. G., 1991).

† John Frank was originally employed at the Tennant Creek Telegraph Station in 1872.

‡ *Northern Territory Times and Gazette*, 27 February 1874.

next morning, they were seen a short distance from the station, and the men in the station again fired on them—several were seen to fall.

Inside the station, the wounded men lay in great pain. John Franks had been killed outright with a spear to his chest. Ernest Flint was 'speared in the leg, and the wound penetrated to the bone at a distance of seven inches below the hip'.

Flint frantically tapped out a message to Charles Todd in Adelaide. Todd called in Dr Francis Gosse, who sent instructions via Morse code to the men about how to deal with spear wounds.

Jemmy, the 'civilised black boy', had been hit a half inch below the right collarbone in his side, and his right hand was badly torn. Flint told Todd that he thought both he and Jemmy would recover, and under the telegraphed instructions of Dr Gosse, he kept the other wounded men awake all night 'for fear the spears may have been poisoned'*.

James Stapleton was the most badly wounded. He had a spear through his groin that had perforated his bowel. Both blood and faeces leaked from the wound, so it was not long before blood poisoning took hold and he slowly deteriorated. He died at 9.45 p.m. on 23 February, after sending a final message to his wife and children by telegram: 'God bless you and the children', it said.

Both Stapleton and Franks were buried outside the station. Their graves can still be seen, but there are no memorials to other innocent men who died as a result of the 'Barrow Creek outrage'—and there were many. The calls for revenge started quickly. There was a:

> … necessity for prompt and decisive action. In the first place it is incumbent upon them [the authorities] to exhaust every means of bringing the perpetrators of this gross outrage to justice …

And:

> … promptness in punishing the murderous outrage committed by the blacks was the only means likely to be effectual in dealing with the affair†.

---

* *Evening Journal*, 23 and 24 February 1874.
† *Telegraph*, 26 February 1874.

The Police Commissioner, George Hamilton, ordered punitive action. Trooper Gason, a survivor of the attack, was on the spot and he was told to gather together a posse. Teamster Jack Bond and five men were known to be nearby, and a stockman named Cowen turned up unexpectedly with cattle, with two offsiders. Three linesmen, led by Charles Tucker, heard of the attack and immediately travelled to Barrow Creek to help—riding 130 km in 24 hours*. The posse was easy to put together—they were ready to go hunting eight days after the attack.

> … Trooper Gason has received authority to press into service all white men whom he can find, and when he has obtained a sufficient force to proceed to the arrest of the murderers. The blacks in large numbers are still in the neighborhood, and a fight is inevitable. But we need have no fear as to the result. A dozen well-armed Europeans will be more than a match for hundreds of natives with their rude weapons, which are powerless at a distance. We can hardly expect that many arrests will be made, but a punishment will doubtless be given to the blood-thirsty rascals, which will be remembered for years to come.
>
> A heavy blow well struck now may prevent the striking of many blows in the future. We hope Trooper Gason is not hampered by too many instructions. He is a man of experience, who knows the ways of the blacks, and a great deal ought to be left to his discretion. He is on the spot and will probably best know how to deal with the murderers†.

A heavy blow was indeed struck. Gason's posse rode out early to look for the guilty men. They shot several Kaytetye men near Taylor Creek, and more over the next few weeks wherever they found them. Gason admitted to shooting 11 men. Historians have determined that more than 50 people were likely to have been killed by the revenge party‡. Skull Creek, 80 kilometres south of Barrow Creek, is named after the bleached bones found there long after the massacre. In the words of Alex Ross, son of the explorer John Ross, 'they were just

---

* Traynor, 2016.
† *Telegraph*, 26 February 1874.
‡ Hartwig, 1965.

blacks sitting in their camp, and the party was looking around for blacks to shoot". Nobody was arrested.

Ernest Flint had been appointed to Barrow Creek from Adelaide in 1871. Then only 17 years old, Flint recovered from his wound, and his career on the line lasted 16 years. In fact, he spent eight years as post and stationmaster in Alice Springs, until he died there of rheumatic fever, in the arms of his young wife[†], in July 1887[‡].

The murders and the retribution massacres were a travesty, and a blight on the success of the O.T.L. Luckily, there were not many incidents as bad as these. The Aborigines were outgunned and must have known they were in trouble—the destructive changes brought by cattle and the other hard-hooved animals meant that the resources their ancestors had relied on for millennia were degraded. It was already getting harder to live off the land as their ancestors had, and many people had no other choice than to move close to white settlements in search of flour and other goods. In 1883, Todd could report that there were few problems caused by Aborigines to the O.T.L.:

> … The natives, principally about the Newcastle Waters, where they are very numerous and treacherous, at one time frequently damaged the line breaking the insulators, the fragments of which they used for spears; the binding wire was converted into fishhooks, and the iron footplates of the poles were dug up, broken, and made, with much ingenuity, into tomahawks, of which I possess some very creditable specimens. We now distribute fishhooks and a few cheap tomahawks to friendly natives for occasional service rendered, and wilful injury to the line has become a rare occurrence …[§]

Unfortunately, Stapleton's and Frank's murders were not the only killings on the line.

---

[*] Hill, 2003.
[†] Florence Flint (nee Madeley) and Ernest Ebenezer Flint married on 26 January 1887. Florence was the first white woman to live at Alice Springs Telegraph Station (from May until July 1887), but her new husband died of rheumatic fever seven months after they married. She returned to England (Traynor, 2016).
[‡] *North Australian*, 23 July 1887.
[§] Todd, 1883.

Charles Johnston

In the early days, the only accommodation at Powell's Creek was a temporary hut. Eventually, building materials were brought from the Roper River Depot and a stone complex was constructed. The temporary accommodation—little more than a collection of tents and shade structures under a shackle on the line—was ready just two days after the line was joined. Charles Johnston was the stationmaster with a hand-held Morse key. He was assisted by Tom Dyke who had worked as a teamster and linesman on the O.T.L. but was quickly building up skills as a telegrapher. Helping them were general hands Bill Loxton and Andrew Hume*, cook Aveling Wilson, and shepherd George Curtis.

Johnston's diary of the months following their arrival is thin. Life settled into a daily rhythm and the weeks passed as the men cut timber for the station house and thatched grass for its roof. The hut went up quickly. The veranda was completed in the middle of November, just as the wet season arrived. Heavy thunderstorms broke above them, and all the local creeks filled to the banks.

The telegraph line was particularly busy on the day in November when celebrations were held for the O.T.L. in London, Adelaide, and Sydney. The operators knew all about the huge public banquet honouring Todd and the O.T.L. workers held in Adelaide. 'Banquet msgs' were flying back and forth all day†.

When the line broke south of Charlotte Waters a few days later, the operators could rest a little. Johnston walked out after rain and shot a 14-pound bush turkey and started on a vegetable garden. The

---

* Andrew Hume was a rogue with an interesting story. After leaving the telegraph, he was arrested and imprisoned for horse stealing, but released in 1874 because he claimed to know where Ludwig Leichhardt's expedition had come to their lonely end and was willing to mount an expedition to prove it. But 'fifty miles from Drynan station on the Wilson River ... Hume, the explorer ... perished for want of water. O'Hea, another of the party, is also supposed to be dead ...' *Brisbane Courier*, 30 November 1874.

† Johnston, 1872–5.

Figure 54: Powell's Creek Telegraph Station, 1903 (SLSA, B-9854).

workers were sent to bring back their horses, but none were found for three days for they had 'crossed the range' and it was weeks before they were all gathered.

Johnston was asked if Dyke could 'read by sound and manage pocket instrument', and if he was ready to be promoted to stationmaster. He could and was, so he transferred to the temporary Elsey Telegraph Camp near Warloch Ponds*, which was to be opened during the wet seasons. He was paid 7 shillings per day.

Very few of the locals had been seen near Powell's Creek Station, but on 30 November two friendly men turned up. Johnston gave them some bread and mutton, an old axe they could use to get native bee honey, and some strips of 'magenta flannel'. Curtis the shepherd gave them a handkerchief and two old hats.

Johnston made several attempts to befriend local Aborigines. The cultural differences were huge, but with increased traffic along the line, vulnerable flocks of sheep and cattle herds (and a gradual

---

* For aviation history buffs: Warloch Ponds (aka Warlock Ponds) is where Ross and Keith Smith (1919), and other early aviators, first landed after leaving Darwin.

degradation of traditional hunting grounds), it was essential that the white men kept peace with the Aborigines.

He was not always successful:

> ... This morning I rode up to 3 mile camp—and there suddenly came upon 3 darkies at a case of insulators which they had broken open and were employed breaking them up, they made off at a run my dogs intercepted one of them and pulled him down I am sorry to say, they gave him a severe mauling and would have very quickly have killed him had I not beaten them off—the poor devil could not walk away at once, but having tried to make him understand I did not want to hurt him, I left him and went to the horses which I found alright near handy, exchanged horses and returned to where I left the darky but he had gone. I had no revolver with me and the ground being very boggy I did not feel comfortable so near them, as if they chose, they could easily surround me, a horse could not get over the ground faster than a slow walk*.

George Curtis and Johnston did not get on well, and as time went on Curtis refused to do anything more than the bare minimum. Loxton and Johnston began to shoulder most of the work of the station. Hume was still there, but ill much of the time, and off salary anyway as he planned to leave. They built stock yards and planted vegetables and melons, killed the occasional sheep, and hunted ducks, turkeys, goannas, and magpie geese for their dinners. For Christmas dinner they ate teal and mutton, currant, and raisin pudding, with a pale sherry wine and watermelon for dessert.

In January, the line was 'making earth' somewhere between the Tomkinson River and Renner Springs, so Johnston and Loxton rode out to check it and meet up with Thomas Bee†, coming from the other direction with the mail. They were away for three days and travelled more than 160 kilometres (100 miles) in the mid-summer heat. Johnston's dogs followed them, and one nearly died from the

---

* Johnston, 1872–5.
† Thomas Bee was a cadet with Goyder during the 1869 survey of Darwin. The rural area of Bee's Creek is named after him. He became a telegraphist at Tennant Creek in 1876.

Figure 55: Powell's Creek Telegraph Station c. 1895 (SLSA, B-61434).

heat after just 14 kilometres (9 miles). Johnston said he 'bled her & carried her' on his horse to Ringwood's Creek.

Horse troubles continued. They had to be able to graze freely—there were too many to hand feed—but a riding horse could take hours to track each morning, and more than a few of the horses ate poisonous plants. On 15 January, they needed horses to send to Attack Creek to help with bullock hunting and went out to catch some, but 'found none but dead ones' being eaten by wild dogs. They caught some healthy horses the next day and rode to Renner Springs for an overnight stay.

The line was working badly. Dyke caught several men about to cut the wire near No. 1 Well, but no damage was done. Nevertheless, for days the line worked 'very weakly'—often the senders would have to repeat messages before they were understood. 'Humbug on this line intolerable' wrote Johnston on 28 February, expressing his frustration. It was also affected by lightning and once Johnston was driven from his post at 11 p.m. when he considered it too dangerous to be attached by a wire to the electric line.

Rumours and news spread quickly along the line. The remote operators heard that Davies had been 'treacherously' speared at the Roper River landing by 'nigs' when they were caught stealing. On 21 January, they heard that 50 or 60 natives had attacked Tennant Creek station. Fortunately, these were 'false yarns.'

Figure 54: Tennant Creek Telegraph Station, 1933 (A. Ball, SLSA, B-16578-12).

Johnston's younger brother, Joe, was also on the O.T.L. In 1873, he was an operator at Charlotte Waters and Charles kept in regular contact with him. He was distressed to hear that Joe had developed scurvy and needed to return to South Australia as soon as he could be relieved*. The vegetable garden at Powell's Creek was a success, with onions and radishes now joining the melons, so scurvy was not a problem for Charles Johnston.

Everyone knew what was happening along the line. For example, in March 1873 a fault occurred somewhere near the Katherine Telegraph Station. James Stapleton set out along his section of the line to Edith River to look what was causing the problem but found the rivers flooded. He isolated the fault as being between the Fergusson and Cullen Rivers but couldn't get there. He ran out of rations and returned to Katherine without repairing the line, enduring a terrible time with mosquitoes in the bush. He suffered an attack of the 'ague' (malaria) on his return, so it was not until 30 March—over a week later—that he was able to try again. Every other operator along the line had no choice but to wait. It took a few weeks until the problem was solved, and the line then worked 'uncommonly well' or, as Johnston repeated over a few days in his diary, 'splendidly'.

---

* He was relieved by Joseph Bowley, stationmaster at Strangways Springs Telegraph Station, from the end of March 1873.

The operators of the stations and their supporting staff—all men—were isolated indeed, but their diaries are full of information about each other. Jim Aldridge at Daly Waters was a 'near' neighbour of Powell's Creek staff, as was Charles Tucker at Tennant's Creek[*], just 181 kilometres (123 miles) away. Sometimes, when the line needed maintenance, or mail needed transferring, the teams would leave home and meet each other halfway.

Teamsters and drovers continually moved up the line, pushing sheep or cattle, and they would rest for days at each station en route. Within the 318 kilometres (198 miles) between Powell's Creek and Daly Waters was a 130-kilometre (80 miles) dry stage, so animals needed to be in their best condition to cross it. As the road improved, drays were used to carry water tanks for the men and horses, but the bullocks and sheep had to last the distance.

Thomas Hassell was a drover who took stock up the line in April 1873. He stopped at Powell's Creek for several days and played cards and chess with Johnston. His drove was slowed down by rain when the ground became too heavy for his wagons, but he was 'a very pleasant fellow' and a 'very welcome & agreeable acquisition to the limited but select society of WK!'[†]. He was sorely missed when he moved on.

Abram Daer was a teamster and linesman based at the Daly Waters Telegraph Station from May 1873. He arrived there after being stuck at the Strangways River for some days, carrying news of a man drowning in the Roper River:

> ... James McEwen[‡] was drowned while crossing a creek which flows into the Roper about two miles from the Depot camp. He was in front of his horses, and it is not known if he was

---

[*] Charles Tucker was later stationmaster at Barrow Creek.
[†] Johnston, 1872–5.
[‡] James McEwen was listed in the original group sailing from Adelaide with Patterson in 1871. At the time of his death, he was a part of Richard Knuckey's metal poling and maintenance crew that arrived at the Roper Landing on the Lord Ashley in March 1873. His body was buried next to Daniel Kavanagh's, and 'Mr. Ellis read the burial service at the grave' (*The Adelaide Advertiser*, 14 July 1873).

taken with cramp, or if he was kicked or knocked down by the horses; but he fell down, and before help came, he was drowned*.

Daer carried the mail from the Roper south towards Newcastle Waters while Loxton travelled north to meet him. They arrived in time to help Thomas Hassell, who had become bogged in the corduroy crossing at Newcastle Waters. He then returned to his chess games with Johnston, to wait for the road to dry out.

Charles Johnston's diary stops at the end of 1873—its sequel is perhaps lost—but several loose pages pick up his story on 16 June 1875. He had been sent to Katherine in November 1873, after James Stapleton was transferred to Barrow Creek to replace Richard Watson. A year or so later, he transferred to Daly Waters Telegraph Station, where the staff included Abram Daer and general hand Charles Rickards. His career on the O.T.L. had already lasted more than four years. His brother Joe had returned to work as the stationmaster at Yam Creek, and Matilda (Mattie), their sister, was married to Postmaster-general John Little. The O.T.L. was therefore a family affair.

In late June 1875, Johnston, Daer, Rickards, and two Aborigines travelled to the Roper River area 'in order to look after some Government horses and cattle which were known to be straying in that locality'†. Johnston's last entry on the diary's loose pages was written in the afternoon of 28 June 1875:

> … Good start made reached McMinn's Table 12 o'clock—met a great number of natives & more of them joined us at our camp—very friendly—dist' about 13 miles.

The next entry was written in a different hand—either that of Daer or Rickards:

> Monday 29 June. Came on the Bar Charlie went for a swim when the Blacks speared him his entrails came out did all I could for him, but he died.

Daer and Rickards were also speared. Daer survived long enough

---

* *The Adelaide Advertiser*, 14 July 1873.
† *Observer*, 17 July 1875.

Figure 57: Daly Waters Telegraph Station, undated (Carl Schultz Collection, LANT, ph0315-0065).

to write a report on the happenings on the river that was published in the *Times* on July 14, 1875:

> Had a pleasant trip down to McMinn's Table, where we met the natives. Went into the Roper bar on June 19; natives very quiet to all appearances, some of them riding on waggon [sic]. After dinner Mr. Johnston and one of the black boys he took from here went to have a swim, leaving Rickards working about the camp. Whilst I was down for water, one of the natives in the camp suddenly speared Rickards without the slightest warning. Heard him shout out, and ran to Mr. Johnston, who was in the water, to tell him to look out.
>
> I was too late; he had already been speared by a black named Pompey and was trying to wrest a second spear from the natives. I rushed at the former, and on seeing me he bolted. Unfortunately, I had not any revolver; the pouch of mine having broken that day, I had to leave it in the camp. Seeing the natives apparently so friendly, I did not think it necessary to carry it. While rendering assistance to Mr. Johnston, who was severely wounded, a native—I believe the one that had speared Mr. Johnston—came round with his spear shipped to throw at us. I got Mr. Johnston's revolver, but it missed twice.

He then threw the spear at me, and I dropped on the ground, thinking it would pass over me. Unfortunately for me it did not but struck me on the bridge of the nose. I was now able to get a shot, but from excitement missed him. He then bolted.

Rickards had also come at once to Mr. Johnston's assistance; his revolver was unfortunately on the waggon. The natives tried to intercept us, but on firing at them with Mr. Johnston's revolver, they bolted and did not show up after that.

In regard to the black boys who went down with us, one I believe was quite innocent; but the other, the youngest I think, was aware that an attack was going to be made on us, but I believe he was afraid to warn us. They were forced by the others to leave us. The youngest took all his things away during the attack, but the other took nothing, and I think was beaten by the natives to get him away. After getting to the dray, I stitched up Mr. Johnston and Rickards's wounds as well as I was able; but being badly wounded myself, could not do much. Mr. Johnston suffered a great deal during the night and threw up a good deal of blood. Gave him some tea in the morning, which he drank. He also drank a deal of water during the night. About a quarter of an hour after he had the tea, he asked me to fill his pipe, and smoked a little, but gave me back the pipe, remarking he could not keep it alight, and a few minutes afterwards he died very quietly.

It is a matter of great grief to us that we were unable to bury him, neither of us being able to use a pick or shovel. We rolled him in two flys and an oilskin and left him at the foot of a tree, which was all we could do for him. We immediately started back for the Daly with seven horses—three we left at Cotton Creek—bringing the waggon and everything else up except a gun and an axe, which the natives got[*].

Daer and Rickards were both severely injured, and travel by cart back to Palmerston must have been excruciating. They:

> … had great trouble in getting back, every jolt of the waggon giving Daer intense pain. He can scarcely move, as all the muscles in the back of his neck have contracted, and his head is very sore; he can hardly bear his hat on. The spear went in just by the bridge of his nose, penetrating about three

---

[*] *Northern Territory Times and Gazette*, 14 July 1875.

inches. He extracted a piece of the spear through the roof of his mouth. Rickards's wound is about three inches long, just below the right nipple. The spear, a stone one, went into the cavity of the chest, and there is still a small discharge and small hole at one end of it[*].

A *Times* correspondent screamed for revenge:

Much sorrow is felt here at the murder of poor Johnston and spearing of his companions by the Roper natives, and we look to the Government to take immediate and stringent measures to punish his cowardly murder. They would be equally as bad here if it were not for our numbers, and they could get the opportunity, as it is, we have constantly to be on the watch, as they keep prowling round the camps, and rob our tents every chance they get. If the Government would grant us a few weeks' carte blanche, just to impress upon their minds and bodies the rewards they may expect for murdering and plundering their white brethren, I fancy it would be some time before they would forget the lesson or require a second teaching[†].

Inspector Foelsche sent out Corporal George Montagu to track down the murderers. He could not officially take revenge, as the press desired, but was happy to permit his officers to use any force they required. He told Montagu to 'have a picnic with the natives':

… I cannot give you orders to shoot all natives you come across, but circumstances may occur for which I cannot provide definite instructions …[‡]

Arrest warrants were carried for four named suspects. There was also a warrant for 'those unknown', which Foelsche included to act as a loophole, permitting the party to arrest anyone they thought guilty. No one thought that there would be prisoners. As the *Times* went on to say:

… Nevertheless, we have no fear of the result. The corporal is armed with warrants for the arrest of four blacks on a charge of murder—Pompey, Alligator Johnny, Jemmy Miller, and

---

[*] *Northern Territory Times and Gazette*, 17 July 1875.
[†] *Northern Territory Times and Gazette*, 24 July 1875.
[‡] Reid, 1990.

Ural. This sounds very English, but we fear the grandeur of English law will strike very little terror into these sable vagabonds. We feel quite sure that they will not deliver themselves up, and we feel equally sure that the party will save themselves the trouble of bringing them prisoners such a distance to serve no sensible purpose.

The police party was joined by a posse of O.T.L. workers who went under the authority of Charles Todd, who was shocked that three of his staff had been attacked. John Little led the posse himself, and it grew to consist of more than ten heavily-armed men, all of whom were intent on revenge.

Charles Johnston was John Little's brother-in-law. Little was the senior telegraph officer in Palmerston, responsible for the northern section of the line and the employment of the telegraph workers. Nevertheless, he made time to be involved in a lengthy campaign of revenge.

A third group of nine white men had already passed through the area before the official parties arrived. They were travelling drovers returning to Queensland, led by George de Latour and William Batten. These men took it upon themselves to 'teach the natives a lesson'.

The official parties met at Warloch Ponds, near the Elsey Creek. They then rode overland from the O.T.L. to Leichhardt's Bar on the Roper River where Johnston's body had been left wrapped in a tarpaulin under a tree. They found his remains:

> ... in a small gully, about 200 yards from the camp, the bones being picked quite clean by wild dogs. They were able to recognise the skull by the teeth. They burnt all the long grass, and made a strict search, but only succeeded in finding part of the bones. These they buried on a rise near the camp. They also found a pair of his trousers, saturated with clotted blood, and torn to pieces with wild dogs.*

Little found a letter buried by de Latour and Batten, and in a public telegram from Daly Waters a few weeks later, informed everyone that they:

---

* *Northern Territory Times and Gazette*, 18 September 1875.

... arrived at Leichardt's [sic] Bar, August 2nd, all well, and without seeing any natives on the way down. Found notices dated July 10th and 24th from Wm. Batten and party (9) en route to Queensland, stating that they found Daer and Rickards' notice notifying murder of Mr. Johnston also that they found natives mustered strongly at Mount McMinn. They dispersed them and did their best to avenge Johnston's death.*

The 'dispersal' must have been a shocking sight. In the nearby camp, Corporal Montagu found 'a large quantity of human bones ... lying in a heap'†. They also found a body with a bullet wound through the chest. De Latour, Batten and their seven colleagues had apparently surrounded the camp, shot every Aborigine they could, and burned the bodies‡. There were no official reports of how many died—but surely someone must have counted them ...

The *Flying Cloud* made a slow trip of four weeks from Port Darwin and arrived on 20 August, about a week after Montagu and Little's party. At the mouth of the Roper River, Captain Marsh met two Aborigines—Ural and Peter—and welcomed them on board as guides. They 'rendered Captain Marsh great assistance in pointing out rocks and other difficulties in the river'. Nevertheless, and unfortunately, because the name 'Ural' had been mentioned by Daer as one of the murderers, Ural was arrested on 21 August, and chained to the front of the *Flying Cloud*.

In the meantime, Little's party joined the spree. They tracked and gunned down two 'chiefs named Abareeka and Harry Byng' at

---

* *Border Watch*, 25 September 1875.
† *Advertiser*, 24 December 1874.
‡ Despite their apparent involvement in this massacre, George de Latour (aka de Lautour) and William Batten both have streets named after them in the Territory because they were two of the first drovers bringing cattle into the Territory. But perhaps justice was done: George de Latour became a government agent in Queensland's 'Kanaka' slave trade in the New Hebrides and was killed by Aore Islanders in 1890, and Batten was clubbed to death by Aborigines on 2 December 1877, near the Calvert River in Western Queensland (*Morning Bulletin*, 22 January 1888).

Harris Lagoon, about 11 miles below the old depot. They were killed because, Little said in justification, they were 'attempting to escape'. Others were 'dispersed'. They:

> ... were seen a little lower down, but they got away in the long grass. Some lubras and children were found same afternoon near Mount St. George, but they were not molested ... on 22nd natives were seen twice, but they got away in long grass on banks of river ... on August 29th a party on foot attacked a native camp on the north side of the river under Calder's Range, and dispersed the natives, but none were killed. A lot of spears were obtained, and camp burnt ... On August 30th nine lubras were captured east of Hawk's Nest Island but were released immediately without being molested*.

Not surprisingly, any surviving Aborigines in the area disappeared into the bush.

Not everyone was happy with Little's report. Government Resident Scott, who had been away at the Adelaide River when Little's party set off from Palmerston, later considered laying charges of murder on the shooters, but nothing ever came of it.

Ural's treatment after his arrest suggests his punishment started immediately. He:

> ... was leg-ironed and handcuffed, and a large chain was then put round his neck and made fast at both ends to the deck, the weight of which he had to bear day and night. He lay on the deck, exposed to the fierce rays of the sun by day and the heavy dews by night, without the slightest effort being made by the police to afford him relief in his torturous position; and had it not been for Captain Marsh's kindness and the attention of the volunteers, I doubt if the man would have reached Port Darwin alive.†

The *Times* had no sympathy, even for the man chained to the deck in the tropical sun. Rather, they lamented the cost of bringing back a prisoner:

> ... It is a great pity an arrest should have been made, for the trial of Ural will put the country to expense, and give him a

---

* John Little, 13 September 1875.
† *Northern Territory Times and Gazette*, 1 January 1876.

chance—a slight one, it is true—of escaping punishment. It would have been better to have made an example of him on the spot, in the presence of the niggers themselves*.

Abram Daer died of his wounds on 7 August 1875, 39 days after he was speared. Luckily for Ural, Charles Rickards recovered and stated at Ural's trial that he did not recognise him. In fact, Ural was a short man who did not even slightly resemble the spear thrower, who was taller than six feet. It seems his name was common in the region—there were at least four men called Ural—and it was clear the police had arrested the wrong one. The prisoner was released by the court immediately and then had to find his own way home. He had lived in chains for five months before his case reached trial.

Women on the Line

Women were few and far between on the O.T.L. Photographs occasionally show women and children living in the telegraph stations, but in general, the more remote a station, the less likely this was, although Alice Springs Telegraph Station was an exception.

Visiting women, naturally, were of great interest to the men. In 1885, Jack Kelsey was stationmaster at The Shackle, which meant he was stationed closer to the settlement in Palmerston than most of his inland colleagues and had a better chance of meeting eligible ladies. She was Miss Crawford, and for a short while, when she was employed by the Murrays at Katherine as governess to their two small daughters, she certainly caused a stir down the line. Fred Goss, then at Daly Waters (D.W.), and a great friend of Jack Kelsey, was among the lonely men who managed to meet her. More than half a century later he recorded his memories of the time:

> … news flashed along the wire that the Stationmaster at The Katherine had imported a governess from New Zealand, for his two small daughters. It caused quite a flutter amongst the young male population, although beyond wistful speculation,

---

* *Northern Territory Times and Gazette*, 18 September 1875.

the event could have no interest for us … Governesses were scarce in that country. So much so, that this one was the first.

However, my star, lucky or unlucky, did not desert me. I received orders to report to The Katherine on official business …

'What-oh, Governess!' I was going to see her. But, I expected, or tried to convince myself that nobody but a lonely, hard up old maid would accept such a job in such a locality. Still, I hoped for the best. In the meantime, I made a new bridle for my mare with an ornamental forehead band, made a new coloured check saddle cloth, trimmed with red braid, and polished up all of my equipment. This part was all O.K., but my wardrobe rather troubled me. We did not own to fashion plate goods at D.W. Having a few days before starting, I set to work to make a pair of trousers out of saddle serge, and unripped a pair of old ones for a pattern. Although I say it myself, I made a real good job and was intensely proud of my work. But alas, it never occurred to me to shrink the serge before cutting it up. When I had them washed, they would not have fitted a boy of twelve. In the line of shirts, I had only one cotton one with a collar on. (We all used only singlets.) It looked dreadfully crumpled, and it wanted ironing and we had no irons. I had heard of the fastidious bushman who ironed his linen with a bottle of hot water. That method did not commend help to me. I decided to try a method of my own. We had a teapot, a tin one with a flat bottom. It held half a gallon or more, so I got the cook to fill it with boiling water, and to put a cork in the spout. It ironed my shirt as well as any ordinary iron. After I had taken it nearly 200 miles in a pack bag, I am afraid all my ironing labour was lost.

I arrived at the KN [Katherine] and all of my hopes were justified. The lady was highly attractive, highly educated, and a good musician (there was a piano at The Katherine). To put it baldly, I fell in love right off. I found out that she was used to horse riding. Mrs. Murray had a side-saddle, which she never now used (ladies did not ride astride then) and I was welcome to it. I tried my pet mare with a blanket and skirt, and she took it like a lamb. The governess was only engaged with the scholastic duties in the morning. Her afternoons were free. What would you do? I had been on the point of starting

Figure 58: Riders at The Peake. Note the women are riding side-saddle on both the horse and the camel, 1889 (SLSA, B-25183).

back, when I was desired to wait the arrival of a Chinese cook from Darwin for Powell's Creek. He would be there in a week. 'Hoorah!' Later I was advised that the Chinese cook refused at the last minute to go. The agents had to find another. I was asked to wait for further instructions. 'You bet!'

Now let me go back a little; by this time (1885) the Stationmaster at The Shackle was a very close friend of mine. He had been my predecessor at Southport. Jack Kelsey had been an assistant at Daly Waters, when I joined up. A very fine fellow in every way. There was a weekly mail from Southport to The Shackle, but from the latter place the Department had to supply its own transport. Then I got notice of another cook, who would reach The Shackle in ten days, from there another two days would bring him on to me. On the 10th day I got a note from Jack that he would be at The Katherine with the Chinaman on the following day at about 4 pm. This news naturally was not calculated to cheer me up. I was surprised at the effect it had on Miss Crawford (sister of the Crawford at the Southport Store). Out on our ride that afternoon—our last—I elicited the information that she and my friend, Jack, were engaged to be married, and were only waiting for a clergyman who was expected there soon.

'Ye Gods!' I had never heard a word of it and was surprised that the Murrays had not given me a hint. They surely must have known. Well, there was a bit of a scene, but not much, only sufficient to convince me that The Katherine was not big enough for Jack and me just then, so I got everything ready to start on my trip back to Daly Waters at 4 pm the next day. Jack tried to put his foot down on the plan. However, my excuse that I had been absent from my Stationmaster so long and was needed there worked.*

Charlotte Waters

The Charlotte Waters Telegraph Station was built just a few kilometres north of the current border between South Australia and the Northern Territory. It can be a desperately dry country. The operators knew the station as 'Bleak House' because of the desolation. In 1878, 'Joss', a roving correspondent, wrote his impressions for the *Northern Argus*, after he had completed a 4-day ride from Dalhousie Springs:

> … we arrived at Charlotte Waters Telegraph Station, a bleak, solitary-looking place. Looking to the south and west, we see nothing more picturesque than a vast stony plain, with a range or two in the distance; to the north and east the view is a little more pleasing, but very limited. Poets or romantic young ladies would not exist here a month … Scarcity of water is the great drawback to this country … The Telegraph Station stock are in time of drought sent 25 miles away from the station, there being no water nearer. In such seasons the station is entirely dependent upon a tank, which holds about 10,000 gallons of water.†

The first stationmaster at Charlotte Waters was Christopher Giles‡, who first came to the Northern Territory as a cadet on the *Moonta* with George Goyder in 1869. Like several other cadets (John

---

* Goss, 1956.
† *Northern Argus*, 28 February 1878.
‡ The name of Giles is found repeatedly in the history of the O.T.L.—Christopher was one of six siblings, and three of them were involved as surveyors, explorers, and drovers on the O.T.L.: Alfred and Alan Giles were Christopher's younger brothers.

Figure 59: Charlotte Waters Telegraph Station in 1900 when Patrick (Paddy) Byrne was stationmaster (John Blakeman Collection, LANT, ph0057-0002).

Brooking, Thomas Bee, and Charles Sprigg*), Giles completed his surveyor's exams en route, although he only 'scraped through'†. Both Christopher‡ and Alfred were employed by Charles Todd during the surveying of the O.T.L. route. Like all the stationmasters, Giles would share any news from his region along the line, such as this from 1873:

> … Mr. C. Giles, Stationmaster, Peake: Strong shock earthquake felt here at about 7.45 p.m. Saturday. Apparent direction, S.W. to N.E., with dull sub terranean thunder. Noticed also by Mr. J. Bagot and party at a camp 15 miles to westward, where shock overturned their quart pot pannikins, which were placed on top of quart pots. The most violent shock I ever experienced.§

Christopher and his brothers were not related to Ernest Giles, although they may have been good friends, as the explorer stayed at Charlotte Waters Telegraph Station for extended periods in both 1872 and 1874. Ernest named Christopher Pinnacle and Lake Christopher after his host.

---

* Alfred Giles married Charles Sprigg's sister, Mary.
† Pugh 2018.
‡ Christopher Giles was assisted by Joe Johnston who developed scurvy after only a few months and transferred to Yam Creek after recovering. Joe was Charles Johnston's brother. Both were brothers-in-law to John Little.
§ *Chronicle*, 26 July 1873.

Alice Springs

The list of stationmasters at Alice Springs includes men whose names are household words in the town: Francis (Frank) James Gillen and his successor Thomas Bradshaw. Both have suburbs named after them.

Frank Gillen first arrived in Alice Springs in 1875 as an enthusiastic 19-year-old assistant to Johannes Mueller. He transferred to Charlotte Waters in 1879 and worked there for 13 years with Patrick (Paddy) Byrne and others, before returning to Alice Springs to replace Joe Skinner as stationmaster in 1892. He became famous for his photography, his anthropological travels with Baldwin Spencer, and several books he wrote about the Aborigines of Central Australia. Gillen was granted a year's leave with pay to undertake studies of the local tribes with Spencer. His book, *The Native Tribes of Central Australia*, quickly became a classic, and is probably the most famous book ever published about Aboriginal culture.

Gillen returned to his position in Alice Springs in early 1899. However, he had applied for a transfer to Moonta, hoping to get a job in Adelaide and be with his wife and children. That came through within months.

The end of Gillen's employment in Alice Springs coincided with a technological advance that hastened the end of the usefulness of some of the other repeater stations on the line—copper wire. In April 1899, Gillen opened the new copper line as it arrived from Adelaide:

> … Hanley is here with the copper wire which I officially! fixed to the terminal pole amidst whiskey and rejoicing yesterday evening. Today we are working through to Adelaide on the new wire and without the aid of another repeater station. This wire will quadruple the carrying capacity of the line …*

Gillen handed over to Thomas Andrew Bradshaw, an experienced telegrapher who had first started work in Victoria in the early days of telegraphy, after its introduction by Samuel McGowan in 1853. Bradshaw moved to South Australia in 1878 and was therefore a

---

* Letter, 19 March 1899, Frank Gillen to Baldwin Spencer.

twenty-year veteran by the time he won the position in Alice Springs. He arrived with his wife, Atalanta*, and their four children. He then stayed for nine years, transferring at last, as Gillen had, to the Moonta office. Attie had three more children in Central Australia, Don, Edna, and Alan. Their eldest daughter, (Winifred) Doris Blackwell, wrote a best-selling autobiography of her time in Alice Springs with Douglas Lockwood, titled *Alice On the Line*. Thomas was a keen photographer, and his numerous photographs, and Doris's book, give us an excellent record of life in the centre at the beginning of the last century.

Attie was a true pioneer, and for many years the only white woman in the centre. She had no medical training but:

> … Wild blacks used to come into the settlement with those partly civilised, and the pitiable condition of the frightened, sick, and starving creatures caused Mrs. Bradshaw great distress. Having no trained medical knowledge, she could do little for the sick natives, for whom her invariable prescription was a mixture of ground ginger, sugar, and hot water. She comforted herself with the thought that it could do them no harm. The blacks who could speak English pronounced it very good …†

Post offices

As life on the line progressed it was inevitable that a sensible expansion of the mail system would follow. From 1878, The Peake received mail directly from Adelaide every two weeks. It would be loaded into a mail service for all stations north along the line every six weeks. The government planned this as an improvement for those on the line, but howls of outrage quickly followed because the post office replaced a system that was already working well:

> 'J.K.' from Alice Springs summed up the problem in June 1879:
> We were not satisfied before and fancied we should get on better if we had a regular mail like other white folks. The

---

* Atalanta Hope Bradshaw (nee Allchurch) was named after the ship she was born on and the land the ship was passing at the time: the Cape of Good Hope.
† *Chronicle*, 22 August 1929, Mrs Atalanta Hope Bradshaw's obituary.

experience of the last twelve months ... has shown us that we had better have held our tongues and allowed things to go on as they were, for we are worse off now than before ...

The sorest point perhaps is that in the old days before our present mail was granted, we used to get our letters on an average about every three weeks, and sometimes oftener, as any respectable person travelling up the line from The Peake was always entrusted with the mails, and travellers were always glad to oblige by bringing on the letters at any rate, even if they could not bring on the papers, &c. Now the case is different. However, many parties may pass The Peake on their way up, whether telegraph officials or police-troopers, it makes no difference; there the letters must lie till mail-day comes round—once in six weeks—and there is no chance of a letter between whiles.

It was also an issue of volume, and how well it could be transported on horseback:

... The Adelaide mail arrives at The Peake every fortnight, and as most of us take in papers and magazines of some sort there is always a heavy bulky accumulation of reading waiting for our mailman, which must try his temper and his horses' backs considerably ...*

As the population in the Alice Springs area grew, the calls for an improved mail service also grew. By 1887, mail was delivered monthly. This was still an issue for 'subscribers' and a deputation of leading citizens and pastoralists met with Education Minister J. C. F. Johnson 'to ask that the mail service from the present railway terminus to Alice Springs might for the future be fortnightly instead of monthly'.†

In 1889, David Lindsay surveyed the Todd River valley a few kilometres from Alice Springs and laid out the town of Stuart. The first blocks of land were sold to settlers later that year. The tiny town, which changed its name to Alice Springs in 1933, appears to have been an immediate success, but it was not until April 1898 that a fortnightly mail service was begun. The mail contractor, Bob Wells,

---

* *Adelaide Chronicle*, 14 June 1879.
† *Express and Telegraph*, 12 August 1887.

Figure 60: The mail being carried by Bob Wells' camels, Stuart (Alice Springs), 1907 (Bradshaw Collection, LANT, ph0756-0021).

Figure 61: Joe Tilmouth's camels bring the mail into Alice Springs, 1921 (SLSA, Laver Collection, PRG1365/1/141).

would leave Stuart with his camels carrying the mail and meet a colleague from Oodnadatta at Horseshoe Bend on the Finke River*. He would then collect letters, packages and newspapers and return to Alice Springs to deliver them.

* It was at Horseshoe Bend [Engoordina Station] where Pastor Carl Strehlow died and was buried, during a rushed journey to Adelaide for medical treatment from Hermannsburg Mission to the Oodnadatta railhead in 1922 (Strehlow, 1969). Horseshoe Bend had a small hotel beside the river.

Twenty to the Mile

Figure 62: The B.A.T. Offices on the Esplanade in Palmerston, taken from The Residency, 1873 (Foelsche, LANT, ph1060-0034).

Oodnadatta was another new town. It was a busy cluster of buildings around the head of the Ghan Railway. Naturally, as the railway line was built, the telegraph line was moved to run beside it and The Peake Telegraph Station, 95 kilometres south of the new town, was superseded and closed in 1891.*

Palmerston

The £6,000 B.A.T. offices and accommodation complex was built on four acres of prime sea-front land in Palmerston on the Esplanade across the road from The Residency. It was a site recommended by Charles Todd and, on the beach below it, the undersea cable from Banyuwangi came ashore. The location's legal status was shaky because the Esplanade was designated a reserve by Goyder in 1869, but there was never any comeback. No one was surprised when it became a social hub for the elite of the new society. They were attracted by parties, billiards, lawn tennis, and social activities such as the annual 'B.A.T. Ball'.†

Some of the buildings were the offices and quarters for the staff of the British Australian Telegraph Company, and the company footed the bill, but Charles Todd also set up offices and quarters for the government staff who would operate the telegraph. He ordered a very large complex:

> … consisting of a central building and two wings. The central building comprises three offices, one of which is used by the British Australian Company. The other two are used by the Department, one for an operating-room, the other for the public on the business of the Telegraph, Post-Office, and Customs. The South Australian quarters comprise a house of five large rooms, a detached kitchen, and bathroom for the Stationmaster, and two detached rooms for one assistant operator, the men being accommodated in adjoining huts of wattle and daub.

---

* The Peake is now known more to visitors as 'Freeling Springs'.
† *Northern Territory Times and Gazette*, 14 June 1901.

Figure 63: The B.A.T. offices cost £6,000 to build on the Esplanade reserve, facing the sea. They had 22 rooms including offices, a ballroom and a billiard room, a well, showers, a carriage house, stables, a tennis court, and punkahs for cooling, 1875 (Foelsche, SLSA, B-10096).

The British-Australian quarters consist of a long range of buildings, containing 10 rooms in all, being quarters for the Resident Superintendent and five (5) assistants. The rooms are large, one being a billiard-room and library, a handsome billiard-table and a good collection of books being provided by the Company, who have also given their officers a light rowing gig (Todd, 1873).

They were attractive stone buildings, roofed with corrugated iron, with wide verandas that faced fabulous views of the harbour. There were also several outbuildings, such as a stable, and outhouse toilets—these fronted Mitchell Street, much to the disgust of some of the residents who complained of the smell*. They also had two large underground water tanks that held 12,000 gallons each.

The Palmerston complex was just one of the offices in a telegraph line that stretched 20,350 kilometres across the globe. It was one of the greatest feats of telegraphic engineering in history.† Newspapers

---

* Pugh, 2019.

† The B.A.T. Company men were required to monitor the international transmissions and the undersea cable. A second cable was laid between Darwin and Banyuwangi in 1880. The cables remained the only telegraphic connection to the rest of the world (except for a cable that was laid under the seas to New Zealand in 1876) until

listed its route (in miles):
> Adelaide to Port Darwin (land) 2,200
> Port Darwin to Banjoewangie (sea) 970
> Banjoewangie to Batavia (land) 480
> Batavia to Singapore (sea) 560
> Singapore to Penang (sea) 381
> Penang to Madras (sea) 1,213
> Madras to Bombay (land) 600
> Bombay to Aden (sea) 1,664
> Aden to Suez (sea) 1,308
> Suez to Alexandria (land) 224
> Alexandria to Malta (sea) 819
> Malta to Gibraltar (sea) 981
> Gibraltar to Falmouth via Lisbon (sea) 1,250
> Total 12,650*

John Little

The government officer in charge of the O.T.L. in Palmerston and nearly 1,000 kilometres south to Attack Creek, was John Archibald Graham Little. The 'Old Man', as he was known to many, was appointed telegraph stationmaster on 1 August 1871. Remaining in the position for the next 34 years, Little became the most senior public servant in South Australia (after Sir Charles Todd†). As well as the 'Senior and Inspecting Officer' of the line to Attack Creek, Little was also sub-collector of customs, deputy sheriff, and justice of the peace.‡

    1889, when a third undersea cable was laid through to Cable Beach in Broome, Western Australia.

* *Journal*, 24 August 1872. (12,650 miles equals 20,350 kilometres.)

† John Little clearly preferred the Top End town to the southern capital. William Crowder overheard him calling Adelaide 'a stinking dirty little hole' (Crowder, 1871–2). John Little died on 21 May 1906, age 63, and his marble gravestone lies in the Pioneer Cemetery on Goyder Road in Darwin. It is embellished by a large cross, about 10 centimetres thick and it lies flat on the ground. The marble is stained by lichen, but it remains a reminder of the 35 years of service Little gave the telegraph office.

‡ Carment *et al*, 1990.

Little was not universally liked. As Fred Goss wrote in 1956:

> … Perhaps I had better describe the Chief. His name was Little, his weight eighteen stone. He was a secretive man who would not let his left hand know what the other did. A most observant man, with a wonderful memory. He would notice scores of things that would not appear to be of interest to anyone, store them away in his mind and perhaps never use them. He had many good points. Being human, he had what we considered many bad ones, not the least of which was having a favourite, a white-headed boy, for whom, whilst he was in favour, nothing was too good. But the day would inevitably come and then great would be the fall thereof. I had never seen much of the OM, as he was generally referred to in the office.*

He lived in the complex of offices in the Palmerston headquarters with his wife, an ex-schoolteacher named Matilda Cecily Johnston and two daughters, Edith and Blanche. John and Matilda had two more children, Egbert and Maud in Palmerston. Unfortunately, Matilda died of 'erysipelas of the brain' in 1877, leaving Little with four young children to rear. He chose to stay in Palmerston and send the children to be cared for in Adelaide.†

John Little was a driven man, and few could stand up to him. For instance, he made many demands of the first government resident, William Bloomfield Douglas, who hated him for treating him as 'a mere storekeeper to the OT'. In the beginning, Little's role was to find telegraph operators for the repeater stations being built along its length and to aid Patterson's team. Some would call his arrogance and bullying tactics strength, efficiency, management, or leadership skills, but a few events darken his reputation. The worst was the month-long punitive hunting trip from Daly Waters for the murderers of his brother-in-law that led to the deaths of an unknown number of Aborigines.

---

* Goss, 1956.

† Edith Little returned and lived in Palmerston through the 1880s—she is listed often in the newspapers as a champion archer.

Other dubious practices were sorted out by the court. On one occasion he was sued by an ex-employee for 76 shillings for wages he had not paid, because according to Little, the employee, Mr Grahame, had no right to quit his service. Little was cross-examined at considerable length and produced an agreement by which defendant was bound to remain in the service until he was no longer required, but it was:

> ... submitted that there was no naturality in the agreement ... It bound the plaintiff to work all his life for the telegraph authorities, which was absurd. Judgment for wages due to 9th August.*

Every year, Little inspected the full length of the line to Attack Creek. This took several months, and his slow movements were tracked by the telegraph operators along the line, so he never appeared unexpectedly. Telegrams about his progress occasionally appeared in the newspapers: 'J. A. G. Little has reached Powell's Creek on his return journey', readers were told in the *Times* of 30 June 1899.

Fred Goss recalled Little's routine on these journeys:

> ... Daily travelling routine with the Chief would be as follows: after breakfast, when all was packed up, two men would get the OM [Old Man] on his horse, one to give him a leg up, and the other hanging on to the offside stirrup to prevent the saddle turning. The chief had a riding whip, with which he would tickle the horse's shoulder all day long. The horse soon ignored that, so the pair wandered along at not over three miles an hour. A day of twenty miles of this would be a hard day's work ...

> Now the Chief was a very conscientious man and would not have missed travelling over every foot of those 600 miles. The detailed inspection of it was more or less theoretical. The Old Gent would perhaps travel a mile or two lost in thought, then suddenly come to himself and say, 'Mr. Goss, I don't think I quite saw the sky through that last pendant clearly.' 'Well, I did, Sir,' I would say. 'Ah'm, I think we had better go back and make sure.'

---

* *Northern Territory Times and Gazette*, 7 November 1873.

Back we go. He would walk around the pole squinting up from the wrong side and then say, 'No. I can't see it clearly. You had better have a look at it.'

I would have to shin up the pole, and this would happen perhaps a dozen times a day.*

Little would then write an annual report of his observation of the journey, and he commented on everything from droughts and rains to the need to extend the railway line. Every year, his reports were similar: 'The overland telegraph line as far as Attack Creek was found to be in the very best of order and reflects great credit on all officers and men concerned'. Changes in the line, such as the installation of the second wire in 1899, staff movements, and stock movements, sales, and purchases gave some variation. For example:

> ... eleven hundred large-framed fat wethers from Avon Downs Station on the Tablelands were purchased by The Post Office and Telegraph Department, and were delivered in good order and condition at Powell's Creek, for distribution between Daly Waters, Powell's Creek, Tennant's Creek, Barrow's Creek, and Alice Springs telegraph stations on the overland line, it may be mentioned that up to three years ago sheep for rations for these stations were purchased in the settled districts in South Australia and then trucked by railway to Oodnadatta, and from there driven to their respective destinations.†

---

* Goss, 1956.
† *Northern Territory Times and Gazette*, 30 June 1899.

Gallery
Alice Springs

Figure 64: Alice Springs Telegraph Station, 1894 (Boerner Collection, LANT, ph0764-0006).

Gallery

Figure 65: Alice Springs Telegraph Station, 1899 (Boerner Collection, LANT, ph0764-0007).

Figure 66: Tom and Atalanta (Attie) Bradshaw are seated centre with their children and staff of Alice Springs Telegraph Station, 1901 (SLSA, B-22491).

Figure 67: Alice Springs Telegraph Station staff. Thomas Bradshaw on right, 1902 (SLSA, B-22490).

Figure 68: An unnamed worker at Alice Springs Telegraph Station in 1907 (Bradshaw, SLSA, B-70589-3).

Chapter 8
Explorers

The 1870s and 1880s were the golden age of exploration of Central Australia, and the Overland Telegraph Line played a pivotal role in the planning of the expeditions, and sometimes their salvation. The remote telegraph stations were centres of European civilisation. They were superbly suited to hosting either small groups of travellers or large horse or camel caravans, as they prepared for the travelling ahead. Explorers would camp near the stations, reshoe their horses and repair equipment, send telegrams to newspapers, their sponsors, or families, muster their resources, store, or leave equipment and livestock, and play chess with the station staff.

Then they would load up their animals and head into the unknown, perhaps to return half-starved and near dead from thirst—or perhaps never to be heard of again.

A few of the highest profile explorers on 'official explorations' are introduced in the following pages, but there were many more travellers who could also be called explorers. Some parts of Australia previously unknown to white men were first visited by adventurous individuals who were seeking gold, land, or direct routes across the country[*].

Some were men like William Nation, who perished 100 kilometres from Daly Waters from thirst, after eating all his horses. He had 'left Queensland at a bad time of year … and this, together

---

[*] Alan Powell, 1982.

with misunderstandings, and the loss of cattle, will no doubt account, to a very large extent, for the misfortune which has taken place". Nation's mate, Leonard Elvoy, made it to the telegraph station seeking help, and Richard Knuckey rode out, only to find Nation dead and decomposing. He had lived long enough to write requests for the dispersal of his belongings and to farewell his friends:

> … Farewell, dear friends, all. I bid you an eternal farewell. I am in my senses at present, by the blessing of God and Jesus Christ. (Signed) W. NATION

There were men who passed by the O.T.L. and left no record of their passing, like teamsters carting freight or hawkers selling their wares. We only ever hear of them if they got into trouble and telegrams were picked up by the newspapers. For example:

> … Barrow's Creek, September 16, Afternoon. George Thomas Doherty, who has been travelling through the continent from Palmerston with two teams and three other men, arrived here to-day. He states that at Sawpit, forty miles north of Barrow's Creek, he lost some horses, and searched for them unsuccessfully during two days and nights; then was himself nearly dead with hunger and thirst, and his horse the same. He next sent two men in search of the missing animals, and in their absence, during a boisterous night, blacks came to the camp and stole his belt and pouch with £138 from his side in addition to clothes and rations from a wagon. Doherty appears to be much exhausted. He left two men at Sawpit[†].

North of The Peake Telegraph Station a journalist was surprised to meet strangers on the track:

> … About 32 miles back we saw a hawker[‡] with a lot of goods in two carts. It was rather a curious thing to encounter such a travelling store as this fully 780 miles from King William Street, and we imagined he could do little or no trade hereabouts, but we were soon undeceived. It seems he has had a regular run of

---

[*] *Northern Territory Times and Gazette*, 10 July 1874.
[†] *Adelaide Observer*, 18 September 1875.
[‡] I can find no information about this individual, but it is possible he was Mr Chawner, who had so much trouble at Newcastle Waters six months after this meeting.

business all the way up, and when we left him, he was driving a roaring trade with one of the construction parties*.

There were very few white women on the line in the early days—men in the remote stations would go years without seeing any. In fact, white women were so rare that Emily Creaghe claimed the local Aborigines near Powell's Creek 'had an idea there was no such thing as a woman among white people, they thought we were all men'†.

Cattlemen moved west into the Territory from Queensland. The Proust brothers disappeared somewhere near the Barkly Tablelands in 1878, but Nat Buchanan made it across to Tennant Creek Telegraph Station. Another was Frank Scar, who found Buchanan's tracks and followed them safely. Other travellers were men like Barney Lamond and his stockman mate Jack Horrigan, whom we know of because Lamond wrote a memoir. They were bored with life in Queensland during the drought of the 1880s, so in 1885, they took a mob of about 20 horses to the Kimberley, looking for work with the Duracks who were busily developing new stations. To get there they crossed the Barkly Tablelands to Tennant Creek from Queensland, and were lucky, because it was a good season. Lamond wrote that there was always plenty of water, and the seeding spinifex gave his horses a feed as good as oats. They arrived when the annual horse races were starting up, and shepherds and cattlemen from hundreds of miles around converged on Tennant Creek. A grand time was had by all, and later, nursing sore heads, Lamond and Horrigan followed the Overland Telegraph Line north as far as Newcastle Waters, planning to turn west from there. Wisely, Lamond scouted ahead, across the dry country to the west, because it was mostly unknown to white men. From him comes information on one way that Aboriginal knowledge was used:

> ... We went out to the Thirty Mile camp, left our pack and spare horses there, went for a ride around to the west, and cut a well beaten pad, evidently made by blacks, leading into the

---

* *Register*, 15 December 1871.
† Creaghe, 1883.

desert and back west for water. We followed the pad until it came out on a bit of a plain, about a mile or so across. There were about twenty black women and children walking in a line along the track carrying water coolamons. Each woman had one under each arm, full of water, and fastened in a loop around her shoulder by a rope made from their own hair. Each coolamon held a gallon of water.

We cantered up towards them—the wind was against them, and they did not see or smell us till we were right beside them. They rushed into a heap, one on top of the other. The water went into the air—the children, boys, and girls on top of the women, all trying to hide their heads. Such a heap of arms and legs! After a few minutes they commenced to untangle and some of the old women could understand what we wanted. They had been used to mixing with the station blacks and were a bit civilised. We explained that we wanted two boys to go out with us to find water, so that we could get across to the big river. We promised them, if they would go with us for a few days, to bring them back to the waterhole and give them some tea, sugar, flour, and tobacco. They seemed quite willing to come, so we went back to where we left the horses, accompanied by two boys about fifteen years old …

The boys guided the drovers to several 'native wells' but they were dry. Luckily, the horses drank heartily from a trench filled by a sudden thunderstorm, but the men decided that there was not enough water to get their party across the plains. Back at the waterhole, they paid the boys off, as promised, and returned to their main camp. They then followed the O.T.L. north as far as Katherine and travelled west from there, along better-known tracks*.

William Gosse, 1872

William Gosse (1842–81) began a career in the surveyor-general's department in Adelaide when he was 17 years old. He had planned to be an explorer but missed out on joining the high-profile journey that became the tragic Burke and Wills expedition. Instead, he undertook

---

* Lamond, 1885 (published in 1986).

trigonometric surveys in the far north of South Australia.

The government needed a leader to explore a route from the O.T.L. in Central Australia to Perth. The role was first offered to both Alfred Woods and Gilbert McMinn, but they refused. Colonel Warburton was keen to take it on, but the government sought out William Gosse, who was nearly 30 years younger than the colonel, because of his experience as a surveyor.

Figure 69: William Christie Gosse, 1875 (SLSA, B-5941).

Gosse took a selection of camels and horses, some of which pulled a dray (later, his tracks were easy to find by Giles) and headed to Alice Springs with provisions for eight months. Gosse hated the camels: 'The camel travelling is very tiring' he said. 'It is more like riding a knocked-up cart colt than any other animal I have ever mounted'—but by employing three Afghan cameleers to manage them, he persevered. Like Warburton, he waited out the wet season that never came, near Alice Springs. Then, on 23 April 1873:

> … Started for the Reynolds Range. My party consisting of five whites, viz.: Mr. Edwin Berry, second in command; Mr. Henry Gosse [William's brother], collector; Henry Winnall, and Patrick Nilen; three Afghans—Kamran, Jemma Kahn, and Allanah; also, a Peake black boy, 'Moses'. All in good spirits at getting started, after such a long stay at the MacDonnell Ranges. Only a short stage to-day, six miles to Todd Crossing*.

They travelled north along the O.T.L. for about 150 kilometres to avoid the MacDonnell Ranges, then turned west. They found it was a waterless, difficult country, and the heavy sand and needle-sharp spinifex took a toll on the horses.

---

* Gosse, 1874.

In the middle of June, near Mount Liebig, the men were already on half rations when they came across the track of three bullocks that had run away from Alice Springs months earlier. Ten days later they found fresh tracks, so Gosse followed them easily and brought them in. The same day one of the camels had a calf. 'My stock is increasing very fast, three bullocks (which were in splendid condition) and a camel in one week' Gosse noted wryly.

The party needed to change tack. It was clear that getting further west from Mount Liebig was too difficult, so they turned south towards the ranges where Giles had found water and skirted the edge of Lake Amadeus. On 19 July, Gosse was then the first European to see the monolith that has astonished visitors ever since:

> ... it was one immense rock rising abruptly from the plain; the holes I had noticed were caused by the water in some places forming immense caves ... I have named this Ayers Rock, after Sir Henry Ayers.

The next day Gosse and Kamran climbed Ayers Rock, Uluru, *barefooted,* via a ridge near the springs they called Maggie Springs. From the top he could see east to Mount Connor, which he named after a politician, and southeast to the Musgrave Ranges, which he named after the State Governor.

He regretted not wearing his boots for the climb:

> ... how I envied Kamran his hard feet; he seemed to enjoy the walking about with bare feet, while mine were all in blisters, and it was as much as I could do to stand ...

From Uluru the party travelled 150 kilometres to King's Creek, then west to the Mann and Tomkinson Ranges and into Western Australia, near where the community of Warburton is today. There was so little water available that Gosse wisely decided to turn back towards the O.T.L. It took them another three months to get there, but they finally met the line near Charlotte Waters, and were 'received very kindly by Mr. C. Giles, Telegraphmaster'.

Gosse had failed to reach the western coast but had mapped and provided information on over 155,000 square kilometres of a part of the country previously unknown to white men. The next year, his maps helped John Forrest complete his successful crossing from east to west

Gosse returned to Adelaide and continued to work for the survey department. In 1875, he became deputy surveyor general but, in July 1881, not being well, was granted a year's sick leave. A few weeks later, on 12 August, he had a heart attack and died, aged 38, at his home in Adelaide*.

Peter Egerton Warburton, 1872–3

Figure 70: Peter Egerton Warburton, 1874 (SLSA, B-7938).

In 1872, 59-year-old Peter Warburton was an ex-Commissioner of Police in South Australia and then a Colonel in the Volunteer Military Force. He had wanted the government position of exploration leader, won by the 30-year-old William Gosse, but was unsuccessful. He was more successful when the Honourable Thomas Elder and Sir Walter Hughes agreed to work with the government and help finance an exploration that they felt Warburton was uniquely qualified to lead:

> … Major Warburton has been appointed to the command of the expedition, it being thought that he is peculiarly well fitted for the position from his knowledge of the Afghan language and having had a good deal of experience with camels†.

Warburton's party included his son Richard; J.W. Lewis, an experienced bushman; two Afghan camel drivers, Sahleh and Halleem; a cook named Dennis White; and, an Aboriginal tracker

---

* Gosse, 1972.
† *Sydney Morning Herald*, 7 September 1872.

named Charley. The plan was to explore the unknown lands between the Overland Telegraph Line and Fremantle, on the coast of Western Australia. Elder provided seventeen camels, bred on the 2331 square kilometre Beltana Station, and six months supplies. Camels* had been used by Burke and Wills, and by John McKinlay† in 1862. The latter found their height particularly useful to keep stores dry when crossing the flooded 'channel country' in Queensland‡.

Warburton's expedition was the first to use camels without horses. His camel train arrived in Alice Springs on 21 December 1872. William Gosse and his party were already there and both groups did their best to ignore the other. Both also decided to wait near Alice Springs for the wet season to pass before heading west. They were mis-informed about the climate—that year rain never fell in the centre of Australia—and months were wasted 'sitting out a wet season that never came'§. Warburton wrote that:

> … I had much reason to regret this measure; for, instead of long-continued tropical rain, as prognosticated, there was none at all, and I might as well have started at once¶.

Both parties set off from Alice Springs during April 1873. Warburton's party endured long periods of extreme heat with little water and survived only by killing the camels for meat (several escaped and were recognised later as they passed by Alice Springs). By the time they reached the Oakover River in Western Australia, Warburton

---

* John Ainsworth Horrocks (1818–46) first used a camel (named 'Harry') in Australia during an expedition in South Australia in 1846 (see p. 199). Sir Thomas Elder imported 124 camels in 1866 from 'Kurrachhee' (Karachi), 121 of which landed in Adelaide alive, with a dozen Afghan cameleers. They were perfectly suited to Australian conditions and successfully bred immediately. Eventually strings of 'more than sixty travelled with an average load of 600 lbs… making from seventeen to eighteen miles per diem and enduring four- or five-days' thirst easily' (Eden, 1875).
† McKinlay may not have survived without his camels—at the end of his journey his party were barely living off horse meat jerky, camel feet stew, and Burdekin plums (Pugh 2018).
‡ Lockwood, 1995.
§ Traynor, 2016.
¶ Warburton, 1875.

needed to be strapped to his saddle. On 11 January 1874, they struggled into Charles Harper's De Grey Station, having conquered the formidable Great Sandy Desert to become the first Europeans to cross the continent from the centre to the west. Warburton was emaciated and blind in one eye, and he wrote to the Governor of Western Australia for help:

> ... We are in great distress from want of provisions and means of moving. We have lost everything but our lives and have only two camels (for seven men) out of seventeen we started with[*].

Later, at a public banquet in Adelaide, Warburton attributed their survival to his Aboriginal companion, Charley[†].

Warburton was awarded the Patron's Medal of the Royal Geographical Society in London, received the 'Companion of St Michael and St George', and the South Australian Government granted him £1000 and a share of £500 to his party. He had contributed much useful information to the colony and to later explorers about some of the driest and most difficult areas of the continent.

Ernest Giles, 1872

Ernest Giles (1835–97) learned his skills in exploration searching for pastoral country west of the Darling River in New South Wales. His first exploration in Central Australia was from the O.T.L. at Charlotte Waters in 1872.

Giles was a romantic—no one knew what lay to the west, but he was full of hope:

> ... there was room for snowy mountains, an inland sea ... for races of new kinds of men—for fields of gold and Golcondas of gems ... and above all the rest combined, there was room for me![‡].

---

[*] *Northern Territory Times and Gazette*, 10 April 1874.
[†] Deasey, 1976.
[‡] Ernest Giles, 1877.

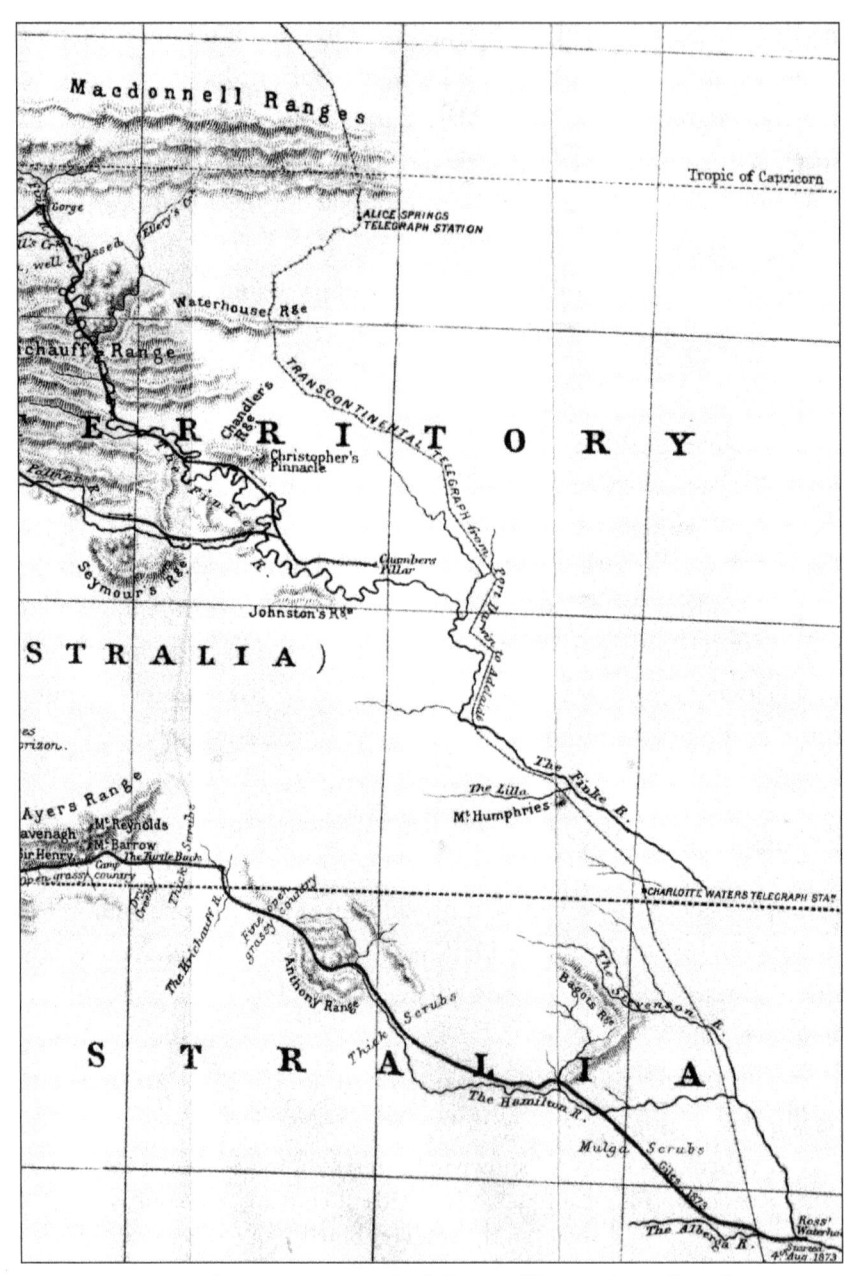

Map 10: The eastern section of Giles's map of his expedition from the O.T.L., departing from Chambers Pillar in 1872, and returning to Ross's Waterhole in August 1873 (Giles, 1877).

There were only three in the party: Ernest Giles, Samuel Carmichael, and Alec Robinson. Giles had wanted a fourth but could find no one willing to brave the unknown lands. He had already lost a constant Aboriginal companion of three years for fear of 'wild natives':

Figure 71: Ernest Giles, Explorer, 1875 (SLSA, B-7546).

> ... my little black boy Dick ... came to me from Queensland; he had visited Adelaide, Melbourne, and Sydney, and had been with me for nearly three years, but his fears of wild natives were terribly excited by what nearly everybody we met said to him about them ...

Giles and his party had a leisurely trip north, camping at The Peake Telegraph Station with Stationmaster John Henry Blood* for several weeks, while they reshod their horses and prepared for the interior. On 14 August 1872, they were welcomed to Charlotte Waters, four days ride away, by Joe Johnston. It was just under a week before the line was joined at Frew's Ironstone Ponds.

> ... In consequence of their kindness, our stay was lengthened to a week. My horses were all the better for the short respite, for they were by no means in good fettle; but the country having been visited by rains, grass was abundant, and the animals improving. The party consisted only of myself, Carmichael, and Robinson; I could not now obtain another man to make up our original number of four.
> I inquired of a number of the natives for information concerning the region beyond, to the west and north-west. They often used the words 'Larapinta and plenty black fellow.'

---

* John Henry Smyth Blood was born in County Clare, Ireland and grew up in Kapunda, South Australia. He worked on the southern construction team on the Overland Telegraph and later became the Postmaster and Telegraph Officer at The Peake Station. He married Mary Enock and they had five children. He died at Auburn aged 49.

> Of the country to the west, they seemed to know more, but it was very difficult to get positive statements. The gist of their information was that there were large waters, high mountains, and plenty, plenty, wild black fellow; they said the wild blacks were very big and fat, and had hair growing, as some said, all down their backs; while others asserted that the hair grew all over their bodies, and that they eat pickaninnies, and sometimes came eastward and killed any of the members of the Charlotte tribe that they could find, and carried off all the women they could catch …*

The first few days after leaving Charlotte Waters were spent following the O.T.L. When they reached the bed of the Finke River, 60 miles north, they camped with Gilbert McMinn and Harley Bacon, who were busy building firm footings for the telegraph poles that had been washed away on the banks of the river. Giles and his party then turned west and began their exploration.

They followed the Finke valley south of the MacDonnell Ranges until lack of water, and the saltpans of Lake Amadeus, blocked their way. Giles wanted to continue, but his travelling companions, especially Samuel Carmichael, resigned and wanted to turn back. Giles had no other alternative than to go with them. He travelled slower than the others and was alone for a day or two before reaching Charlotte Waters, but he met a great number of friendly Aborigines. He related an extraordinary story that demonstrates the cultural arrogance of the times. Giles met several Aboriginal boys who helped him get sweet water from a bitter soak:

> … these little imps of iniquity took my tin billy, scratched a hole in the sand, and immediately procured delicious water; so I got them to help to water the horses. I asked the elder boy, whom I christened Tommy, if he would come along with me and the yarramans [horses]; of these they seemed very fond, as they began kissing while helping to water them. Tommy then found a word or two of English, and said, 'You master?' The natives always like to know who they are dealing with, whether a person is a master or a servant. I replied, 'Yes, mine

---

* Ernest Giles, 1877.

master.' He then said, 'Mine (him) ridem yarraman.' 'Oh, yes.' 'Which one?' 'That one,' said I, pointing to old Cocky, and said, 'That's Cocky.' Then the boy went up to the horse, and said, 'Cocky, you ridem me?' Turning to me, he said, 'All right, master, you and me Burr-r-r-r.' I was very well pleased to think I should get such a nice little fellow so easily*.

Presently 'Tommy's' father and brothers arrived, and Giles asked them if he could take the boy. He was told no, but the next morning the father changed his mind and:

> … thought better of my proposal, thinking probably it was a good thing for one of his boys to have a white master … The boys brought up the horses, and breakfast being eaten, the father led Tommy up to me and put his little hand in mine … I gave the old fellow some old clothes (Tommy I had already dressed up), also some flour, tea, and sugar, and lifted the child on to old Cocky's saddle, which had a valise in front, with two straps for the monkey to cling on by … The boy seemed quite delighted with his new situation and talked away at a great rate.

> As soon as we reached the road, by some extraordinary chance, all my stock of wax matches, carried by Badger, caught alight; a perfect volcano ensued, and the novel sight of a packhorse on fire occurred. This sent him mad, and away he and the two other packhorses flew down the road, over the sandhills, and were out of sight in no time. I told the boy to cling on as I started to gallop after them. He did so for a bit, but slipping on one side, Cocky gave a buck, and sent Tommy flying into some stumps of timber cut down for the passage of the telegraph line, and the boy fell on a stump and broke his arm near the shoulder. I tied my horse up and went to help the child, who screamed and bit at me, and said something about his people killing me.

> Every time I tried to touch or pacify him it was the same. I did not know what to do, the horses were miles away. I decided to leave the boy where he was, go after the horses, and then return with them to my last night's camp, and give the boy back to his father. When he saw me mount, he howled and yelled, but I gave him to understand what I was going to do,

---

*   Ernest Giles, 1877.

Map 11: Ernest Giles returned to The Peake from Western Australia on his 5th expedition in 1876 (Giles, 1877).

and he lay down and cried. I was full of pity for the poor little creature, and I only left him to return. I started away, and not until I had been at full gallop for an hour did I sight the runaway horses. Cocky got away when the accident occurred, and galloped after and found the others, and his advent evidently set them off a second time. Returning to the boy, I saw some smoke, and on approaching close, found a young black fellow also there. He had bound up the child's arm with leaves and wrapped it up with bits of bark; and when I came, he damped it with water from my bag. I then suggested to these two to return; but oh no, the new chap was evidently bound to seek his fortune … at the Charlotte Waters Station. Off I went and left them, as I had a good way to go. I rode and they walked to the Charlotte. I got the little boy regular meals at the station; but his arm was still bad, and I don't know if it ever got right. I never saw him again*.

At Charlotte Waters, Giles met Colonel Warburton and his son Richard. They were going into the regions he had just come from, so he shared everything he knew and showed them his map. He was also surprised to hear of another expedition that was ahead of Warburton. It was funded by the government and led by William Christie Gosse. Both Warburton and Gosse led their expeditions west from Alice Springs and both mentions crossing each other's tracks in the bush. Giles was worried that the South Australians might beat him to the west coast and observed that their camels gave them an advantage. However, he took credit for the genesis of the two South Australian journeys:

> … The fact of two expeditions starting away simultaneously, almost as soon as I had turned my back upon civilisation, showed me at once that my attempt, I being regarded as a Victorian, had roused the people and Government of South Australia to the importance of the question which I was the first to endeavour to solve—namely, the exploration of the unknown interior, and the possibility of discovering an overland route for stock through Central Australia, to the settlements upon the western coast. This, I may remark,

---

* Ernest Giles, 1877.

had been the dream of all Australian explorers from the time of Eyre and Leichhardt down to my own time. It also showed that South Australia had no desire to be beaten again (Burke and Stuart), and in her own territories, by 'worthless Melbourne's pulling child'[*].

Giles found support for a second expedition the next year, and he planned to initially follow the Musgrave Ranges, where Gosse had gone, but then go further. On this expedition he was accompanied by William Henry Tietkins, and James (Jimmy) Andrews[†].

Passing through Beltana, Giles was reunited with his Aboriginal friend:

> ... Mr Chandler had got and kept my black boy Dick, who pretended to be overjoyed to see me, and perhaps he really was, but he was extra effusive in his affection, and now declared he had been a silly young fool, that he didn't care for wild blacks now a bit, and would go anywhere with me ... Leaving Beltana, in a few days we passed the Finniss Springs Station, and one of the people there made all sorts of overtures to Dick ... some promises must have been made to him, as when we reached the Gregory, he bolted away, and I never saw him afterwards ...

At The Peake, a third young man joined them. Alfred Gibson had met Giles years before on the Murray River and was desperately keen to go exploring.

Giles' route west of the O.T.L., started at Chambers Pillar. It went through the Musgrave Ranges and led him to Uluru, named 'Ayers Rock' by Gosse after the premier of South Australia, and Kata Tjuta, that Ernest Giles named 'Mount Olga'[‡] after Grand Duchess Olga Nikolaevna of the Russian Imperial family. Trailing behind the party were 24 packhorses, each carrying a 200-pound load (91 kg)—Giles stubbornly refused to use camels. The party then spent months

---

[*] Ernest Giles, 1877.
[†] Plus Alex Ross, an 18-year-old son of the explorer John Ross (Doris Blackwell, 1965).
[‡] Grand Duchess Olga Nikolaevna became Queen consort of the Kingdom of Württemberg. 'Kata Tjuta' means 'many heads' in the local Anangu language.

looking for a stock route into Western Australia. Giles's wordy journal describes the huge effort and the desperate, final attempt to cross a desert that he named Gibson, because poor Alfred Gibson got lost in it and was never seen again. Giles, at death's door himself, again retreated to the safety of the O.T.L. near The Peake.

In 1875, Giles made a third attempt to cross to the west coast from South Australia. This time he left Beltana and used camels bred at Beltana and provided by Thomas Elder. The camels allowed him to cross the Great Victoria Desert, including a dry stage of 502 kilometres, and he finally made it to Perth. He then returned to South Australia via Gibson's Desert and the Rawlinson Ranges on a fifth expedition, ironically finding good waterholes that would have saved Gibson and his horses on the previous expedition (see Map 10). The Overland Telegraph Line was again their destination and salvation. On 23 August 1876, they

> … reached The Peake Telegraph Station … and were most cordially received and welcomed by my old friend Mr Chandler, Mr. Flynn, the police trooper, and everyone else at the place*.

Ernest Giles's reward, apart from several entertaining books that have stood the test of time, included a knighthood from 'the crown of Italy', honorary membership of several European societies and a gold medal from the Royal Geographical Society of London, presented in 1880. The South Australian government granted him £250 for each of his expeditions and a lease of some 2000 square miles (5,180 km²) of the Northern Territory. Unfortunately for him, he was refused an official appointment because Governor Sir William Jervois was not impressed by him socially: 'I am informed that he gambles and that his habits are not always strictly sober' he said†. But then, as Giles mentioned several times in his books—he *was* from Victoria.

---

* Ernest Giles, 1877.
† Green, 1972.

Ernest Favenc and the Creaghes, 1883

Ernest Favenc was another man whose explorations would have been very different without the Overland Telegraph Line. He came west from Queensland and reached Powell's Creek Telegraph Station on 14 May 1883, after a torrid dry crossing of the tablelands, the last 80 miles or so completely without water*. His party included Lindsay Crawford and Harry Creaghe and his wife Emily. Emily Creaghe was the only female explorer of the 1880s in central and northern Australia.

Fred Goss at Powell's Creek was astonished. When Lindsay Crawford, who had been a stationmaster himself, rode ahead to warn the men of the station:

> ... One evening, after tea, we were sitting by the fire ... We were suddenly startled by the sound of a horse being ridden or driven. It was the former. It turned out to be Lindsay Crawford, my former boss in the store at Southport. He had come from Queensland with a party, one of whom was a woman. Knowing something of outback ways in the matter of clothing, he had ridden ahead to warn us— 'A woman!'—we were galvanised into life. When others of the party arrived half an hour later, all was well. Our clothing had been donned and we felt quite respectable again†.

Favenc's party split up at Powell's Creek and the Creaghes took the weaker horses north to Katherine along the O.T.L., while Favenc and Crawford explored the McArthur River area. The track next to the O.T.L. was easy to travel on, compared to the unknown country, and the Creaghes were accompanied by Fred Goss with a dray that carried three tanks of water as far as Daly Waters Telegraph Station. This easy travel was a relief to Emily, because by this time she was pregnant and not feeling well on most days. Her diary records her impressions of some of the distant stations along the way. Daly Waters Telegraph Station, wrote Creaghe, was not as grand as the Powell's

---

* See Creaghe, 1883, *The Diary of Emily Creaghe*.
† Fred Goss, 1886.

Creek complex. The house was made of slabs, and beams of light streamed through the cracks. When she was there, it was manned by Mr Johns and Mr Kemp. They had not seen a white woman for three years and Harry wisely rode ahead to warn them of the approach of a woman, as Crawford had at Powell's Creek.

The next stop was Elsey Telegraph Station, which was manned only in the wet season 'with the object of being able to effect repairs to the line far more promptly than could have been done from the Katherine'*. It was a simple affair, consisting of little more than a log hut. The operator, Mr Tuckfield, kept the telegraph equipment in his bedroom.

In Katherine, the Creaghes stayed a few nights at the Katherine Telegraph Station with the Murrays and their three children in a house that was a 'very poor affair'†. They also stayed with the managers of Springvale Station, Alfred and Mary (nee Sprigg) Giles‡.

The Forrest brothers, 1874 and 1890

In 1874, on his third expedition, John Forrest used the Overland Telegraph Line as his final destination. The party included Forrest's brother Alexander, Tommy Windich and three others. The expedition

---

* Todd, 1884.
† By 1891, the Murrays lived in a new house: A visitor reported that 'the Telegraph Station is another insignificant building, but the quarters occupied by Mr. Murray seem to be ample for all present needs' (NTTG, 19 June 1891). Incidentally, the Murrays experienced tragedy when their son, Henry Hammond Murray, died at the age of 4 years and two months in 1880. He was buried in the Knott's Crossing Cemetery on the banks of the Katherine River. In 1893, Robert Murray fell ill and travelled to Burrundie to see Dr. Lynch. Unfortunately, he was delayed for three days by the flooded Fergusson River, and he died, aged 43, a few hours after he arrived. Murray served on the O.T.L. for 20 years (Obituary, *Northern Territory Times and Gazette*, 3 February 1893).
‡ Alfred Giles drove sheep and cattle northwards along the O.T.L. in 1871. He was later station manager for Dr William James Browne, but subsequently he bought Browne out on his retirement. He then owned both Springvale and Delamere Stations.

started in Geraldton, Western Australia, and travelled through the centre of the state to the O.T.L. near Mount Alexander and reached The Peake Telegraph Station three days later, on 30 September. Forrest proved that there was no inland sea in Australia but identified good pastoral land near the Murchison River. They also found a lot of desert—which nearly killed them.

John Forrest made a significant plant collection during his travels and was knighted for his exploration work by Queen Victoria.

Figure 72: Sir John Forrest, explorer and Western Australia's first premier, 1874 (Talma & Co).

In 1880, Alexander Forrest became an exploration leader in his own right. He led a party of explorers through the northern part of Western Australia, and as before, struggled through to the O.T.L. when his party were nearly dead from the effort. As most of the men were weak and ill, Forrest left them in a camp and moved forward to meet the line to get food and other supplies quickly. He knew the O.T.L. was about 100 miles east of the camp and finally, nearing the end of his energy:

> ... I could hardly believe the evidence of my own eyes, and forgetting our thirst, out through the night rang our cheers ... had Hicks and I not reached the line safely, the whole of our party must probably have perished of starvation[*].

Forrest found tanks of water, and a sign pointing to other water sources within a mile of the line, but it took him four more days to find a maintenance party, led by a Mr. Woods, who gave them food and resources to return to pick up his colleagues[†]. Two weeks later

---

[*] Forrest, 1880.
[†] A memorial to Alexander Forrest sits beside the highway south of Katherine. Fenced by sections of Oppenheimer poles, it reads: 'Alexander Forrest reached the Overland

Figure 73: Alexander Forrest n.d. (Anon., undated, Canberra Times Collection, ACT Heritage Library, 003613).

Figure 74: Katherine Telegraph Station, c. 1895 (SLSA, B-24181).

they all arrived at Katherine Telegraph Station, and Robert Murray* and his family received them 'with the greatest kindness' …

Telegraph Line near this point on August 31st, 1879, after he and his party had made an epic journey from de Grey on the W.A. Coast. Erected by the Royal W.A. Historical Society and Katherine Historical Society, August 31st, 1979'.

*   Twenty-five-year-old Robert McKellar Murray arrived in Katherine in May 1875 and replaced C.H. Johnston as stationmaster. He was married to Jane Louisa Hammond and had already spent a year as stationmaster in Port Darwin. Jane was the first white woman to live in the Katherine region. Incidentally, Murray was a South Australian champion swimmer.

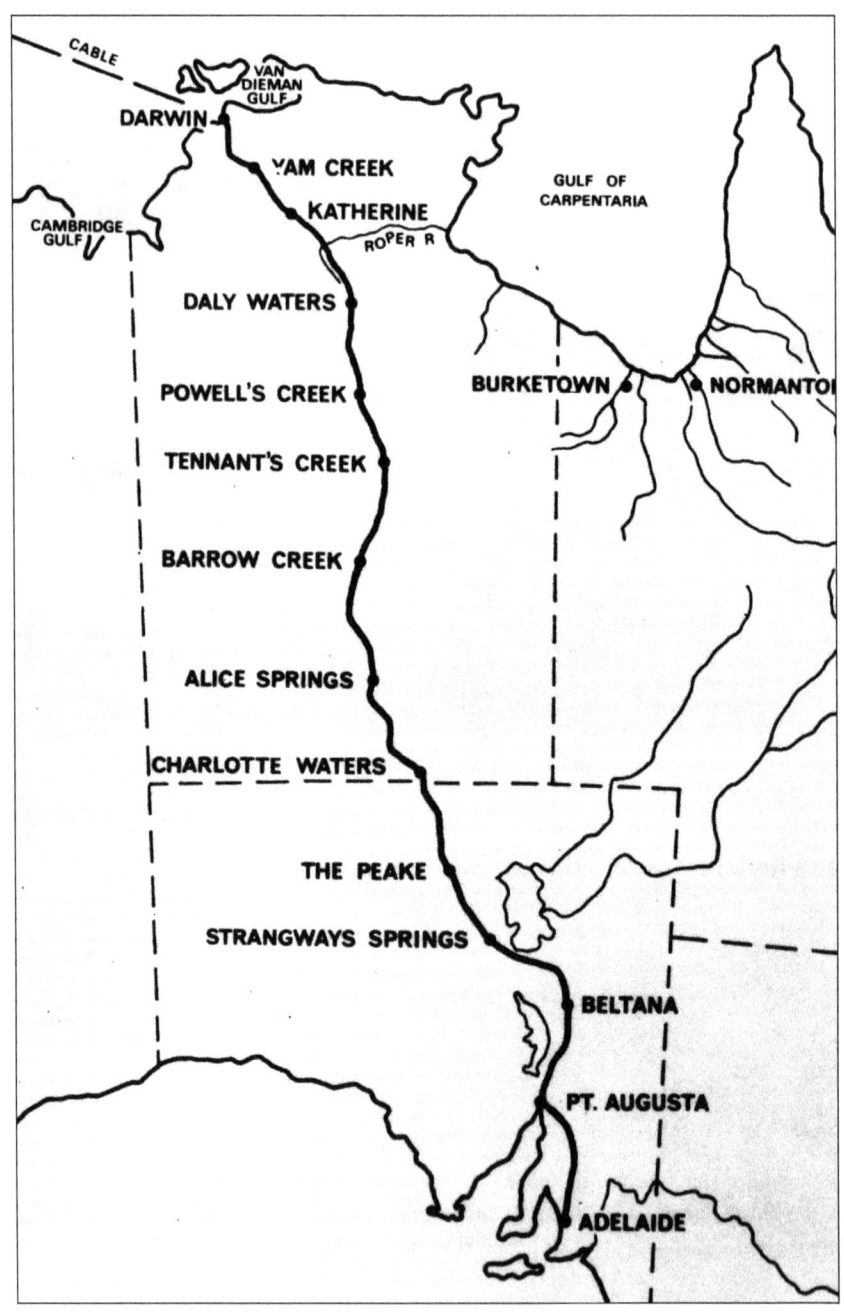

Map 12: The route of the Overland Telegraph Line and the original stations, c. 1900 (NT Heritage).

Chapter 9
Along the O.T.L.

The final reports of Charles Todd and Robert Patterson were published in the *Express and Telegraph* on 7 January 1873. Patterson went into great detail with a mile-by-mile explanation of what poles they used through his section, the difficulties in finding them, how they crossed the rivers, the problems with the wet season floods, and where the government should build wells to limit the dry stages for travelling horsemen.

In May 2021, I was not expecting to need the wells, or have any difficulties crossing the rivers, but the *Express* gave me the route to follow along the old telegraph line:

> … On the line there are twelve stations erected, some of them good substantial stone buildings, and others of a more temporary character. These stations are at Beltana, Strangways Springs, The Peake, Charlotte Waters, Alice Springs, Barrow Creek, Tennant's Creek, Powell's Creek, Daly Waters, The Katherine, Yam Creek, and Palmerston*.

I knew that the list was not complete. An O.T.L. pilgrimage would need to include other important sites along the route to fully appreciate the feat. The *Express* did not mention Farina, Chambers Pillar, Renner Springs, Elsey, Pine Creek, Southport, or a dozen other places of interest; but I added them to my list.

Then, early on a Sunday morning, I stood before information board number 7 on the Port Augusta Heritage Trail, across from

---
* *Express and Telegraph* on 7 January 1873.

the post office. A solid brick telegraph station had once stood here. Nowadays rows of letter boxes, shaded by ornamental grape vines, lead people into a modern store that sells everything from stamps to jigsaw puzzles and passport photos.

Ahead of me, lying between the windy Spencer Gulf and the warm brown waters of Darwin Harbour, lay the ruins of eleven telegraph repeater stations and other places that saw the events recorded in this book. They were the focus of white civilisation across the continent for decades, and they were about to celebrate their sesquicentenary. Patterson smashed the brandy bottle against the joining pole near Frew's Ironstone Ponds on 22 August 1872. On the same date in 2022, 150 years will have passed.

I had a long way to go.

Port Augusta (Barngarla)

Winter was exploring the streets of Port Augusta, just like me. I was propelled by cold winds as I followed the marked heritage trail that points out reminders of the old town sitting among the modern supermarkets and self-cleaning toilet cubicles. Port Augusta is now billed as the start of 'The Explorers' Way'—a three-thousand-kilometre tourist route that follows the trails north to Darwin. The footsteps of John McDouall Stuart and other explorers are faded, but numerous memorials can be found dotted along the highways. More than coincidentally, The Explorers' Way not only follows the highway named after Stuart, but also the routes of the old Ghan Railway and the Overland Telegraph Line to Alice Springs. The famous unsealed road along this route is known as the Oodnadatta Track.

The O.T.L. was there first of course, but the Ghan Heritage Trail has more pulling power. Perhaps few of us follow old telegraph lines—but railway buffs from across the world come to marvel at long-disused bridges, huge metal water towers that still stand on long-forgotten sidings, and ruined stone-walled dormitories where

Along the O.T.L.

Figure 75: Port Augusta Post Office in 2021.

railway workers spent their downtime. Some of them may notice the remnants of the O.T.L., but as I stood in front of the Port Augusta Post Office, I wondered how long it had been since anyone had set out to travel the whole of the line for its own sake.

I would probably meet other 'line pilgrims' on my route of a different breed. The first half of the journey north shares the road with the Ghan Railway Line, and railway enthusiasts know no bounds. I would see what they see on the track north, but with a focus on the O.T.L., perhaps I would see more.

Port Augusta revels in its history and is particularly proud of its derelict wool wharf, but the best place to travel through its history is the 'Wadlata Outback Centre'. Its extraordinary 'Tunnel of Time' takes hours to fully explore. Communication is the focus of one section, and the O.T.L. is there, of course, and visitors can try their hand at sending Morse code messages to each other, without the high cost the telegrams incurred in the 1880s. Moving forward in history, they can join a party line, pedal the wireless to join the School of the Air, and then visit the gift shop to buy history books ...

Port Augusta Telegraph Station was fully established before the O.T.L. was built. A line arrived from Adelaide in 1866 and was opened on 30 August by Charles Todd and James Phillips. Phillips was then the chief telegrapher, without complaint, for a dozen years. When he retired to become publican of the Wharf Hotel, his successor, James Beatton, was loud in his demands for a larger space to work, a 'proper domestic accommodation', and a small heater for the wintertime. Rightly so, said the *Advertiser*, because there was by then a staff of 12, and '100 telegrams are received and dispatched daily'*. For the month of July 1882, the Port Augusta Telegraph Office held receipts worth £964 6s.6d. The staff also had to deal with 387 bags of mail each week, run the money order office, and the savings bank. It was a busy place.

It is still busy. The modern post-office is in the centre of town. It is Number 7 on the Heritage Walk around the port city.

From here the O.T.L. stretched northwards, built by Edward Bagot's two construction teams†, following a pattern that would stretch across Australia. The first repeater station was established several hundred kilometres away at Beltana. Bagot was lucky—much of the land he crossed was already well known and mapped. He was a station holder on the Murray River, and he was familiar with the bush, so he knew what to expect.

These days, Beltana is the first stop in a modern traveller's odyssey along the O.T.L.

---

* *Port Augusta and Flinders Advertiser*, 21 August 1882.

† Edward Bagot was a busy and wealthy man. His contract for constructing 500 miles of the O.T.L. paid £38,000. In 1872, he leased 1489 km² near the Ross River that he called Undoolya Station and invested in Northern Territory gold mines—though they had failed by 1876. In 1870, he built a boiling-down works at Thebarton, which handled over 70,000 sheep per year. He manufactured 'Bagots'—a popular processed meat product, and had interests in wool-washing and fellmongery. He also bred racehorses: in 1873, his thoroughbred, 'Don Juan', won the Melbourne Cup).

Figure 76: The Beltana Telegraph Station now occupied as a private home.

Beltana

Beltana Station was leased by Thomas Elder, and settlers began arriving in the area in the 1850s. It is the country of the Adnyamathanha people. The town of Beltana was surveyed in 1873 and it has been occupied ever since. All the buildings in the area, including the original stone structures, are privately owned. However, visitors are encouraged to wander around and read the interpretive signs.

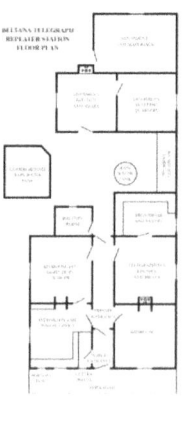

Figure 77: Beltana Telegraph Office Floorplan (www.environment.sa.gov.au).

Many of the buildings are still in use, though some are in ruins. Apparently 30 people live in Beltana, but they must have all been at work, as I saw no one. The telegraph station was built in 1875 and it

Twenty to the Mile

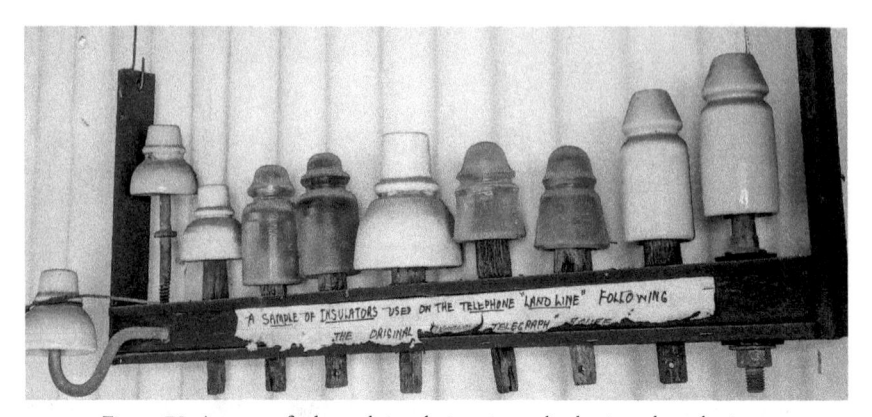

Figure 78: A range of telegraph insulations is on display in a dusty heritage display in Beltana.

housed the staff of six, but it is now a private house and looks to be in great condition. I would have liked to have a sticky beak inside, but no one was home. The station was built across the road from a temporary premise that operated on the banks of the Warioota Creek when the line first opened in 1872. The office was particularly important for the local copper mines, sheep barons and railway workers from the region.

It is especially notable because it became an early experimental station with the telephone. The first phone call to Beltana came from Strangways Station, 200 kilometres (125 miles) north, on 22 April 1878—a year after the telephone was patented by Alexander Graham Bell*. The house operated as a telegraph office until 1940, when the

Figure 79: A camel is delivered to Port Augusta in 1893 via the *Bengal* (SLSA, Port Augusta Collection, B-68916).

equipment was moved to the railway station about a kilometre away, which is also now a private house.

Beltana was also important as a staging post for the O.T.L. workers, railway builders and explorers.[*]

Australia's first camel herds were bred here. Thomas Elder (later Sir Thomas) imported them as a solution to the problems confronting the transportation of goods to the interior of the state.

They were not the first camels in Australia—John Ainsworth Horrocks brought Harry the Camel to Adelaide in 1846 to help with his expedition north. Unfortunately, when near Lake Dutton on 1 September, Harry was kneeling down, and the movement caught his pack on the trigger of Horrocks' shotgun. The pellets hit Horrocks and blew off half his upper jaw and a finger. The expedition then wisely returned home, and Horrocks took three weeks to die. In a pique of vengeance during his final breaths, he ordered Harry to be shot.

Other camels soon arrived. Burke and Wills used camels on their fateful expedition in 1860, and so did John McKinlay, when he was looking for them. McKinlay found the height of his camels useful, particularly when crossing the flooded 'Channel Country' in Queensland. It kept his equipment dry, but by the end of his journey he was heartily sick of camel-feet stew[†].

About the same time, Thomas Elder sent Samuel Stuckey to British India (now Pakistan) to purchase a breeding herd, and to engage experienced cameleers. Stuckey was unable to charter a suitable ship that year and had to return to Adelaide empty-handed. However, he went back to India in 1866 and bought 124 camels and shipped them all to Port Augusta with 11 cameleers to care for them. About 3,000 cameleers eventually came to Australia and they were collectively known as 'Afghans' or 'Ghans', despite being recruited

---

[*] Beltana was also the first posting of the Reverend John 'Flynn-of-the-Inland' Flynn after his ordination.
[†] See Pugh 2018 *Escape Cliffs*.

from many different areas, such as Pakistan, Afghanistan, Kashmir, Punjab, Egypt, and Turkey.

The camels that survived the trip were taken to Elder's station at Beltana. They were successfully bred and were ready for sale to transport companies and explorers by the time the O.T.L. was being built and more than 100 were used to carry wire, insulators, and supplies.

Beltana remained the most important breeding station for camels and a depot for supplies through the 1870s. Camels were an essential tool for any successful exploration of a continent that was without the 'inland sea' everyone had hoped for. In 1872, Warburton's exploration expedition used them exclusively, instead of horses:

> ... Until Sir Thomas Elder took the field, camels were not generally popular as travelling companions ... The prejudice yielded very quickly, however, before the test of practical experience. Warburton would never have reached Roeburn with horses, whose slender lives were only too ready a sacrifice to the rolling sandhills where there was no water. Forrest knew the value of camels sufficiently to deplore his own early methods (with horses). Ernest Giles needed no convincing. His own camels had taken him where horses were useless, carrying for the frailer animals the water which they themselves were not allowed to drink ... In 1876 [camels] were more indispensable than damper, bully beef, or blackfellow*.

The town of Beltana lives on. Judging by its neatness and welcoming interpretation signs, the small community is proud of the history of their home.

The old Ghan Railway passed by, and Beltana benefited from its regular route. All too soon, however, the next settlement along the line became more important to the railway. Beltana eventually lost most of its population, and its telegraph station became 'non-official' in 1913.

The new settlement at Government Gums became an important staging post when the railway reached it in 1882. It was the place

---

* *Threadgill*, 1922.

Figure 80: The Farina Post and Telegraph Office, First Street, Farina, with an Oppenheimer pole standing beside it.

Figure 81: A camel train arrives at the Farina railhead, carting bales of wool in the 1890s (SLSA, B-23999).

where the train changed from standard to narrow gauge, and where bales of wool were delivered by long strings of camels from the outlying sheep stations.

Government Gums changed its name after it was surveyed into more than 400 half-acre blocks in 1883. It became known as Farina.

Farina

Farina was not one of the original overland telegraph stations, but it has a place in this story because the remnant ruins, of what is now a ghost town, are a worthy stopover for any O.T.L. traveller. Farina reached the height of its importance in the 1890s. It was home to more than 300 people and was particularly important to the cattle baron, Sir Sidney Kidman, to move his beasts to markets in Adelaide. It had two hotels, a school, a telegraph and post office, a bank, a brewery, two churches, several shops, and an underground bakery (which is again operational, selling bread to tourists). Farina lived long—and tried its best—but the school closed in 1957, and the store in 1967. By the time the last train passed by on its way to Alice Springs, only the pastoralists of Farina Station lived in the area.

Unfortunately for Farina the railway continued north, and when it reached Hergott Springs, and the town of Marree was built in 1884, the writing was already on the wall.

The ruins nowadays are a delight for visitors. They are being restored or maintained by a small group of volunteers who call themselves the Farina Restoration Group Inc. The post office walls and chimneys still stand, and it was here that a 'spur-line' connection to the O.T.L. was installed and opened in 1878. It was an offshoot, rather than a repeater station, as the line actually passed by three or four kilometres to the west. It operated as an 'omnibus' circuit that used two letter codes so that each operator on the line would know if he had to respond. The codes would also identify which direction the message was travelling.*

The next repeater station was built beside some peculiar mound springs in otherwise very dry country. The springs were named Strangways, after the premier of South Australia in 1868, Henry Bull Templar Strangways (1832–1920). I would get there via Hergott Springs, now called Marree, at the start of the Oodnadatta Track.

---

* Richard Venus, personal communication 2021.

Figure 82: The Marree Hotel

Marree (Mari)

When Marree became the railhead in 1884, it took the wind out of Farina's sails. However, unlike Farina, Marree is still a vibrant village with its history riding proudly on its sleeve. The Marree Hotel is magnificent. Built in 1883, it still operates and has a healthy flow of locals and tourists alike propping up its bar and sleeping in the upstairs rooms. The park across the road displays railway memorabilia, and the village has grown to include dozens of demountable houses and two caravan parks. I was here 30 years ago, when the hotel was fairly isolated. The railway had closed, most of the workers' houses had been trucked away, and the barman was a lonely man. As his only customer one afternoon, he complained to me that he'd had no one to tell a story about the previous night's guests. A strong wind was blowing across the plains, and the man decided to pitch his tent in the dark outside the pub. He needed to turn his Land Rover around to use its lights, and did so, but the tent had disappeared. He drove down wind, swinging his lights left and right, thinking the tent had blown away. It was only when he heard his wife calling out that he looked behind to see the tent tied to the back of his car, with his helpless wife inside, being dragged all over the paddock!

About the same time, my old mate Pat visited the Marree Pub. He was offered wine by an old man sitting in the bar, and they had a merry time sampling a number of bottles. The man quizzed Pat for his opinions and it was only after he had left that Pat learned that it was Mr Wolf Blass* himself, carrying out market research. Country pubs always have the best stories.

When the O.T.L. came through Marree, it was called Hergott Springs. The latter name was used until World War One, when ill-feeling towards anything German caused its name to be changed to *Mari*, the local Diyari name for possum.

In 1871, a camp was established near Hergott Springs to support the O.T.L. workers, and many of the Afghan cameleers employed on the line lived with their families in 'Ghantown' where they built the first mosque in Australia.

Marree was not one of the original stations, but a telegraph repeater station was built in 1884, as the town was developed for the railway. It was opened by 20-year-old Jim O'Brien who had already served several months as post-master in Farina. He was accompanied by his wife Annie, who was just 15. She took over the licence of the Great Northern Hotel (called Marree Hotel since 1989), and they remained there for 18 years, raising their children†. In its heyday, Marree grew to be a town of about 600 people.

Strangways Springs (Pangi Warrunha)

Like Beltana, Strangways was already settled by the time the O.T.L. passed by. The homestead was bought by the South Australian

---

* Wolf Blass is a famous vintner from the Barossa Valley.

† The O'Brien's story is told by their granddaughter, Colleen Hines, in her book *Jim and Annie on the Overland Telegraph* (Hines, 1997).

Along the O.T.L.

Figure 83: Strangways Springs Telegraph Station c. 1880. The water tank is on the right behind a telegraph pole (SLSA, B-11945).

Figure 84: The rear of the Strangways Springs Telegraph Station as it is now. The buttressed water tank is on the left.

Government in 1870 and the O.T.L. repeater station was built next to it in 1871–2. These days, the area is a part of Anna Creek Station*.

---
* Anna Creek station is the biggest pastoral station in the world. This is impressive, but so too was the tiny honesty-box I found beside the highway at the station's entrance road, tens of kilometres from the homestead—$7 for a dozen of the

The mound springs are reached by a short trail off the Oodnadatta Track and are worth visiting in their own right. They are 'a large group of nearly extinct springs'* that were once a reliable source of water. For two decades—until 1896, when it was closed and moved to William Creek—the telegraph station sat beside them.

Mound springs were once found all over this part of South Australia. They were places where water from the Great Artesian Basin bubbled up to the surface and left deposits that grew into large mounds—hence the name. George Goyder discovered many of them in the 1850s. He described spectacular fragile natural hillocks but, unfortunately, most were quickly trampled and decimated by cattle as white settlement overtook the country. Some still exist— Coward Springs† has active springs called *Wabma Kadarbu*, about 40 kilometres to the southeast. The most famous of them all is Dalhousie Springs, far to the north.

The mound springs at Strangways‡ were fenced by the cattle station owners, S. Kidman and Co, in the 1980s. They have been protected from cattle since then, and more recently, the 'Friends of Mound Springs' group (FOMS) have constructed two interesting sign-posted walks through the springs and around the ruins, both of which I was happy to follow.

I found the Strangways ruins to be evocative. A dozen or so ruined stone buildings are still surrounded by the rock walls of sheep pens. The telegraph station was converted from the original sheep

---

    whitest eggs I've ever seen. Even kids who live on the world's largest station need to earn a little pocket money.

*   Social and Ecological Assessment (SADEP, 1986).

†   In the 1890s, Coward Springs had a hotel. Ned Ryan died there of appendicitis in 1893. Ryan worked on the Overland Telegraph Line by sinking wells and 'Ryan's Well' near Ti Tree is named after him. Ryan originally arrived in the reinforcement party to Escape Cliffs in 1865 under Finniss and was included in McKinlay's exploration party to Arnhem Land. He was back in the north with Goyder in 1869, and in 1870 was a stonemason who worked on the first walls of The Residency, now called Government House, in Darwin (Pugh, 2018).

‡   *Pangki Warrunha* in the local Arabana language.

Figure 85: Albert Hewish's Overland Telegraph Line maintenance party.
L–R: George Hablett, Albert Hewish (foreman), George Ross, and Bernie
Supple, 1907 (LANT, ph0756-0024).

Figure 86: Mary Hewish's grave at Strangways Springs. A lonely and
evocative place.

station manager's house. It sits next to a large, buttressed stone water tank that looks more like a doorless church. There was also a police station, storerooms, workers' quarters, a woolshed, a smithy, and other buildings. Once they made up a small village.

There are several graves in the Strangways Springs cemetery, but only two have headstones. The earliest belongs to Walter David Randall, whose death notice in the *Register* says he died suddenly at Strangways Springs on 7 November 1893. He was the 'third son of William Randall, late of Port Pirie, aged 41 years. Universally beloved'*.

Randall was the telegraph and postmaster, and it seems likely that he was replaced immediately by his assistant, Albert Hewish, whose wife lies in the second grave. Albert had lived at Strangways Springs since 1886, when his brother, Andrew, was the boss. By 1893, Andrew was in charge of Oodnadatta Telegraph Station.

Albert Hewish and his wife Mary (nee Paterson) had married on 4 December 1890. They seemed happy to raise their family in Strangways Springs, although the subsequent events did not go their way. A son was born on 5 August 1891, and a daughter in early 1895, but sadly, Mary died soon after her daughter was born. Her grave lies next to Randall's and her headstone reads:

> 'In memory of Mary, beloved wife of Albert Hewish, who died
> at Strangways Springs, March 2nd, 1895, Aged 32 Years'.

I could not find a death notice for Mary, but perhaps she died in childbirth. Further tragedy struck when a baby girl, Hester Maud Hewish, died of 'bronchitis and convulsions' 11 months later.

It was not always so tragic at Strangways Springs. In the heat of January 1888 for example, an 'entertainment' went over very well with the small 'sympathetic but applausive audience':

> ... An entertainment, consisting of vocal and instrumental
> music, was given at the telegraph station here, on Monday
> evening, January 2, by lady and gentlemen amateurs ... The

---

* *South Australian Register*, 9 November 1893.

performers included Mesdames Bennett, Bailey, and Gentle, and Messrs G. Bennett, Hewish, John Besley, and Whitters, all of whom acquitted themselves in a creditable manner. On the termination of the concert a dance took place and was kept up till early morning[*].

Albert Hewish died in 1928, but he lived long enough to warrant an obituary. Strangely, it does not mention Mary at all:

… Mr. Albert Hewish, of Main Northroad, Prospect, whose death occurred on September 19, at the age of 65, had retired from the Post and Telegraph Department on August 15 after faithful service of 42 years, most of which time was spent in the north, where he was well-known along the overland telegraph line. He joined the service at Strangways Springs in May 1886, where his brother, the late Mr. Andrew Hewish, was in charge. At that time Strangways was a repeating and busy station. Later he was transferred to Oodnadatta, where he was for some years assistant operator.

In 1906 he was given charge of a repair party consisting of three men, horses, waggons, &c., and during the next few years made three trips into the Northern Territory as far north as Powell's Creek. On many occasions he came in contact with blacks, and at no time did he have trouble with them, although precautions were always taken. In fact, it was a common occurrence for blacks, who knew by their 'bush telegraph' that the overland telegraph party were approaching, to leave timber ready to make camp.

His last few years were spent in Adelaide, but bush life always appealed to him. He left a widow, three sons, and three daughters. One son, Ernest, made the supreme sacrifice in the Great War[†].

Wandering around the extraordinary landscape of the mound springs, with the dead-flat treeless horizon shimmering in the heat, I tried to imagine what it was like living here 150 years ago. Some men and women must have revelled in it. Many stayed out here their entire careers. I stood for a while where the telegraph station verandah used to be. Long ago, there were dances and concerts here, and judging by

---

[*] *Port Augusta Dispatch*, 10 January 1888.
[†] *Chronicle*, 6 October 1828.

the ubiquitous piles of broken bottles* around the village, good times were had by all. I listened for a minute. The only sounds were flies, the wind, and the occasional twitter of a distant bird …

The Peake (Kalturruka)

The Peake Telegraph Station was built above the extraordinary Freeling Springs (Yardiya) that still flow out from under the hill. It was named after Peake Creek, which honoured a politician named C.J. Peake. Most sources describe the station as *The Peake*, but its Arabana name was *Kalturruka*, which translates as 'breaking up a windstorm by means of incantations'†. To get there is to follow a rough, 15 kilometre (the sign says 21) public access track through Anna Creek Station. The track crosses country that is increasingly more interesting geologically. Large swathes of brilliant white quartz stones and pebbles lay across sections of the land like snow, each stone standing on a little pillar of protected dirt as if they have been pushed out of the ground.

It comes as no surprise to learn that miners moved into the hills around here in the 1890s to mine copper.

The springs run across flat rocks into reed beds that seem out of place in the desert. A journalist for the *Northern Argus* described what he saw in 1878:

> … The Peake station is the first government building met with after leaving Beltana. It is a substantial stone structure containing eight rooms. There are also several substantial stone outhouses, besides Messrs. J. & G. M. Bagot's station buildings. These buildings are situated at the base of the Dennison Range, and just above a fine cluster of freshwater springs. The Peake Creek, from which the place takes its name, is two miles north of the station. The surrounding country, within a radius of five miles, consists of soda flats and stony tablelands. Spring waters are liberally distributed over this run,

---

* I won't go on about it, but the ruins of every telegraph station on the line are remarkable for the sheer volume of broken bottles lying around them.

† Luise Hercus, 2009. (Hercus, 2009)

Figure 87: The Peake Telegraph Station

which is certainly one of the most valuable properties in the far north-west. The Peake is not a pretty place, but it possesses attractions which my friends in the interior appreciate more highly than scenic effects*.

As you approach the springs nowadays, the first ruin you pass is a single building on the flat, with a sign stating that was the Hammer and Gad Eating House. With a good water source and herds of cattle and flocks of sheep being staged nearby by drovers in the 1870s, perhaps it was the 'roadhouse' of the day.

Todd placed the main depot for the central section of the line here and the first wagons arrived on 28 October 1870. The springs had been discovered by John McDouall Stuart in June 1859, eleven years earlier. The Peake was soon the furthest outpost of pastoralists in South Australia. Philip Levi leased 155 square kilometres of the area in 1863 and, after a drought, Christopher and John Bagot took it over in 1870.

Charles Todd required explorers to map and plan the best route from here on. He sent John Ross northwards from the tented camp that had established itself beside the creek. In the meantime, construction of the telegraph station soon started. The buildings were substantial, so their ruins are extensive. Some of the ruins date back to the pastoral days of the early 1860s. Others date from the telegraph station built in 1871, when the builders used and extended several of the pastoral buildings and built new structures.

---

* *Northern Argus*, 20 August 1878.

The telegraph station operated here for 20 years. In 1891 the line was moved to run alongside the railway and the station was transferred to the new railhead at Oodnadatta, about 70 kilometres north.

However, near the turn of the century the buildings had a new lease of life. In 1870, the O.T.L. workers discovered copper ore in the hill above the station and a mine was planned by a public company called The Copper Top Proprietary Mining Company, formed in 1898. Mining started in 1900, and the visible lode suggested there was enough to invest further and instal a smelter. It was expensive infrastructure but, unfortunately, there was never enough copper to make a profit. The mines closed in 1904 and the investors lost their money. The mineshafts and black slag piles are still there and a signposted walk around the site has been installed by the Friends of the Mound Springs. It is well worth following and despite being nearly carried up the valley by the flies, I was happy to gaze down the vertical shafts into the earth without venturing further.

In August 1873, the station hosted Ernest Giles and his exploration party after their return from exploring west of the line. The party had hit the line some 60 miles from The Peake on the Neales River, and it had a been a simple task to follow it south to the telegraph station. The news of his arrival was immediately transmitted to the waiting ears of the Morse readers in Adelaide, as was the news in October 1874 of the safe arrival of John Forrest and his party from Western Australia. They were then 'most hospitably entertained by Mr. Blood and Mr. Bagot'.

Forrest was unimpressed by the country he had witnessed. He wrote from The Peake:

> ... On reviewing the long time, we have spent upon the march, I often wonder how we managed to get through such a miserable country, as for over six hundred miles we travelled through nothing but a spinifex desert[*].

---

[*] *Border Watch*, 7 October 1874.

Figure 88: A roll of telegraph wire and broken insulators still lying beside the old Ghan Railway route.

Perhaps he had forgotten that he still had another few hundred miles of similar country before reaching 'civilisation'. It wasn't so bad for me—a few hours drive along the famous 'Oodnadatta Track' gets a modern traveller to Oodnadatta, where The Peake's replacement was built.

Oodnadatta (Utnadata)

I camped overnight at Oodnadatta's iconic Pink Roadhouse—and it sure is pink! Oodnadatta is the biggest town on the 'Oodnadatta Track'*. With a population of 180 people, it has a school, a police

---

* There are other towns, such as William Creek, population 12. Today it is an important airport for tourist flights over nearby Lake Eyre. It has a pub, phone communication, and a display of old stuff in its park. Most other railway siding 'towns' have perished. You can see ruins of the fettlers' accommodation in in several

Figure 89: The 'Angle Pole', Oodnadatta.

station, and a hospital. It also has a small railway museum set up by the community in the delightful old railway station building. Visitors to the museum need to pick up a key from the roadhouse or the town shop, and then visit it unassisted. It is full of information about the Ghan Railway and the school, which opened in May 1892*, but there is little on the O.T.L.

South of Oodnadatta, four telegraph poles stand on either side of the road. Two are metal Oppenheimer poles and two are cypress pine. They were placed there as a memorial to the line, but obviously are not in their original positions—they are less than ten metres apart—a far cry from their original 80 metres. Other remnants can be seen often beside the old track of the Ghan Railway. White insulators gleam in the sun like scatterings of mushrooms near where telegraph poles used to stand. They were cleared away in 1982, but any that were

---

places along the line.
* *South Australian Register*, 29 April 1892.

broken were left on the ground, and there they remain, worthless. At one point I found a roll of telegraph wire they had forgotten to take with them.

A few kilometres on the other side of the town is the 'angle pole'. It is a crooked bit of wood surrounded by an ancient timber fence. It has a hand-painted sign declaring it to be a monument to the men who made the O.T.L. Its strange proclamation reads:

> This plaque and monument depicting the angle pole used extensively in the district, stands in recognition of a great achievement won through hardship and endurance.

Whether the pole was actually *the* angle pole or not is unclear. It is far from straight, so the word 'angle' may refer to this particular pole's crooked dog-leg shape. There was an actual 'angle pole' here in the beginning because the O.T.L. changed direction here, creating an angle, but I am not convinced this pole is it, although the timber is certainly ancient.

'Angle Pole' was also a placename before Oodnadatta* became a town. It was near the last waterhole on Neales Creek, and travellers north faced an 80-kilometre dry stage from it. A parliamentary party was escorted there from the rail head by camel because it was 'the extreme point to which the construction of the Transcontinental railway has so far been authorised'[†]. They were not impressed. They concluded that the line would end up as a 'railway to nowhere' and it would be a 'farce'[‡]. Much better, they said, to push on to the MacDonnell Ranges and the town of Stuart (Alice Springs), which they did, albeit 40 years later. In the meantime, a 400-metre bore was sunk, Oodnadatta grew out of the dust, and the railway arrived.

The Oodnadatta Telegraph Station replaced the station at The Peake. It was managed by Andrew Hewish [aka Hewitt] J.P.—the brother of Albert Hewish at Strangways. He had wide-ranging roles

---

* *Utnadata* in Arrernte.
† *The Express and Telegraph*, 15 October 1889.
‡ *The Express and Telegraph*, 23 October 1889.

that included responsibilities not usually expected in a telegrapher. In 1892, for example, there was a murder at Dalhousie Springs, and Hewish was required to travel north with Mounted Constables Stewart and Holland to perform the inquest[*].

Hewish also tried an 'Afghan' who was suspected of arson, held an inquest on the body of Charles Frost, a suicide who had swallowed strychnine, and another on the body of David Boland, who had fallen from a train near Hergott Springs[†]. Plus, he was the officiating registrar of marriages, a commissioner for taking affidavits in the Supreme Court and, in 1876, he collected £30 from railwayman George Lawrence after he attempted suicide during an attack of *delirium tremens*. Lawrence would get his money back, he was told, but only if he kept the peace for three months[‡].

Andrew Hewish's career was cut short in 1898 when he died 'from failure of the heart's action, after influenza', in Oodnadatta. Andrew was 44 and 'respected by all who knew him'. His death was a surprise because although he 'had been suffering from influenza for a few days, he was not in a serious condition and no importance was attached to his illness'[§].

Oodnadatta became the mail-sorting centre for the region, and it was from here that a mailman would set out every two weeks to transfer the mail to his Alice Springs colleague at Horseshoe Bend on the Hugh River. At least, this meant that the next station north, Charlotte Waters, had a visitor once a week, as the mailman went back and forth. All visitors were welcome in those days. Travelling the road between Oodnadatta to Charlotte Waters, I got the feeling that I was about as remote as it is possible to get in Australia.

---

[*] *Evening Journal*, 29 September 1891.
[†] *Port Augusta Dispatch*, 15 April 1887.
[‡] *The Port Augusta Dispatch*, 23 November 1886.
[§] *Chronicle*, 18 June 1898.

Charlotte Waters (Arlyernpe or Alkngulura)

> … Mr. Knuckey formed his main camp on the Charlotte Waters*, on the Wall, a little north of latitude 26°. which he recommends as a suitable site for the first station after leaving The Peake, where we have already erected a stone station now used as our first depot. The waterholes are large and deep and are supposed to be permanent; at all events, I should think a permanent supply could be obtained by sinking. The surrounding country is described as very fine and well grassed[1].

It wasn't fine and well-grassed when I was there. A more desolate place is hard to imagine. The country is mostly flat and stony. Of the telegraph station, there is nothing but a scattering of stones and an inground water tank that descends about three metres into the plain and acts as a deep pit-trap for snakes, lizards, and careless kangaroos. The road passes by the front gate, but few people stop, as there is little to see.

Its near total destruction is a shame. The station stood in its extraordinarily countryside—and if the ruins were more substantial, they would be an attractive stopover for modern travellers to visit. Nowadays, even the information signs that are scattered over the site are cracked, faded and nearly illegible. In 1874, Charlotte Waters consisted of an eight-roomed stone dwelling with the underground tank in a courtyard, a blacksmith's shop, cart shed, harness room, paddock, and stockyard. There were also 583 sheep, 32 horses, 100 cattle and 150 goats. The two camels supplied to the station had wandered off into the bush.

In 1887, Simpson Newland of the South Australian Railway Commission, toured Central Australia. He was not impressed by Charlotte Waters:

> … The site of the telegraph station is an unfortunate one. It is dry, bare, and desolate, with the hot stony land all round

---

* Ernest Giles wrote that Charlotte Waters was named by Knuckey after 'Lady Charlotte Bacon', a character in a long narrative poem titled *Child Harold's Pilgrimage*, by Lord Byron.

† Charles Todd: *South Australian Register*, 29 March 1871.

Figure 90: Charlotte Waters Telegraph Station in 2021.

Figure 91: Charlotte Waters—the grave of a blacksmith's dog …

... disconnected and forlorn ... chiefly remarkable for its ugliness and heat ... Not a verandah exists, and old Sol must have a rare grilling within those walls during the long summer months. Think of sweltering in there listening to the tick of the instrument! Oh, the monotony of such an existence!*

Baldwin Spencer described Charlotte Waters in 1896:

... The station is placed close to the northern edge of a wide plain. The main buildings form three sides of a quadrangle, the fourth side being closed in by strong gates—or rather it used to be in the early days when it was first built, and it was necessary to have protection against the blacks. At that time, the doors all opened on the quadrangle, and every room had loopholes through which, if necessity arose, the officials could defend themselves ... Charlotte Waters looks out upon a great open, stony plain without a sign of human habitation. North and south runs the line of telegraph poles, streaking away to the horizon, and the ticking of the instrument, as the message passes through, only serves to heighten the feeling of isolation ...†

The station's heyday appears to have been during the early 1900s, but it limped on until 1938, when the police were transferred to Finke. The buildings were condemned and abandoned by all except one old man, Scotty McKenzie, who had lived there for three decades, and chose not to move on. His desiccated corpse was found in one of the rooms by an Andado Station worker long after he had died, in December 1938.

In 1945, Jim Davey of Andado Station bought the buildings by tender, and removed the tin and roofing materials and they were re-used at Andado. Several of the walls collapsed in 1947, and the stones were then taken for use at New Crown Station. There are said to be stones bearing initials carved by Charlotte Waters staff, or their visitors, still visible in the walls at New Crown‡.

There is a grave behind the site and a sign that says it belongs to a blacksmith's dog. The fine metal work of the fence and cross

---

* *South Australian Advertiser*, 15 July 1887.
† Spencer, 1896
‡ Kimber, 1992, cited by Heritage NT.

above it suggests that indeed, it was built by a blacksmith. Nearby is a 1993 plaque commemorating Stanley Percival Hocking, a telegraph operator, and the senior postal assistant from 1922 until 1928. He died in 1993, so perhaps relatives installed the plaque in his honour.

The Charlotte Waters Telegraph Station opened on 31 August 1872. The local Arrernte mostly accepted their arrival, but relationships were strained at times. When Richard Knuckey and his party were camped there in April 1871, a fracas occurred between Knuckey and an Arrernte man that resulted in a spear being thrown. It struck Knuckey on the left elbow, and in retaliation Knuckey shot the spear thrower in his right shoulder. There the matter seems to have ended. There were certainly never any attacks here like those at Barrow Creek.

This was where Mueller, Watson, and Kraegen, excited at the thought of settling into their new station-master roles further north were to impatient. They departed ahead of their guide, Ray Boucaut, in December 1871, and this proved foolhardy, of course, when Kraegen perished for want of water. Mueller and Watson only survived by drinking the blood of their horse.

An important scientific expedition organised by W.A. Horn, and led by Charles Winnecke, visited Charlotte Waters in 1894. The party included Dr Edward Stirling, who had travelled with Governor Kintore across the continent a few years previously; Professor Baldwin Spencer, a well-known ethnologist remembered for his early photographs of Aborigines; and Professor Ralph Tate, who had accompanied the 1882 Parliamentary Party to the gold fields near Darwin. From Charlotte Waters, they were able to relate:

> … since leaving Alice Springs the party has obtained many additional objects of interest*, and the trip has been a success. Mr. Winnecke has succeeded in filling up a large amount of

---

* It was during this expedition that Winnecke stole items from a major repository of Aboriginal sacred objects, helped by an Aboriginal guide who was later killed by local elders for his crime of leading Winnecke to their hiding place. Some of these objects have recently been returned to Central Australia.

Figure 92: Paddy Byrne (seated right) worked at Charlotte Waters for nearly 50 years. Frank Gillen is seated in the middle. Photo by Government Geologist Henry Yorke Lyell Brown, c. 1880 (SLSA, B-11607).

space that was vacant on the maps and has corrected a number of inaccuracies in the maps. Professor Spencer's biological and photographic collection is an extensive one, and Professor Tate has made a fine botanical collection. Dr. Stirling has been amply and successfully employed in ethnological work, and Mr. Watt has accumulated an interesting collection of geological specimens and fossils. Mr. Heartland's ornithological specimens include over 200 skins, representing nearly 100 different species[*].

Charlotte Waters almost sits on the Northern Territory–South Australian border of the 26th parallel, so it was once a major entry point into the Territory and the government established a customs station there to gather information about exports and imports[†]. But there is precious little to see now.

---

[*] *Melbourne Leader*, 4 August 1984.
[†] *Northern Territory Times and Gazette*, 24 August 1889.

Christopher Giles[*] was the first stationmaster, with Joe Johnston as his assistant—before his attack of scurvy. Frank Gillen spent 13 years at the station, and his brother-in-law, Paddy Byrne, nearly 50. A police station stood nearby for many years too. Mounted Constable W. Walkman was stationed in it for years, primarily to curtail the illegal sale of liquor[†].

Isolation is a strange thing. City folk wonder at people who choose to live so far from 'normal life'—especially in a time when travel in either direction was risky and took weeks to complete. However, the characters who chose these stations as their homes often stayed for years. Perhaps the reason why was best summarised by Bertha Strehlow in the 1930s. She visited Charlotte Waters when only policemen and their staff lived there:

> ... I was impressed ... They were all brave, cheerful people. Even the children. The homestead served also as the police station. It was a large, sprawling building standing in isolation—out on gibber plains, hundreds of miles from nowhere. When I first saw it, I thought it was the most desolate place I had ever set eyes on. I remember thinking that only utter loneliness could exist out there. But, after a few hours, I realised the people there really cared for each other more than I had believed possible, and there was a wonderful sense of belonging to each other. I remember watching an off-duty policeman and his son going off with a wagon and horses to collect mulga stumps for the kitchen stove and for the fires that kept the homestead warm in winter, because the nights could be very cold. They were gone for hours. When they returned, the wagon was loaded, and the man and boy were dirty and tired, but there was a look of satisfaction on their faces that I hadn't seen before[‡].

---

[*] A full list of station staff can be found on www.ntlis.nt.gov.au/heritageregister/heritage_register.
[†] NT Heritage
[‡] McNally 1981, cited by NT Heritage.

Along the O.T.L.

Figure 92: Chambers Pillar was visited by John McDouall Stuart in 1860. Stuart chose not to carve his name into the soft stone.

Figure 93: John Ross and the members of the 'Adelaide–Port Darwin Overland Telegraph Line Exploring Party' carved their names or initials on Chambers Pillar on 3 October 1870. His was the second party of Europeans to visit the pillar after Stuart's discovery a decade before.

Chambers Pillar (Ildracowra)

Chambers Pillar is a point of interest on the O.T.L. route, not because it was on the line—that passed by some 30 kilometres to the east—but because John Ross, Alfred Giles, and surveyor William Harvey visited it while exploring for a route north during October 1870:

> ... The next day we started at 8 o'clock in the direction of the Pillar, and upon gaining the top of a high sandhill we presented to our view three of the grandest sights probably we have ever seen.

One was Chambers Pillar, named by Stuart after a sponsor of his expedition. The explorers were so impressed that:

> ... We all carved our names an inch deep on the western face of the pillar, and also the date of our visit ... Ours was the first party to visit it since [Stuart] discovered it*.

The names are still there, of course—along with a hundred others carved by Mounted Constables Willshire and East, members of the Hayes family who arrived during the 1880s, other station workers, and more recent idiot tourists who could not resist the temptation of graffiti. I climbed up the stairs and skirted round the modern walkway installed by NT Parks and Wildlife. I easily found the name J. ROSS on the western face, just as Giles said it would be. 'TC' was carved under it by Thomas Crisp and Hearne's name was there in full, except the H had dropped off. Not far from it was the initials 'AG, 1870' where Giles had left his mark.

I camped not far from the pillar, thankful that I had carried enough firewood in on my roof rack to keep me warm. The night was crisp and as dark as it can get in the desert. The stars were magnificent, and I watched a procession of satellites make their way through them. Apart from two other hardy campers on the other side of the park, it was strange to think that some of those satellites were closer to me than any other humans.

I needed the rest. The road between Charlotte Waters and Alice Springs, via the community of Apatula/Finke, follows the old Ghan Railway track and is about as corrugated as roads can get. It was made more exciting by the occasional metal dog-spike (a remnant of the rail line) sticking straight up out of the road. Several desert racing cars passed me on the Alice Springs to Finke racetrack that runs beside the road. Their teams were practicing for the upcoming annual race.

---

* Giles, 1878.

Along the O.T.L.

Figure 95: The children of the Alice Springs Telegraph Station in 1906, the Bradshaws and their donkey wagon: Donnell and Edna are passengers, the driver is Jack, and watching is Consie and Mort (Smith Collection, LANT, ph0763/0038).

Figure 96: The same donkey wagon now on display at the Alice Springs Telegraph Station.

Figure 97: Ernest Flint's grave near the Alice Springs Telegraph Station.

And practising well—some of their buggies passed me at double my speed or more. There were motorbike riders too, defying death on the corrugations. For me, it had not been an easy drive, and I had already shredded one tyre, so I marvelled at their skills.

The highpoint of the journey was caused by the good rains that had fallen here in the previous year. Vegetation was everywhere, and though I had missed its brilliant flowering, everything now had seeds, and they supported huge populations of birds. There were birds of many species everywhere, looking fat and healthy, and budgerigars in particular. Budgies are ubiquitous in the Australian desert and flock in huge numbers during good seasons. At one point, I startled several thousand that sat beside the road. I drove into an emerald-green cloud as they took to the skies. My vision was filled with the colour as birds fled in every direction.

It was an image I carried with me as I came back into civilisation. I thought I might treat myself to a hotel in Alice Springs. The nights were cold, and I'd been in the bush a few days … a shower would be welcome.

Alice Springs (Mparntwe Ampere)

I hadn't counted on Alice Springs being the epicentre of a post-covid tourist boom in Central Australia. Every hotel was full, and by the time I got out to the caravan parks, their offices were closed because of staff shortages—at 6 P.M.!

Homeless, I ended up driving 30 kilometres out of town and camping on the banks of Jay Creek, which meant I was woken before dawn by the heavy footsteps of wild horses coming to the creek to drink, but this, in turn, allowed me to be at the gates of the Alice Springs Overland Telegraph Station the moment they opened.

I paid the $15 entry fee and being early, I had the place to myself for an hour or two, before hordes of bright-eyed grey nomads appeared. It was worth it—the Alice Springs Telegraph Station is now a museum of fully renovated station buildings set among beautifully kept gardens, with an excellent display of the history of the O.T.L. in the station rooms. It is a jewel in the crown of attractions to the centre of Australia, and the locals are justifiably proud of it.

In the stables are several old drays and light buggies, harnesses for horses, and other old equipment on display. The smithy is so fully stocked with tools, it looks like it could be fired up easily. Other buildings have displays of rooms furnished as they were 120 years ago, and when the telegraph office is manned visitors can send messages in Morse code, or have their names spelt out in dots and dashes. I was too early for this, so was spared the temptation.

The station museum holds several items of great interest. From 1899 until 1908, Thomas Bradshaw was stationmaster and he lived here with his family. They were all regularly photographed over the

Figure 98: Barrow Creek Telegraph Station in 1926 (Captain Bagot, SLSA, B-71884-11).

Figure 99: Barrow Creek Telegraph Station in 2021.

years, but the image that most appealed to me was of the children playing in a cart that was pulled by a donkey. In the museum is the actual cart, a direct link to the Bradshaw children of more than a century ago, near the place they played with it.

A short walk took me out to the cemetery. Ernest Flint lies there after eight years' service as the stationmaster, forever 33 years old. His near-death experience at the end of a Kaytetye spear at Barrow Creek may have taught him much, but he failed to conquer rheumatic fever. How sad, I thought, for his widow. He died after just seven months

Figure 100: A wagon in the shed at Barrow Creek Telegraph Station.

of married life. I recalled that Carl Kraegen hadn't even got this far. Johannes Mueller, the first stationmaster at Alice Springs (Flint's predecessor), was only there because of Kraegen's death by thirst on the way to take the role. Their deaths, as deaths always do, provided a fork in the road of history, promotional opportunities, and a turnover of staff. Mueller particularly benefited—he became the senior office of the line from Attack Creek, south to Beltana[*].

After an excellent coffee at the cafeteria, and a rummage through the Overland Telegraph tea towels, enamel mugs and racks of T-shirts, I hit the road again, but left the dirt tracks behind. I was now on the Stuart Highway, and, not far out of Alice Springs, I passed a 'Teamster's Memorial'. It remembers Charles Palmer, who died of 'palpitation of the heart' on 4 July 1871. According to Smith 'he was warming himself over the fire and fell backwards lifeless'[†]. The memorial reads: 'Buried in this vicinity—C. Palmer, teamster, died August [sic] 1871 while serving with a survey party during the construction of the Overland Telegraph Line'.

---

[*] Todd, 1883.
[†] Crouch 2020: Smith's diary. Todd later said that Palmer had died of consumption (1883).

Figure 101: Barrow Creek Telegraph Station.

The next telegraph station along the line was the place where Stapleton and Franks were murdered, and Flint received his wound. It was on a creek named by Stuart after a South Australian Parliamentarian in 1860, John H. Barrow.

Barrow Creek

A temporary stone hut with a thatched roof was erected here while the foundations for the Telegraph Station were laid in December 1870. The station was completed by August 1872, and it was here that Charles Todd chose to spend the moment of the joining of the cable. As the long-winded, dull message, penned by John Little in Palmerston, passed through Barrow Creek Station, as it did with all stations along the line, Todd must have felt a supreme sense of satisfaction. He had seen the project through from its beginning, Australia would soon be connected to Europe, and his knighthood was assured.

Visitors can easily call in on the station. It is next to the Barrow Creek Roadhouse, and the doors are unlocked. The building is in good repair, the covered well in the courtyard still holds water, and there are even fly screens on some of the doors.

It looks as if little has changed here since that momentous time in 1874, when Stapleton and Franks were speared as they sat chatting in the cool of the evening. The main building still looks fit to live in, the wagon shed holds an old wagon, and the smithy looks like it could be used again. Only the smithy was locked, but I could see through the bars of the door.

By today's standards the building must have been crowded in the early years—a staff of seven lived here, plus a police officer. In 1883, the latter was Constable John Charles Shirley, and it was his rescue party of eight men, including Alan Giles, who set off on a search from here, only to have most of them perish for want of water.

The station became a post office and maintenance depot in 1910, without telegraph duties, and then a police station in 1930. A new roof was installed in 1941, so the walls have always been protected from the weather. In 1942 it was a staging camp for army convoys travelling north to Darwin and it continued to be used up to 1980 as a line depot by Telecom. The last linesman, Tom Roberts, finally left in 1986. Now it is being managed by the Parks and Wildlife Commission as an historic site, and the interior walls look freshly whitewashed.

Tennant Creek (Jurnkurakurr)

The Tennant Creek Telegraph Station is another that is well-restored and maintained. The doors are locked, but visitors can collect a key (on a healthy deposit) from the museum in town and enter the buildings. Its halls echo with past events. During the nineteenth century it was a busy place, particularly during the annual Tennant Creek races. Barney Lamond happened across them in 1885 when he was transporting horses to the Kimberley, and he and others spent a lot of time at the station:

Figure 102: Tennant Creek Telegraph Station.

Figure 103: Tennant Creek Telegraph Station.

…there were continually a lot of us up at Tennant's Creek Telegraph Station for news of the world, which the operators hear. At the station there were Allen [sic: Alan] Giles (Telegraph Master), Billy Abbott (Second Operator), a mechanic, two line-repairers, and also a cook. They had good buildings, a well, and good food which was sent up from Adelaide. Mr. Giles and all the telegraph men treated us splendidly. Abbot told me he had been fourteen years there and on other telegraph stations and had never been down to Adelaide or up to Port Darwin. His salary was paid to his credit in the bank at Adelaide. The others living at the station were two men who used to travel up and down the line every week (one hundred miles north and south to keep it in repair and cart water when necessary) and the cook who never left the station. Their rations were of the best and were sent up from Adelaide by the Government. They were passed along the line on their repair wagons of four horses each. These people were also kept in rifles and ammunition to defend themselves in case of attack by the blacks. A few years before we were out here, at Barrow Creek Telegraph Station (two hundred miles south of Tennant's Creek) there had been an attack, the station surrounded and three of the staff killed. Since then, a police patrol rides along every few months. Most of the Telegraph Stations are two hundred miles apart[*].

Renner Springs

The springs that became known as Renner Springs were discovered by Dr Fred Renner in 1872, after he followed birds to its waters. The springs were an important water point for the Warumungu people, of course, but they had also stopped there for generations to quarry stones to make axes and knives[†]. It was a handy 30 kilometres from Powell's Creek to its north, so it became an important watering point for horses and cattle, and the O.T.L. passed by. It was later used as a staging post for army convoys during World War Two. The roadhouse and 'Desert Inn' were built by the Doyles in 1947, and both still operate.

There was never a telegraph station here, but it is an interesting stopping point for a part of the O.T.L. story.

There is no evidence left of the early huts, but part of the wall in the shop is constructed of Oppenheimer poles and old glass insulators, which may be of interest to visitors. When I was there, the owners were excited to tell me that the entire Renner clan—descendants of the doctor from South Australia—were about to descend on the pub

---

[*]   Lamond, 1885, published in 1886.
[†]   Spencer and Gillen, 1912.

and celebrate their own sesquicentenary—150 years since Renner discovered the springs.

Across the road from the roadhouse there is a tiny cemetery with two gravestones lying flat on the ground. One belongs to Alan McFarlane Giles, J.P., the survivor of Shirley's tragic search party for Henry Readford. Giles, who had been telegraph stationmaster at Tennant Creek, died of 'brain fever' at Renner Springs on 24 November 1888, aged 39.

The *Evening Journal* announced his death to the world:

> ... News was received on Saturday that Mr. Alan M. Giles, J.P., Manager of Tennant's Creek Telegraph Station, was dead. He was the only witness in the Renner Springs murder case[*]

Reading this, of course, sent me on another hunt. What murder case? I found it in the *North Australian* of 24 November 1888, under the heading of *Murder in the Interior*:

> ... On the 19th instant the local police authorities received a telegram to the effect that a man had been shot at Renner Springs cattle station, about 20 miles south of Powell's Creek, on the overland route to Adelaide. The telegram was sent down by Mr. Allan [sic] Giles, and through the courtesy of the officials we have been able to secure the following abstract reference to the circumstances as given by Mr. Giles:
>
> 'A man named James Anderson shot the cook, Walter Hammond, early this morning with a 450 revolver. The ball went in about the middle of his chest and came out of his side. They had a quarrel over some money transactions. Hammond is in a very precarious condition. I saw the firing done. There is only a white lad on the station, the manager and all other white men being away ... '
>
> Mr. Giles was instructed by Dr. Wood by wire as to the course to adopt in treating the injured man, but he was unable to save his life, and the unfortunate fellow died on Wednesday. As soon as the circumstances were made known Mr. Inspector Foelsche instructed Constable Stott, of the Katherine, to proceed to Powell's Creek and arrest Anderson, who will be

---

[*] 26 November 1888.

brought on for trial as soon as possible*.

Giles must have felt desperately unprepared, but he tried save the man with instructions from a doctor coming by telegram!

Anderson, who was 'a man of low stature, about 45 years of age, and not very taking in appearance', was found guilty of manslaughter at the end of December and sentenced to 10 years hard labour. After sentencing he feebly remarked:

> 'Thank you, your Honor [sic]; we'll both be ten years older when I come out!'†

Alan Giles's cracked gravestone lies flat on the ground as a result of vandalism in 1952:

> … the lonely grave of a man named Giles—which has been there since the Overland Telegraph construction days—has been badly damaged by vandals recently. The iron railing round this pioneer's resting place has been torn down, and the headstone which his relatives had brought thousands of miles to mark his memory, has been knocked over‡.

Renner Springs is 11 kilometres north of Attack Creek, and two memorials have been raised beside the Attack Creek bridge. The first is to John McDouall Stuart. It was here, on 25 June 1860, that he, William Kekwick and Benjamin Head turned back on Stuart's unsuccessful fifth attempt to reach the north coast. The party were already suffering badly from poor diet and long exposure to the elements, and when they were attacked by hostile Warumungu on this spot, they turned around and began the long walk home.

In the attack, Stuart and his men dodged spears and boomerangs and fired their pistols back at the Aborigines, but it is not known if anyone was shot. Stuart uses euphemisms in his diary such as we 'stayed their mad career for a while', 'gave them another reception' and 'took steady aim, to make an impression'. Stuart's biographer, John Bailey, concludes that casualties and deaths *must* have occurred§.

---

* *North Australian*, 24 November 1888.
† *North Australian*, 29 December 1888.
‡ *Centralian Advocate*, 15 February 1952.
§ Bailey, 2006.

Twenty to the Mile

Figure 104: Powell's Creek Telegraph Station.

Figure 105: Powell's Creek Telegraph Station and staff accommodation.

Figure 106: Powell's Creek Telegraph Station.

How else could three white men escape from several hundred angry Warumungu warriors?

But there is an alternative possibility. Baldwin Spencer and Frank Gillen visited the Tennant Creek in the early 1900s and met an old man who had 'actually taken part in the attack on Stuart's party, and from what he told us, we came to the conclusion that Stuart rather exaggerated the capacity of the natives to hinder his progress northwards'*. The altercation seems to have been over dwindling water supplies. Perhaps the Warumungu people were concerned about how much water was taken by the white men and their horses.

The other memorial at Attack Creek is to Mounted Constable John Charles Shirley, who 'perished in the performance of his duty in this vicinity on 7 November 1883'. Shirley's story is told in Chapter 7. He is commemorated as the first policeman to die in the Northern Territory while on duty.

Powell's Creek (Pamayu)

Powell's Creek Telegraph Station is about 30 kilometres north of Renner Springs. There is a small sign on the highway marking a track west to 'Powells Ck†', but that is the only tell-tale. The telegraph station sits alone in the bush five kilometres down this road, again on the left. There is no sign, but the station is visible from the track, about 400 metres from it. There is a rarely used access trail across grasslands—a car needs to cross the raised soil left by the grader, but apart from that, a two-wheel-drive vehicle shouldn't have any trouble‡.

I arrived at sunset and camped outside the fence. I was alone, and far enough away from the highway to hear nothing but the sounds of the bush during the night, and the faint crackle of my fire.

---

* Spencer and Gillen, 1912.
† Modern place names do not use apostrophes.
‡ Visitors should remember that the station is on private land—Newcastle Waters Station—and it is good manners to call ahead or email the station before you go in.

The station buildings still have their roofs, but everything else has been pillaged. There are no doors, taps, or anything left that can be unscrewed or unbolted. In parts, the ceiling has collapsed—it was originally insulating straw-thatched panels. Other more recently installed ceiling panels look like asbestos. There is a lot of broken glass. Bottle collectors were here in the twentieth century, so there is nothing left that is not already broken. Still, what remains of the buildings is salvageable—a tourist site of the future, perhaps?

But what a great place to camp! The atmosphere created by the long-abandoned buildings, glowing in both the sunset and sunrise was extraordinary. Here, generations of telegraph station staff planted vegetable gardens and herded cattle and sheep. Huge numbers of beasts passed here in droves. On the plains behind the station, I found signs of them in horseshoes and bullock shoes (known as *cues*), wire bent in innovative shapes for a purpose I could only guess at, broken pottery, broken telegraph insulators, and even more broken glass.

In the creek there were rusted metal pots and anonymous bits of metal. The well, once a walled structure near the creek, still holds water, albeit with a dark and rancid look. The creek was not flowing, but a duck swam on the billabong among the trees, and fish swirled in its waters. Charles Johnston had shot teal here for their Christmas dinner in 1872. With sheep, ducks, turkeys, goannas, and magpie geese, and good melons and corn from their gardens, the station folk dined well. They had watermelon for dessert that Christmas.

In the early 1900s, when Baldwin Spencer and Frank Gillen visited, the telegraph station was managed by the hospitable Mr and Mrs Kell*. The station's gardens were full of banana palms, *Bauhinia* and 'bean trees', and some of the local 'Tjingilli' (Jingili) tribe were camped nearby. Spencer wrote that it was 'a wonderful relief, after six month's camping out, to have a meal properly served and everything as nice as possible'†

---

* Walter James Kell and Mrs Isabella Jane Kell.
† Spencer and Gillen, 1912.

Near the station is the grave of Alfred Pybus. A pipe frame surrounds the old wrought iron grave marker. Pybus was a member of the Overland Telegraph Construction Team, and from 1885, was a linesman based at Daly Waters. He was at one point a justice of the peace and a manager of various teams on the O.T.L. It was Pybus's party that installed the second wire on the O.T.L. poles in the Top End in 1889. He died at Powell's Creek on 10 April 1900, aged 49[*].

The Joining Point (near Frew's Ironstone Ponds, Warlirra)

There is a roadside memorial to Charles Todd on the highway, about 20 kilometres south of Dunmarra Roadhouse. In 1954, when it was erected by the Line Training School, P.M.G.'s Department, of South Australia, it was a marble sheathed obelisk that gleamed in the sun. The marble is long gone. These days it is naked, pitted concrete in need of care. Its plaque announces that the O.T.L. joining point is one mile to the west.

NT Heritage recently built a road through the lancewood forest to the pole. A rusty weathered sign attached to the pole incorrectly says the time of connection was 3:15 p.m. rather than 12:10. A second sign, like the 'National Heritage Marker' beside the roadside memorial, was installed by Engineering Heritage Australia in 2012. It labels the pole as 4E28 and lists those present at the joining in 1872.

I first visited Pole 4E28 around midday one October. It was already nearly 42°C when my sons and I started walking the track but fortunately, we realised the foolhardiness of that before we'd gone a quarter of the way, so we turned back and chose a cooler time of day to return.

It was an exciting place to see. The lancewood is thick here. It must have been almost impenetrable for men on horseback leading

---

[*] *Advertiser*, 12 April 1900.

Figure 107 (above): The O.T.L. still runs through the lancewood (*Acacia shirleyi*) forest at the point where the north and south sections were joined by engineer Robert C. Patterson, near Frew's Ironstone Ponds, at 12:10 p.m. on 22 August 1872.

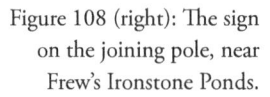

Figure 108 (right): The sign on the joining pole, near Frew's Ironstone Ponds.

packhorses. But the line still exists. Oppenheimer poles disappear into the bush both to the left and the right. I followed them for a while on my second visit, in cool weather, and found the bush closes in on them within a few hundred metres. However, the line carries on, stretched between large white insulators on top of the poles. It is well worth visiting if you're an O.T.L. pilgrim.

Daly Waters

I called in at Daly Waters looking for anything left over from the O.T.L. days. This tiny village has an interesting history of its time during World War Two, and its airfield is renowned as one of the first international airports in Australia—on the Batavia to Brisbane route—with the oldest hangar in the Northern Territory, dating from 1930. The first fare paying passengers to visit included Lady Mountbatten, in 1935.

Nowadays, it is a tourist haven with a character pub, a number of rusting old cars and ancient petrol bowsers, and a large caravan park. There were hundreds of caravans on site the day I passed through, many of them from Covid-ravaged Victoria, the grey nomads within them congratulating themselves on escaping another lockdown at home.

I asked a barkeep if she knew where the old telegraph station was. I got a blank look, then she brightened. 'There's a post outside,' she said.

And indeed, there was—an Oppenheimer pole with eight insulators on a cross beam stood proudly outside the door. A small sign screwed onto it commemorated the O.T.L.

The original telegraph station did not survive the test of time. In 1984, Earl James reported a set of concrete steps 400 metres south of the town that belonged to the station. I assume they are still there somewhere, but I failed in my brief search for them. Earl also said 'the town is riddled with OT poles' and near the police station there were

Figure 109: The only remnant of the telegraph line I could find at Daly Waters is outside the pub.

two cypress poles with copper wire lying on the ground. Nearly 40 years later there is no sign of them.

The original station was built of timber slabs and corrugated iron, two substances not known for longevity in this climate. Once the timber rotted away, the iron was probably either cleared away as a storm hazard and buried or recycled on a chook shed somewhere.

Also lost, somewhere on the other side of the creek, is the old Daly Waters Cemetery. In 1914, the surveyor A.B. Scandrett marked it on a map in his field book, but by the 1980s no sign of the graves existed*.

There is a more recent post-office building a hundred metres from the Daly Waters Hotel. A signboard in front of it told me that it was constructed in 1951 to replace the old telegraph building, and it was shared with the police station and telephone exchange in the 1960s. Out the back are police cells from 1964, complete with a skeleton sitting at rest on a plastic chair, still rueing the day …

The first stationmaster at Daly Waters was Isaac Roach. He had also been in charge of a construction party here during the erection of the line and he remained for a year or two. His successors were the team that would be attacked at Roper Bar—Johnston, Daer and Rickards. Roach transferred to Mount Gambier Post Office and then Terowie. His obituary reveals that he was 55 years in the public service†, and as he was 67 when he died, he probably started work as a 12-year-old telegram boy.

Elsey

In 1873, Charles Todd reported that a 'temporary station' was constructed on Elsey Creek, a tributary of the Roper River, between Daly Waters and Katherine. It was manned by two operators during the wet season, when faults along the line were difficult to access, or more likely to happen. It was near the current town of Mataranka, which is a tourist destination these days because of the nearby hot springs, but the actual site is lost. Earl James found broken glass and other rubbish on a site near Warloch Ponds in 1984 but was not successful in his search for the 'temporary' station. It was a log hut originally manned by E. J. Kemp, with a cook (Atkins) and two

---

* James, 1984.
† Roach died in 1930 (*Chronicle*, 20 March 1930).

Aboriginal workers (Johnny and Larry). The telegraph equipment was kept in the bedroom of what may have been a two-room hut.

Elsey Telegraph Station was closed in 1885 to save £700 per year, despite complaining letters to the editor*. The nearby Elsey Station homestead, made famous by Jeannie Gunn in *We of the Never Never*, was dismantled and moved 42 kilometres to its current position on the Roper River, some time before World War Two†.

Elsey, or 'Elsie', Telegraph Station appears rarely in the record, but a telegram from there in June 1881 informed the Government Resident of the murder of a drover named Patrick MacNamara. He was of 'medium build, black whiskers and hair, slightly bald, 40 years of age, 5 ft., 6 in or 7 in high'. MacNamara was apparently 'speared through the head by Aborigines near Limmen's Bight' and all the drovers' rations had been stolen‡. Oddly, the murder was never mentioned by the media again. Perhaps it never happened.

Short of time and unwilling to spend hours looking for shards of broken glass and rusty tin cans on the banks of Elsey Creek, I pushed on to Katherine. But my thoughts turned to Jeannie Gunn, who had spent a year at Elsey Station, within a few miles of the O.T.L. at the turn of the twentieth century. It doesn't take long, reading the text of *We of the Never Never*, to find her description of how important the line had become:

> ... Being within four miles of the Overland Telegraph—that backbone of the overland route—rarely a week was to pass without someone coming in, and at times our travellers came in twos and threes, and as each brought news of that world outside our tiny circle, carrying in perhaps an extra mail to us, or one out for us, they formed a strong link in the chain that bound us to Outside .... Two hundred and fifty guests was the tally for that year, and earliest among them came a telegraph operator, who as is the way with telegraphic operators out-bush invited us to 'ride across to the wire for a shake hands

---

* *North Australian*, 17 April 1885, 12 June 1885.
† *West Australian*, 4 August 1951.
‡ *Northern Territory Times and Gazette*, 2 July 1881.

with Outside'; and within an hour we came in sight of the
telegraph wire as our horses mounted the stony ridge that
overlooks the Warloch ponds, when the wire was forgotten
for a moment in the kaleidoscope of moving, ever-changing
colour that met our eyes.

Jeannie Gunn and her party were at a particularly beautiful section of the line near the waterholes that had been named after a horse*:

> Two wide-spreading limpid ponds, the Warloch, lay before
> us, veiled in a glory of golden-flecked heliotrope and purple
> waterlilies, and floating deep green leaves, with here and there
> gleaming little seas of water, opening out among the lilies, and
> standing knee-deep in the margins a rustling fringe of light
> reeds and giant bulrushes …

> But the operator, being unpoetical, had ridden on to the 'wire'
> and presently was 'shinning up' one of its slender galvanised
> iron posts as a preliminary to the 'handshake'.

> … With the murmuring bush about us, in the clear space
> kept always cleared beneath those quivering wires, we stood all
> dressed in white, first looking up at the operator as, clinging
> to his pole, he tapped the line, and then looking down at him
> as he knelt at our feet with his tiny transmitter beside him
> clicking out our message to the south folk …

> In the heart of the bush, we stood yet listening to the clatter of
> the townsfolk, for, business over, the little clicking instrument
> was gossiping cheerily with us—the telegraph wire in the
> Territory being such a friendly wire. Daily it gathers gossip,
> and daily whispers it up and down the line, and daily news
> and gossip fly hither and thither: who's 'inside,' who has gone
> out, whom to expect, where the mailman is, the newest arrival
> in Darwin and the latest rainfall at Powell's Creek …

> Daily the telegraph people hear all the news of the Territory,
> and in due course give the news to the public, when the
> travellers gathering it, carry it out to the bushfolk, scattering
> it broadcast, until everybody knows everyone else, and all
> his business and where it has taken him; and because of that

---

* Warloch's owner was one of Alfred Giles (Kelsey, 1975), John Ross (Herbert, 1873), or John McDouall Stuart (Hill, 1951).

knowledge, and in spite of those hundreds of thousands of square miles of bushland, the people of the Territory are held together in one great brotherhood …

Roper River

Another important site of O.T.L. history I wanted to see lies about 140 kilometres east of the line. The depot on the Roper River ran for two or three years from 1871. To get there I followed the Roper Highway, which leaves the Stuart Highway just south of Mataranka, and passes through the old Elsey Station.

I spent a day scrambling through riverside vegetation looking for the depot. I was expecting to find swathes of broken glass and other detritus left behind by men who were not known for their tidiness—like on every other O.T.L. site I had visited. The rubbish may still be there, but I didn't find any. Too many wet season floods and shifting sands may have covered it all. I hope to be corrected, but the only signs of the OTL on the river appears to be the remnants of the wreck of the *Young Australian*, 20 kilometres downstream, and a little up from the Tomato Island Campground and boat ramp.*

Alfred Giles described the scene in 1872:

> … It was an immense encampment, and the display of flies and tents, wagons, drays, carts, and buggies, as well as horses and bullocks, and some 300 men, made it a busy as well as picturesque scene†.

Perhaps I was looking in the wrong spot. Unfortunately, the depot seems to be long forgotten on the river today. Seeking information, I asked the lady who ran the nearby Roper Store and camping ground and called in to see the rangers of Limmen National Park. None of them could give me any ideas, but nevertheless, I learned a few things of interest.

---

* A National Heritage Marker sits beside the boat ramp. It was installed by Engineering Heritage Australia in 2011.
† Alfred Giles, 1925.

Just outside the back fence of the campground lies the lonely grave of John Urquardt, who died on 3 March 1885. Urquardt was a stockman from the Diamantina River taking cattle for the Durack family west to the Kimberleys. Mary Durack, in *Kings in Grass Castles*, wrote that he became delirious with fever at the Roper, and shot himself. The coroner of the time, Charles Nash, found nothing suspicious in his death, and his body was released for burial without trouble*. He has lain here ever since, and someone has cared for his grave because the headstone has been repaired.

On the bank of the river near the crossing are the ruins of the Roper River Police Station. Abandoned in 1985, there is nothing left of the elevated house apart from foundations and stairs—the rest succumbed to bushfires long ago, but a few sheds and the lock-up remain and are interesting to see.

On the edge of the rough car park, there is an old wooden stump in which was placed a concrete memorial. Very few letters are visible, but this is supposed to be a grave marker for Charles Johnston, whose

Figure 110: This old memorial near the Roper Bar Crossing is supposed to be for Charles Johnston, murdered in 1875.

---

* *Northern Territory Times and Gazette*, 30 May 1885.

bones were scattered near here by dingoes after he was murdered in 1875. As yet, there is no memorial to the unknown number of Aborigines killed in reprisal.

Exploring the police station site, I met a couple of travellers from down south who were also wandering around the ruins. The man said he was tracing the path of a great uncle, who worked at the depot. 'Who?', I asked.

'His name was Knuckey.'

Richard Randall Knuckey appears regularly in the story of Northern Territory settlement*. He was last at the Roper as the leader of the re-poling parties sent to replace the wooden telegraph poles with metal Oppenheimer poles in 1873. Barry Marshall, his great (X3) nephew, was following him nearly 150 years later. There was a lot to follow: Knuckey was also the overseer for Section A for Todd, and before that a surveyor with Goyder in Darwin. The street named after him is one of the major roads in the City of Darwin.

The enigmatic couple had another secret. Jennifer Marshall also had an ancestor who appears in the Territory story although, unfortunately, he was a less-salubrious character. Henry Searle was a miner during the 1870s gold rush. He made the papers when he was accused of 'salting' a worthless mine with a little gold in order to swindle others†. We can't pick our relatives, but Jennifer, like most of us, was keen to find out more about hers.

Meeting them was a reminder that many, if not most of the O.T.L. men, had families. Their descendants, like the Marshalls and the large Renner family who gathered to commemorate Dr Renner's sesquicentenary at Renner Springs, are numerous and interested in their lives.

---

* For Knuckey, see *Darwin 1869: The Second Northern Territory Expedition* (Pugh 2018), and *Darwin: Origin of a City, The 1870s* (Pugh 2019).

† Searle appears in *Darwin: Origin of a City, The 1870s* (Pugh 2019).

Katherine (Emungalan)

More than 120 years ago, Jeannie Gunn arrived in Katherine* on her way to Elsey Station. It was not a big community:

> ... we discovered the remainder of the Settlement from the cottage verandas, spying out the Police Station as it lurked in ambush just round the first bend in a winding bush track—apparently keeping one eye on the 'Pub'; and then we caught the gleam of white roofs away beyond further bends in the track, where the Overland Telegraph 'Department' stood on a little rise, aloof from the 'Pub' and the Police, shut away from the world, yet attending to its own affairs, and, incidentally, to those of the bush-folk: a tiny Settlement, with a tiny permanent population of four men and two women—women who found their own homes all-sufficient, and rarely left them, although the men folk were here, there, and everywhere ...†

Katherine is bigger now—around 10,000 people call it home. In 1929, the town shifted to its current site at Emungalan, where the railway bridge crossed the river and the Stuart Highway road bridge joined it. This is fortunate, as it means there are a few remnants of the town of the nineteenth century still in existence. The O.T.L. Office is long gone, and so too the police station, but the 'Pub' that Mrs Gunn wrote about is still there, albeit with a few changes brought by occasional renovations, such as the verandas.

It was built by Bernard Murphy in 1887 and called the Sportsman's Hotel and Pioneer Cash Store. When Jeannie Gunn visited, it was owned by P.R. Allen and Co and managed by Tom Pearce, but over the following five decades it was bought and sold several times, until it ceased trading in 1948. Today it sits empty, but it is accessible to interested visitors, and there are several information signboards around it and the accompanying harness shed.

The Overland Telegraph 'Department', as Gunn called it, was about a kilometre upriver‡. The site is now private land, and there

---

* Aka 'Catherine', 'The Catherine', 'The Katherine' and/or Katherine River.
† Gunn, 1907.
‡ Look for it on the left, 1.7 km down Gorge Road past the hospital.

Figure 111: The Sportsman's Hotel and Pioneer Cash Store was built by Bernard Murphy in 1887. It was about a kilometre down river from the telegraph station, at Knott's Crossing.

is nothing to see of the station itself. However, the huge pylons that carried the wires above the river are still there. Built in 1898, they stand on both sides of the river, 400 metres apart, and probably will for a hundred more years without trouble. The telegraph station was a few metres from the eastern side of the pylon on the southern bank.

Travelling north, the first 'original' station that divided the distance between Katherine and Darwin, was built at Yam Creek. But before reaching there, two gold rush towns also had a role to play in the O.T.L. story. They were products of the gold rush of the 1870s and 1880s.

Figure 112. Above: Two 9.1 metre pylons lifted the O.T.L. over the Katherine River with 15.2 metre Oppenheimer poles attached to the top. The main photo (above) was taken from the veranda of the telegraph station during the flood of 1924 (LANT, ph0145-0015).

Left: The telegraph pylons still stand, 400 metres apart, on each side of the Katherine River. Similar pylons remain on the Fergusson River, 50 km north and 9 km east of the highway. The heritage listed pylons date from 1898–9.

Pine Creek and Burrundie

The O.T.L. was in operation for less than a year when it became clear that another station was needed to service miners who were working in the Pine Creek area. The *Northern Territory Times* reported that:

... a temporary station has been opened at Pine Creek in the

Figure 113: Pine Creek Telegraph Station (left) and Standard Hotel (right), 1878 (Foelsche, LANT, ph1060/0046).

Figure 114: The last telegraph office in Pine Creek. Although this building has also had many other uses, it is now the Pine Creek Museum and Library.

charge of Mr. Whitelaw. The office of the Telegraph Gold Mining Company has been kindly lent for the purpose, and the officers and men for the present are living in tents*.

There is, of course, no sign of the temporary station. Early photographs show that it soon had a more permanent structure, but that too is long gone (except for the remnants of a concrete slab that might have been a part of the station). Eventually the O.T.L. office

---

* *Northern Territory Times and Gazette*, 7 November 1873.

found itself in an iron building, which still stands a few hundred metres from the old slab. From 1889, this building was the mining warden's office in Burrundie, but it was dismantled and moved to Pine Creek in 1913. It then went through several incarnations—as a clinic, a 'half-caste home', and as a small hospital for the flying doctor, Dr Clyde Fenton. According to the information sign outside its front door, the building is the oldest prefabricated iron building in Australia. It eventually became the Pine Creek Post Office and Telephone Exchange, and is now the community museum and library, operated by the National Trust. Its link to the original O.T.L. is tenuous, but it is the closest the town has, and is worth a visit in its own right.

Burrundie, the original home of the building, is a half hour's drive away. The town was on the O.T.L. because when it was built in the mid-1880s, the line was realigned to follow the new railway tracks. It was a thriving little town with its own racing club, hotels, and numerous privately owned dwellings. The O.T.L. office was a recycled building. As Southport was abandoned when the railway bypassed it, the Southport Telegraph Station was dismantled, loaded onto drays, and pulled by bullocks south to the new town.

There is little to mark Burrundie's existence these days. Blink and you'll miss them, but worth finding are the remnants of the railway platform, a well, an explosives bunker, and the small concrete floor where the police 'cells' stood—complete with metal rings through which prisoners' chains were locked.

Outside the town, on the road to the Mount Wells Tin Mine, lies the tiny Burrundie Cemetery, with two fenced-in gravestones marking the last resting place of three people who died too young. The first two share a gravestone: George Fitts, post, telegraph, and stationmaster, aged 33, who died of consumption six months after arriving in Burrundie in 1893; and Robert McKellar Murray, aged 43, the hospitable Post and Telegraph Master from Katherine Telegraph Station. Murray was mentioned by every traveller who passed

Figure 115: An 1890s view of Burrundie township. Today there are few remnants left (SLSA, B-9044).

Figure 116: Burrundie Police Station showing the rings through which prisoners' chains would lock.

through Katherine for more than a decade. He fell ill and tried to get to Burrundie from Katherine to see a doctor in 1893. Unfortunately, the flooded Fergusson River delayed him for three days and by the time he arrived, he was too sick to save. Murray's widow, Jane, and their four children returned to Adelaide without him.

The other grave belongs to Ruth Beckwick, who died of amoebic dysentery in 1901. She was the six-year-old daughter of Ralph Beckwick, the railway stationmaster at Burrundie at the time.

Figure 117: Burrundie Cemetery, the grave of G.W. Fitts and Robert Murray.

Apart from these three, any other occupants of the cemetery remain in unmarked graves, hidden in the bush.

Burrundie was in the heart of the gold rush area. Thousands of miners, most of whom were Chinese, passed this way during the rush. In typical Northern Territory style, their stories are as interesting as they are unique (see Pugh 2021). The serendipitous role of the O.T.L. in the start of the gold rush is a part of the story of the next telegraph station up the line, at Yam Creek.

The Shackle, Yam Creek

The Shackle Telegraph Station at Yam Creek was an important link in the line in the 1870s and early 80s. It was particularly famous because it was here, in 1870, that the line parties found gold nuggets in the holes they dug for the telegraph poles.

The Shackle was, as its name suggests, near a 'shackle', which was a junction in the line using two special insulators with an access wire. It was a place where a field operator could easily hook into the line with a handset. The station was initially nothing but a tent and a handset. However, by 1871, Charles Todd could report that:

…At Yam Creek we have put up a substantial three-roomed

hut, built of cypress pine, and roofed with galvanized iron. It is nearly completed*.

Two years later, Todd gave more details:

> … one small room for telegraph office and post office; three small rooms and a detached kitchen for use of stationmaster and assistant, one small room for men, also stables and sheds; one paddock, area about 240 acres; one yard, about half-acre; four 400-gallon iron tanks; one well of good water. The well was circular, 4 ft in diameter, stoned up and 12 ft deep†.

The station remained in operation almost continuously until the line was realigned to follow the new railway line in 1886. By then, the police station, warden's office, and the local hotel had already moved 30 kilometres to the new town of Burrundie. So too, had the telegraph office. Unfortunately, there is little left of the settlements at either location.

The Territory's gold rush started from Yam Creek. It was initially delayed because Government Resident Douglas was ordered to keep the finds quiet so the workers on the O.T.L. would stay at their jobs, rather than join a rush‡.

Even though I had a map, and the site is less than two kilometres from the Stuart Highway, The Shackle was difficult to find. I drove past it twice before I caught sight of a small white NT Heritage sign hidden in the grass. The drying grass was waist high, but the sign provided a small map of the area, and using it, I easily found thousands of pieces of broken bottles, rusting tin cans, hoop iron, horseshoes, and many bits of unidentifiable iron lying on the surface of the ground.

I visited again a month or so later when much of the grass had been burned off. The building sites were easier to spot, as the ground was levelled, with rows of rocks supporting the edges on the downhill side of the slope. One has a row of beer bottles marking its edge.

---

* Todd, 1871.
† Cited in Wilson 1983.
‡ Douglas eventually had a role in the rush after the O.T.L. was complete. At the Roper River Depot, he convinced a group of O.T.L. workers waiting to return south to instead go overland to Yam Creek to seek their fortunes.

Figure 118: The Shackle as it is today.

Which building site was which is not possible to tell. Even the detailed survey by Wilson in 1983 was unable to pinpoint where the telegraph station actually stood. The most likely place, Wilson thought, was the most westerly site actually under the line! Likely, because the station was originally a tent under the wire, and when the office was built there would have been little available land because of the gold rush*. In Foelsche's 1879 photograph of the station (see Figure 45) the poles pass by very close to the building, so he may be right.

In 2014, NT Heritage listed four hectares of the land along Yam Creek as a 'site of considerable archaeological potential'†. For me, the most poignant story from The Shackle comes from the operator Dudley Kelsey. Several years after the tragic 1884 massacre of Woolwonga people near the Daly River‡, a little boy visited the

---

* Wilson, 1983.
† The Shackle, Heritage Assessment Report 2014, Heritage Branch. Use reference 13°34'37.13" S, 131°31'2.33" E to find a corner of the listed site.
‡ For the full story, see *Darwin: Growth of a City*, Pugh 2021.

Figure 119: Detritus of The Shackle at Yam Creek is spread across the whole site. As well as a telegraph station, there was a miners' hospital, police station, and a hotel in the area.

Figure 120: A line of beer bottles marks the edge of a building site at The Shackle (NT Heritage).

station. Kelsey noticed scars disfiguring the boy's buttocks, and asked how he received them:

> … he told us that during the time the shooting parties were out, one came on some of his tribe. He was hit and dived under some thick undergrowth. All his friends were killed, but he wandered about in the bush till he came up with another tribe who took care of him …[*]

Southport

Southport was a river port on the Blackmore River, about 42 kilometres from Palmerston in the South Arm of the harbour. It was a three-hour journey by steam launch from Palmerston, and it quickly became a staging and supply post for Goyder's men during the 1869 survey. Travel by boat saved a day or more of overland travel, and ships could unload directly in Southport and bypass Port Darwin altogether.

The government supported Southport's construction by providing the telegraph station and a police office, which were built side by side in Barrow Street in 1871. A government jetty was built on the river, designed by someone who had never been there:

> … The portion of the jetty now constructed by the Government is one of the greatest follies in the world. It is full 12 feet too high for even the highest tide which can occur, whilst as to medium and low tides, it will be perfectly useless. But at present nothing is being done on the work. It has been commenced in a solid and substantial manner, but there it sticks. Like everything else in the Northern Territory, it is in a state of suspense, hanging midway between heaven and earth, and nobody can say when it will be completed …[†]

Transport by boat relied on the tide. it often took much longer that the three hours promised by the launch operators, and a slow journey through the mangroves was not everyone's favourite event, especially at night:

> … Any person in search of the horrible might do worse than

---

[*] Kelsey, 1975.
[†] *Northern Territory Times and Gazette*, 14 November 1873.

Figure 121: Southport Telegraph Station, 1879 (Foelsche, LANT, ph1060-0067).

spend a night or two on board of Gore's boat in some of her eventful voyages between Port Darwin and Southport. Having the mast blown away by a squall is one of the trifles which occur occasionally, but this is nothing compared with some of the more startling events. You leave Southport at 8 o'clock in the evening; there is not a breath of wind, but you want to be off, so the boat is rowed down the river in the darkness; alligators loudly disporting themselves in the mangroves on each side as you go slowly by … all night in the boat, sometimes being anchored, and sometimes rowing slowly along, waiting for the breeze which is to take us to Port Darwin.

Then, the voyage to Southport, too, is sometimes a stirring one. Men going up to the reefs in various stages of intoxication make things lively, until a sudden downpour of rain saturates all on board, and in five minutes makes them all look like so many drowned rats; some with their shirts off in vain attempts to keep them dry, and others trying to cover themselves with coats and wrappers. Altogether, truly, Gore's boat is a remarkable institution, and deserves to be patronized*.

The gold boom collapsed before the end of 1874 and only

---

* *Northern Territory Times and Gazette*, 14 November 1873.

Figure 122: Adcock's Store and the Southport jetty at high tide, 1876. The ship is the *Estelle* (Foelsche, SLSA, B-5781).

the best of the companies remained operational. Southport had a resurgence when Chinese alluvial miners started arriving in 1876 and 'Chinatown' developed at the southwest end of Kersley Street.

The town survived during the 1880s as a supply station for mines and the developing pastoral industry further south, but when the Palmerston to Pine Creek Railway bypassed it in 1888, the town was abandoned. It came as no surprise—in 1884 it was easily predicted:

> ... Southport is going to die hard. We suppose there can be no suggestion about its dying after the railway line passes it[*].

The sites of the telegraph office and the police station in Barrow Street are signposted, but not maintained. There is little there to maintain: the police station's stone foundations still exist, but nothing of the telegraph office, because the metal walls and roof of the original building, and anything else of use, were taken to Burrundie in the mid-1880s. At the back of the block, hidden in thick scrub, is a single corner of a stone building. Perhaps it was a part of an outhouse or kitchen that once stood behind the station. There is a large well on the site with a pool of water at the bottom, into which the fruit of the

---

[*] *Northern Territory Times and Gazette*, 19 January 1884.

strychnine tree above it drops. My advice: don't drink water infused with strychnine.

In recent years there has been a return of people to Southport, seeking a rural lifestyle on small blocks of land. Access to fresh water has been a problem, but some of the residents are fanatically pro-Southport, and problems are there to be solved.

Darwin

Arriving in Darwin on a pilgrimage along the O.T.L. is, frankly, disappointing. Arguably, the O.T.L. was the most important economic and social development event for the tiny colony of Palmerston in the nineteenth century. Heritage organisations and interested groups are stirring themselves, at the time of writing, to be ready to commemorate the sesquicentenary in 2022. Hopefully, something tangible and long-lasting will be arranged that people can engage with and learn from. There's very little on the O.T.L. in Darwin at the moment.

However, there are memorials. One stands in the gardens of the Administrator's offices, on the corner of Smith Street and the Esplanade. It is the top piece of an Oppenheimer pole with two insulators (concreted in place) standing among the bushes. A faded sign announces that it was near here that Harriet Daly tamped the earth around the first pole in September 1870 and gave her first public speech. If it was not *exactly* here, it was certainly within a hundred metres or so of the site. The pole is visible now because David the gardener helped me get my photograph by pruning the weeping foliage that curtained it from view. He also promised to keep it clear for the sesquicentenary year.

Not far from the pole, on the edge of Liberty Square, across from Government House, sits a larger memorial to the O.T.L., erected on the centenary of the opening of the line and the arrival of Halpin's telegram 'Advance Australia'. The plaque reads:

This Memorial Commemorates The Centenary Of The Laying Of The Overseas Cable To Java On 20th November 1871. The Completion Of The Overland Telegraph Line Between Adelaide And Darwin On 22nd August 1872. And The First Message Between London And Adelaide On 22nd October 1872.

Figure 123: The Palmerston Telegraph Offices were on the site of the current NT Parliament buildings on the Esplanade, 1873 (Foelsche, SLSA, ph1060-0020)*.

Figure 124: The Overland Telegraph Offices in Darwin became the post office, but they no longer exist. They were bombed on 22 February 1942. Nine staff members of the post office were killed, 1961 (LANT, ph0238-0403 and ph0120-0117).

---

* Todd reported that the facilities in 1873 in Port Darwin were 'One large room for operating; one large room for post office mailroom; one room for station-master's office; one room for stationery; station-master's quarters, five rooms and detached kitchen; quarters for operators and clerks, fourteen rooms and one detached kitchen; also, one building containing store, stables, and men's quarters; no paddock; one yard, containing in all about two acres; one underground tank out of repair, capacity about 15,000 gallons; also, fourteen 400 gallon iron tanks, all very old; one well of good water' (Todd, 1 Jan 1873).

Figure 125: The O.T.L. first pole memorial. A top section of an Oppenheimer pole stands in the fabulous gardens of the N.T. Administrator's Offices. David, the gardener, trims back the foliage so it can be seen.

Figure 126: The centenary monument to the O.T.L. on the Esplanade in Darwin has seen better days.

Unfortunately, the memorial is in such poor condition that it really needs major surgery, or replacement. The ceramic tiles are broken, and the concrete is chipped and stained. It's also the ugliest monument in the Territory.

Along the O.T.L.

Figure 127: This memorial cairn once sat on the cliff above Darwin Harbour, 1959 (LANT, ph0238-0402). It now sits next to Parliament House on the edge of Liberty Square.

There is another memorial, but few people these days know of its existence. It is a stone cairn made of telegraph office stones that used to stand on the edge of the cliff overlooking Darwin Harbour. It was built by the Overseas Telecommunications Commission (Australia) in 1959, from blocks that were once part of the original stone telegraph office. It was moved in the 1980s to stand next to Parliament House, near the parking garage. The Institution of Engineers (Australia) added their own plaque to the cairn in 1999.

Other sites an O.T.L. pilgrim might visit in Darwin include the Museum and Art Gallery of the Northern Territory. They hold items from the time and hopefully will have them on display during 2022. Visitors may get to see insulators, perhaps a Morse key, large prints of the photographs you have seen in this book, plus other items. At the National Trust's Roadmasters Museum, there is a display of Goyder's survey pegs and survey equipment, such as a theodolite, an original chain, maps, and other bits and pieces.

One remnant can only be seen at low tide. It lies on the beach below Government House in Darwin, where several straight lines

Figure 128: The heritage listed undersea cable from 1870 still lies on the beach below Parliament House. It heads to Banyuwangi in Java. Parliament House stands on the ground once occupied by the B.A.T. offices and accommodation.

run across the mud. These are the undersea cables that carried Morse signals through Java, and to and from London. One of them is the very first, dragged ashore by around 90 men (and two horses) on 7 November 1871. I waded calf-deep through the soft mud and sliced my bare feet silly with sharp shells and other detritus hidden in it. This cable was in use for nearly 70 years—until 19 February 1942, when it was cut by a naval officer after the bombing of Darwin by the Japanese. The navy did not want the Japanese to have a ready-made telegraph to Java if they invaded (O'Grady, 1972).

Confirming Captain Halpin's message on November 20, the country did indeed advance quickly after the opening installation of the Overland Telegraph Line. Palmerston's success in the early years is owed in no small part to the telegraph. The O.T.L. gave the South Australian colony, now known as Darwin, a reason for being. For at least two decades it held the only northern international telegraphic connection point and enjoyed the fruits of monopoly*. The B.A.T.

---

* The second international route for telegraph was from Sydney to Nelson, on the south island of New Zealand. The cable was laid by the Eastern Extension Telegraph

employees were at the top of the social ladder of the town: they played tennis and lived on the best real estate, held the best parties, and married the most eligible women. Unfortunately, as far as the telegraph is concerned, Darwin's memories of the halcyon days of the B.A.T. are hazy because there is little left. The best experiences of the O.T.L. will be found at the Alice Springs Telegraph Station, the Wadlata Outback Centre in Port Augusta, and the remote ruins in the arid centre of Australia.

Company in collaboration with the Australian and New Zealand Governments and opened for business on 21 February 1876 (McLintock, 1966).

Twenty to the Mile

Appendix
Telegraph line construction parties

Following are lists of the men employed to survey and build the telegraph line. The information comes from a number of sources, but the lists are unlikely to be complete. Some names appear more than once as men were reassigned.

Note that the appendix is not indexed and names that appear here may not be referred to elsewhere.

Central Section

Sir Charles Todd remembered the leaders of his construction parties in 1884:

> … In the selection of good officers, the Surveyor-General afforded valuable aid in recommending Messrs. Harvey, R. R. Knuckey, Gilbert R. McMinn, and W. W. Mills all of whom, as well as Mr. A. T. Woods, whom I subsequently made chief officer on the central section, rendered good service, and carried out the difficult work entrusted to them with a zeal and intelligence worthy of all praise. The five parties were made up as follows:

> Section A.—Overseer, Mr. R. R. Knuckey; sub-overseer, Mr. Christopher Giles, jun.; cadet, Mr. J. H. Aldridge; and sixteen men.

> Section B.—Overseer, Mr. G. R. McMinn; sub-overseer, Mr.

C. Musgrave; cadet Mr. T. Bee; and sixteen men.

Section C.—Overseer, Mr. J. Beckwith; sub-overseer, Mr. W. W. Mills; assistant, Mr. A. G. Burt; and seventeen men.

Section D.—Overseer, Mr. A. T. Woods; sub-overseer, Mr. S. Jarvis; cadet, Mr. C. M. Bagot; and nineteen men.

Section E.—Mr. W. Harvey; sub-overseer, Mr. J. L. M. Roberts; cadet, Mr. A. Y. Forster; and nineteen men.

Mr. Beckwith became so ill that I sent him back to Adelaide on my arrival at The Peake and placed Mr. Mills in charge. Mr. Harvey ... was, in the first instance, attached as surveyor to the exploring party under Mr. John Ross*.

Section A: Richard Knuckey's Party, 27°00′ to 25°30′ S

Richard Randall Knuckey, overseer; Christopher Giles, sub-overseer; J. Aldridge, cadet; W. Ogilvy, blacksmith; C. Almers, carpenter; Fisher, wireman; W. Rowe Jnr., saddler; V. Scotchmere, ganger; A. Warren, head teamster; Rose, H. and Miller, P. Holzerland, teamsters and labourers; Andrew Young, R. Biddle, J. Lowther, George Hughes, W. Houston, and Patrick Kelly, sawyers and labourers; Davis and J. Barnden, bullock drivers; C. Laycock and M. Francis, cooks.

Section B: Gilbert McMinn's Party, 25°30′ to 24°00′ S.

G. R. McMinn, overseer; C. Musgrave†; Thomas Bee, cadet; plus George Ledan, J. Gudge, W. A. Carter, J. Homer, Harrison, D. Johnston, M. E. Fitch, C. Dix, Joseph Dix, E. Burfort, J. Robinson, —? Cocker, Henry Krüss, M. Burke, James Davies, Ed Biggs, J. O'Donnell, P. C. Smith, J. Borrow.

Section C: Mr. Beckwith's (W. W. Mills) Party, 24°00′ to 22°30′ S.

James Beckwith, overseer; William W. Wills, sub-overseer; Plus A. G. Burt, J. Forster, W. Prowse, T. Allen, Isaac Guster, H. Masters, J. Hyde, G. Langford, W. McNicol, M. Hausan, C. Gapper, W. Bonney, J. Anthony, W. Milton, H. Spafford, G. Walker, P. Nilan, J. Wascombe, A. McKenzie, A. Spiller.

---

* Todd, SAPP 191/1884.
† In 1875, Charles Musgrave was one of the victims of the *Gothenburg* disaster.

Appendix

Section D: Alfred Woods' Party, 22°30´ to 21°00´ S.

Alfred Thomas Woods, overseer; Jarvis, sub-overseer; C. M. Bagot, cadet; Thomas Badge, blacksmith; Walter Feast, wheelwright; Charles Smith, saddler; William Arthur Hamp, head teamster; George Chalmers, wireman; William Beal, ganger; plus, teamsters Patrick Moloy and Charles Palmer; W. Crisp and Edmund Quigley, bullock-drivers; George Kersley and A. Powell, cooks; and labourers W. J. Farrant, Michael O'Donnell, Albert Hous, William Stamborough, E. Samson, and John Gerrald.

Section E: Mr. William Harvey's Party, 21°00´ to 19°30´ S.

William Harvey, overseer; J. F. Roberts, sub-overseer; J. Y. Forster cadet; and William Cox, H. Halstead, C. Kelly, J. Hurst, J. Wauchope, S. Dawson, C. B. Frinsdorf, W. H. Sadgrove, H. Threadgold, H. Brumbey, W. H. Tucker, J. Saunders, J. Cleland*, W. Collett, J. Austin, J. Smith, Francis Price, and J. Ewart.

Northern Section

Darwent and Dalwood's party to Port Darwin on board the *Omeo*, September 1870†

Messrs. W. A. Paqualin (in charge), J. Darwent, Stephen King, C. Tymn (officers), and 75 men. Messrs. William McMinn and Robert Burton, superintendents on behalf of the Government, and Messrs. James Stapleton and Andrew Howley, telegraph operators and sub-overseers

Patterson's team on board the *Aldinga*, then to Port Darwin on the *Omeo*, July 1871

The men who travelled with Patterson were listed in the Adelaide newspapers in July 1871 [with occupations added]:

Messrs. Todd, Patterson, and Rutt were met at the station by

---

* In 1875 John Cleland was a hero of the *Gothenburg* disaster and one of three men to receive medals for their efforts in rescuing others.
† *The Adelaide Register* (Supplement) 10 September 1970.

the Hon. the Treasurer (Captain John Hart, M.L.C.). The wharf was lined with relatives and friends of those departing. In about half an hour after the arrival of the train Mr. Rutt mustered the men on board. The following answering to the roll:

Henry Angas [labourer], Richard Ball [teamster], John Brooks [carpenter], Joseph Beckwith [wireman], F. Booder [bullock driver], Thomas Bevan [labourers or blacksmiths], Jas. Bye [teamster or labourer], T. J. Barnett [mason], J. Barnett, Thomas Bacon, A. Bamfield [rough carpenters], J. A. Butler [labourer], W. Bushby [bullock-driver or labourer], W. Barlow, C. Bertrend [teamster or labourer], J. Bastion [teamster or bullock-driver], W. Baldock, and P. Blacking, William A. Crowder [cadets], Thomas Cox [labourer], Tim. Comick [teamster or axeman], J. Connoll [labourer or bullock-driver], and Augustus Caesar [cook]. W. Dempsey [teamster or labourer], and Thos. Dyke [teamster or labourer]. Sydney Ellis [labourer], William Easther [labourer or teamster], C. Ekers [saddler], and Jas. Ellison [labourer or teamster], W. Floyd [labourer] and J. B. Funnell [assistant storekeepers], P. Glackend [teamster or labourer], J. Griffin, W. Garlick [labourers], T. Gilmore [labourer], Alan Giles, and William Garson [carpenter]. K. Helien [labourer], R. E. Holmes[teamster or wireman], P. Hinds [labourer], James Harper [labourer], J. Hollis [labourer or cook], and Charles Hawson [storekeeper], John Jones [well-sinker], Charles Johnston [teamster or labourer, became a telegrapher], and William Jones [labourer], Edward Kirkland [smith or carpenter.] and C. Knight, S. Lisser [maybe aka 'Lizzer'] [cooks], J. Lyons [labourer], T. Langman [blacksmith], and C. Lowther [axeman or labourer.], C. A. Miller [labourer], James McEwen [teamster or labourer], D. Melville [fitter or wireman], G. Medland [teamster or labourer], Thomas Maher [well-sinker], and B. Marchant, Thomas Nimmo [carpenter], John Ockleford [wireman], W. Odgers [wireman], J. Powditch [wireman], E. Privett [wireman—died of scurvy March 1872], Alfred Pybus [labourer or poleman], and Edward Potter [shoeing-smith], J. Russell [teamster or labourer], Edward Riley [teamster or labourer], R. Richards [labourer or seaman], B. Reid [boatman or labourer], and Wm. Reid,

Edward Stirling [shoeing-smith or labourer], William Scadden [sawyer or labourer], G. M. Schinnick [labourer], John Sheedy [teamster or labourer], and R. Smith [wireman], J. Toohey [labourer], Robert Tapscott [cadet], James Thompson [labourer or seaman], E. Trivett, James Troubridge [bullock-drivers], H. Williams [mason or labourer], John Wood [carpenter and teamster], William Witherick [labourer], Patrick Welch [or 'Walsh'—labourer], and S. Whitehead [wireman].

The following are the officers of the expedition: Messrs. Robert Patterson [in charge], Walter Rutt [second-in-charge] and B. Hack [overseer of transport], George Bayfield [overseer of transport], W. G. Masson [overseer of transport], D. B. Wiltshire [explorer], and Dr E. C. Rix [medical officer]*.

Others in Robert Patterson's team in the Northern Territory

This list may include workers left over from Dalwood and Darwent's party:

Robert C. Patterson, leader; Walter Rutt, engineer and second in command; Mr E. C. Rix, medical officer; George Bayfield, overseer of transport; B. Hack, overseer of transport; W. G. Mason, overseer of transport; Harrison Packard, surveyor; Mr. Wiltshire, explorer†, C. Miller, Lowther, Read and (Bob?) Collard ('Collie') (crewmen on *Gulnare* and/or *Bengal*); W. Taylor (resigned in Normanton) and T. Maislet (*Larrakeeyah* crewmen); E. Bowman, bullock driver (deceased 4 Nov 1871); J. Harcus [lost in the bush]; Augustus Caesar, cook; James Stapleton [telegraphist]‡, plus the men listed above who arrived on the *Omeo* with Patterson.

---

* *Advertiser*, 29 July 1871, with first names added. Occupations as listed come from the *Evening Journal*, 25 July 1871.
† *The Argus*, 31 July 1871.
‡ Rutt, 1871.

Other men mentioned in diaries from the Roper River depot and Central Section of the Line

Jack Miller (head man at the Roper camp); W. Jones (assistant storekeeper); E. Bayfield; Daniel Kavanagh (died at the Roper River Camp); B. Williams (cook); Stretton, Chief storekeeper, and H. Davies (storekeeper); Jim Burton; Christopher Giles (sub-overseer, section A): Charles Johnston, telegrapher, and Thomas Dyke (assistant operator, eventually at Powell's Creek and then temporarily stationed at Warloch Ponds as operator); Thomas Hawkins (died of fever, March 1872); Abrahams (member of Ross's expedition) and Abrahams (member of King's team, could be the same man); Andrew Howley, telegraphist.

Members of the King's survey party

Stephen King Jnr and Alexander Ringwood, surveyors; Newton, C. Elborough and Livingstone Chalmers, axemen; William A. Crowder, cadet; Edwards and Moles, wiring party (Moles was accidentally shot on June 30 but survived); Tyrell, stock catcher; Stark, alias 'Bismark'*.

Southern Section

Babbage and Abbot's teams

The southern section of the line was divided into two sections, managed by Benjamin Herschel Babbage and William H. Abbot.

Sub-inspectors: Officer in charge Ray Boucaut and J. Servante, plus ten men: Carl Kraegen (telegrapher, died of thirst, 1872), D. Harris, J. Cook (aka Cooke), J. Anthony, Henry Krüss†, B. Burton, H. Barton, J. Brown, A. Brown, and W. Everett. Mr. Blood, in charge of depot at The Peake, and Harley Bacon in charge of the second depot, at Hugh River. There were also five shepherds led by Mr Jarvis, including the butcher/diarist,

---

* Crowder 1871–2, and Johnston 1872–5.

† Henry (Heinrich Ralfs) Krüss was also a worker on Goyder's survey team in 1869. After the O.T.L. was built, he returned to the Territory as a miner, but died of dysentery in 1873. He is buried at Rum Jungle (Batchelor) (Pugh, 2018).

Thomas Frederick Smith, and Charles Palmer, cook (died on 4 July 1872).

Knuckey's 1873 re-poling team

The Express and Telegraph published the following list of men who joined Knuckey to replace wooden poles with metal Oppenheimer poles in 1873.

> A Government expedition, under the command of Mr. Richard Knuckey, is to start next week for the purpose of partly renewing the Overland Telegraph with iron poles. The party, consisting of about sixty men, who have been selected, will leave Adelaide next week by the *Claud Hamilton* or *Rangatira*, proceeding to Sydney, where they will tranship to the steamer *Lord Ashley*, by which they will be conveyed to the Roper. The *Enterprise*, a steam launch of 25 tons register, will accompany the *Lord Ashley* to convey the poles to the Roper landing place, should the latter vessel not be able to get up the river. At the Roper landing place there are, at the present time, about fifty teams in readiness for carting, and the party will, immediately upon their arrival, commence the distribution of about 5,000 poles, which they are to distribute between a point 20 miles north of Elsie Creek and the middle of Section E, a distance of something like 400 miles. In places where timber is plentiful only ten iron poles will be erected to the mile, but in localities where timber is scarce the wooden poles will all be replaced by iron ones … Appended are the names of the men composing Mr. Knuckey's party:
>
> Officer in command, R.R. Knuckey; Overseers of transport, S. Jarvis and E. Bayfield; Teamsters and laborers, W. Wood, F. Wood, H. M. Jones, O. Dix, J. Barwis, G. Cook, S. Jones, B. Frinsdorf, T. Walker, G. Viccary, J. Lloyd, W. Vile, W. Carter, W. Batton, J. R. Knuckey[*], A. Hart, M. Papps, J. Hockley, J.A. Hewitt, W. Ogilvie, W. Bushby, W. F. Farrant, T. Jones[†], T. Bacon, E. S. Browne, W. Crick, T. B. Crispe, H. Brumby,

---

[*] John Randall Knuckey (1845–90), Richard's younger brother, also worked on the O.T.L.

[†] Thomas Jones remained in the Territory and several generations of his family were raised at Newcastle Waters. His son, Jock, bought Jones' Store at Newcastle Waters in 1936. His grandson, Peter, recorded the family history in 2016 (Jones, 2016).

J. Hunter, J. Lloyd, E. Burford, O. Lloyd, G. Clark, G. H. Langford, L. Chalmers, H. Bayfield, E. Elliott, M. Kowalick, J. Thompson, E. Quigley, J. Cronk. W. Pike, O. Laycock, M. Francis, T, Cooker, J. Cocker, J. Fermee, M. E. Fitch, E. J. Samson, P. Healey, J. Brennan, J. Davies Vannan, T. F. Smith, and E. Judd.

There were about 500 applicants. Most of the men selected have previously been in the Northern Territory, and all are personally known to. Mr. Knuckey, so there is every probability of this proving a good party*.

---

* *The Express and Telegraph*, 3 April 1873.

Bibliography

A Wire Through the Heart. 2007. [Film] Directed by Wendy Hughes (narrator) Darcy Yuille (director). Film Australia: Constructing Australia.

ADB, 1974. McMinn, Gilbert Rotherdale (1841–1924), *Australian Dictionary of Biography*, National Centre of Biography, Australian National University. [Online] Available at: https://adb.anu.edu.au/biography/mcminn-gilbert-rotherdale-4130/text6611 [Accessed 11 March 2021].

Bailey, J., 2006. *Mr Stuart's Track: the forgotten life of Australia's greatest explorer.* Melbourne: MacMillan.

Barrie, D., 1982. *The Heart of Rum Jungle.* Batchelor: Dominion Press.

Bisa, D., 2016. *Remember Me kindly: A history of the Holtze family in the Northern Territory.* Darwin: Historical Society of the Northern Territory.

Carment, D., Maynard, R. & Powell, A., 1990. *Northern Territory Dictionary of Biography*, Vol 1: to 1945. Darwin: NTU Press.

Carruthers, J. & Stiebel, L., 2012. *Thomas Baines: Exploring Tropical Australia 1855 to 1857.* Canberra: National Museum of Australia.

Coltheart, L., 1982. *Australia Misère: the Northern Territory in the Nineteenth Century.* Brisbane: (PhD). Griffith University.

Cracknell, W., 6 June 1870. Letter from Superintendent of Electric Telegrams to Hon. Postmaster-General, Brisbane. Brisbane: in *Sydney Morning Herald*, 15 July 1870.

Creaghe, E. C., 1883. *The Diary of Emily Caroline Creaghe: Explorer.* Edited with Introduction by Peter Monteath: Corkwood Press, 2004.

Cross, J., 2011. *Great Central State: The Foundation of the Northern Territory.* Adelaide: Wakefield Press.

Crouch, A., 2020. *Building the Line: The construction of the Overland Telegraph Line.* Adelaide: Hesperion Press.

Crowder, W., 1871–2. *Diary of W. A. Crowder, cadet* with R.C. Patterson. Adelaide: State Library of South Australia, Kay Anson and Helen Davies.

Cryle, D., 2018. *And Now the Biography: 150 Years of 'Telegraph'*. Telecommunications Association Inc. https://telsoc.org ed. Brisbane: Central Queensland University, ajtde, Vol 6, No 1, Article 143.

Daly, H., 1887. *Digging, Squatting, and Pioneering Life in the Northern Territory of South Australia*, by Mrs Dominic D. Daly. London: Sampson Low et al, London. Facsimile Edition 1984: Hesperian Press, Carlisle.

Deane, G., 1868–69. *Diaries of George Price Deane*, Transcribed by Barbara Deane Wall: SLSA, D 2875, 1868–69. Vols 1–3.

Deasey, D., 1976. *Peter Egerton Warburton.* [Online]
Available at: https://adb.anu.edu.au/biography/warburton-peter-egerton-4798/text7993 [Accessed 12 April 2021].

Debnam, L., 1988. *Men of the Northern Territory Police 1870–1914: who they were and where they were.* Darwin: Genealogical Society of the Northern Territory.

DEH, 2001. *Oodnadatta Track Heritage Survey.* [Online]
Available at: https://data.environment.sa.gov.au/content/heritage-surveys/oodnadatta-track-heritage-survey-2001-13149.pdf [Accessed 10 June 2021].

DeLaRue, K., 2004. *The Evolution of Darwin 1869–1911: A history of the Northern Territory's capital city during the years of South Australian administration.* Darwin: Charles Darwin University Press.

Donovan, P., 1981. *The Northern Territory: A history of South Australia's Northern Territory.* St. Lucia: University of Queensland.

Doris Blackwell, D. L., 1965. *Alice on the Line.* Adelaide: Rigby.

Douglas, W., 1872. *Transcript of the 1872 Private Diary of Captain William Bloomfield Douglas.* Transcribed by Russel G. Pugh 2016. ed.

Duminski, M., 2005. *Southport, Northern Territory 1869–2002.* Darwin: Historical Society of the Northern Territory.

E.A., 2021. Engineers Australia. [Online]
Available at: https://portal.engineersaustralia.org.au

Eden, C. H., 1875. Introduction to Warburton's journal. In: *Journey Across the Western Interior of Australia.* London: Hesperian Facsimile Edition, pp. 1–135.

Erecting an O.T.L. pole in 1925. 1925. [Film] s.l.: https://digital-classroom.nma.gov.au/videos/building-overland-telegraph-1925-silent.

Ferres, J., May 1878. *Report on the Proceedings of the Conference Respecting the Duplication of the Telegraph Lines between Australasia and Europe.* https://www.parliament.vic.gov.au/papers/govpub/VPARL1878No14.pdf ed. Melbourne: Government Printer.

Forrest, A., 1880. *North West Exploration: Journal of Expedition from DeGrey to Port Darwin.* https://espace.library.uq.edu.au/data/UQ_730304 ed. Perth: Government Printer.

Giles, A., 1925. *Exploring in the Seventies: A Pioneer's Interesting Reminiscences XII*. Adelaide: 'Observer', 18 July 1925.

Giles, E., 1877. *Australia Twice Traversed, The Romance of Exploration: Being A Narrative Compiled From The Journals Of Five Exploring Expeditions into and through Central South Australia, and Western Australia 18720 1876*. Adelaide: https://www.gutenberg.org/files/4974/4974-h/4974-h.htm.

Gill, S., 1998. *Storytracking: Texts, Stories, and Histories in Central Australia*. London: Oxford University Press.

Gosse, F., 1972. *Gosse, William Christie (1842–1881)*. [Online]
Available at: https://adb.anu.edu.au/biography/gosse-william-christie-3643
[Accessed 14 April 2021].

Gosse, W. C., 1874. *Report and Diary of Mr W. C. Gosse's Central Australian and Western Exploring Expedition 1873*. Adelaide: http://gutenberg.net.au/ebooks13/1306451h.html.

Goss, F., 2021. *Life In The Never Never Country Of South Australia In The 70s To 90s: By a Telegraph Operator, 1956*. [Online].

Goyder, G., September, 1869. Dispatch. Adelaide.

Green, L., 1972. Giles, Ernest (1835–1897), *Australian Dictionary of Biography*, Australian National University,. [Online]
Available at: https://adb.anu.edu.au/biography/giles-ernest-3611/text5607, published first in hardcopy 197. [Accessed 13 April 2021].

Gunn, J., 1907. *We of the Never Never*. 15th ed. New York: McMillan.

Harcus, W., 1876. *South Australia: Its history, Resources and Productions*. London: Samual Low et al.

Hartwig, M., 1965. *The Progress of White Civilisation in the Alice Springs District and its Effects on the Aboriginal Inhabitants*. Adelaide: Thesis submitted for the Degree of Doctor of Philosphy, University of Adelaide.

Hercus, L., 2009. Aboriginal Placenames: Aboriginal History Monograph 19, *Murkarra, a landscape nearly forgotten*. 2009 ed. Canberra: ANU E Press and Aboriginal History Incorporated.

Heritage, 2011. *Charlotte Waters Telegraph Station*. Darwin: NT Heritage Branch, NTG.

——, 2014. *The Shackle, Heritage Assessment Report*. Darwin: NT Heritage Branch, NTG.

Hill, B., 2003. *Broken Song: T G H Strehlow and Aboriginal Possession*. Penguin, Vintage Australia ed. Sydney: Knopf-Random House.

Hines, C., 1997. *Jim and Annie on the Overland Telegraph*. (2002). ed. Wallendbeem.

James, E. B. M., 1984. *The Overland Telegraph Line: From Katherine to Tennant Creek and Alice Springs*. Darwin: National Trust.

Johnston, C., 1872–5. *Charles Henry Johnston's Diary 1872–1875*. https://archival.collections.slsa.sa.gov.au/d/D7265_Johnston_diary_transcript.pdf ed. Adelaide: State Library of South Australia.

Jones, P., 2016. *Jones Store Newcastle Waters Northern Territory: A Social History of an Outback Store*. McDowall, Queensland: Everbest.

Journal, August 24, 1872. *History of the Overland Telegraph*. Evening Journal.

Kelsey, D. E., 1975. *The Shackle*. s.l.:Edited by Ira Nesdale. Lynton Publications..

Kimber, R. G., 1990. Stott, Robert (1858–1928), *Australian Dictionary of Biography, Australian National University*. [Online]
Available at: https://adb.anu.edu.au/biography/stott-robert-8690/text15203
[Accessed 18 April 2021].

———, 1991. *The End of the Bad Old Days: European Settlement in Central Australia, 1871–1894*. Occasional Papers ed. Darwin: State Library of the Northern Territory.

Lamond, G. H., 1986. *Tales of the Overland: Queensland to the Kimberley in 1885*. Carlisle: Hisperian.

Langford, R., 2008. *Singing Strings: A history of the Cardwell-Normanton Telegraph Line Far Nth. Qld*. Atherton: Undaval Pty Ltd.

Letters, 16 March 1871. *Letters: the Overland Telegraph*. Adelaide: South Australian Register.

Lewis, D., 2004. *A Wild History: life and death on the Victoria River frontier*. Melbourne: Monash University Press.

Lewis, J., 1922. *Fought and Won*. Facsimile copy, Gillingham Printers Adelaide ed. Adelaide: W. K. Thomas & Co..

Lockwood, K., 1995. *Big John: The Extraordinary Adventures of John McKinlay 1819–1872*. Melbourne: State Library of Victoria.

Manser, W. L., 1966. *The Overland Telegraph—Whose Idea?*. Education Gazette (Supplement), Volume Royal Geographical Society of South Australia D4625.

Matthews, J., 1984. *Report to the National Trust on Overland Telegraph from Pine Creek to Katherine*. Library & Archives NT ed. Darwin: National Trust.

McLintock, A., 1966. *An Encyclopaedia of New Zealand*. Wellington: https://teara.govt.nz/.

McMinn, G., 1870. *Diary of G.R. McMinn, Surveyor and Overseer during construction of the Overland Telegraph Line to Port Darwin*. Adelaide: State Records of South Australia GRG 154/9.

Mills, E., 1993. *W. Whitfield Mills: experiences with Darwin survey & overland telegraph parties and discovery of Alice Spring: from SA to WA by camel.* Glenside, S.A: E.W. Mills, 1993..

Mueller, J., 1871. *Diary: Journey from Adelaide to Alice Springs McDonnell Ranges. Commenced September 26th 1871. Finished December 31st 1871.* Alice Springs: Quoted from Traynor 2016, and/or Crouch 2020: copy in National Trust, Alice Springs Branch..

Nesdale, I., 1975. *The Shackle*, D.E. Kelsey. Ira Nesdale, Editor. Adelaide: Griffin Press.

NTTG, 7 Nov 1873. Law Courts. *Northern Territory Times and Gazette*, Issue 1, p. 2.

O'Grady, F., 1972. *The Overland Telegraph Line Technology of the 1870s.* Darwin: from papers presented at a symposium at the 100th anniversary of the O.T.L. (MAGNT).

Palmer, A. H., 12 July 1870. *By Electric Telegraph, Brisbane to Sydney, and Galle to London to J. Douglas, agent Queensland.* Brisbane: Queensland Government Offices.

——, 11 June 1870. *Letter, Colonial Secretary Office to John Douglas, Esq., Agent-General for Queensland.* Brisbane: in SMH 15 July 1870.

Patterson, R., 1872. *Diary of Robert Patterson.* portal.engineersaustralia.org.au nomination: Overland Telegraph Joining Point Nomination, pp. 9–10.

Pike, G., 1971. *The Northern Territory Overland Telegraph: An Epic of Courage — Just 100 Years Ago.* https://espace.library.uq.edu.au/data/UQ_207991 ed. Brisbane: Read at the meeting of the Royal Historical Society of Queensland.

Powell, A., 1982. *Far Country.* s.l.:Melbourne University Press.

Pugh, D., 2014. *Turn Left at the Devil Tree.* Darwin: www.derekpugh.com.au.

——, 2017. *Fort Dundas: The British in North Australia, 1824–29.* Darwin.

——, 2018a. *Escape Cliffs: The First Northern Territory Expedition, 1864–66.* Darwin: www.derekpugh.com.au.

——, 2018b. *Darwin 1869: The Second Northern Territory Expedition.* Darwin.

——, 2019. *Darwin: Origin of a City.* Darwin: www.derekpugh.com.au.

——, 2020. *Port Essington: The British in North Australia 1838–49.* Darwin: www.derekpugh.com.au.

——, 2021. *Darwin: Growth of a City: The 1880s.* Darwin: www.derekpugh.com.au.

Reid, G., 1990. *A Picnic with the Natives: Aboriginal-European Relations in the Northern territory to 1910.* Melbourne University Press.

Rose, A., 1964. *Early Northern Territory Droving Epics.* Alice Springs: Australian Veterinary Journal, Vol 40, March 1964.

Rutt, W., 1871. *Diary kept by Walter Rutt, Overseer of the Overland Telegraph Construction Party, Section 1.* https://digital.collections.slsa.sa.gov.au/nodes/view/2520#idx17492 ed. Adelaide: State Library of Spouth Australia, Digital collections.

SADEP, 1986. *Mound Springs Heritage Survey: Data sheets for Biological Assessment of South Australian Mound Springs.* s.l.:South Australian Department of Environment and Planning.

Searcy, A., 1909. *In Australian Tropics.* London: George Robertson and Co.

——, 1912. *By Flood and Field: Adventures Ashore and Afloat in North Australia.* London: G. Bell and Sons, 1st Edition.

SLSA, 1855. Letter of appointment, Sir Charles Todd. 1826–1910. Retrieved 4 March 2021 ed. Adelaide: South Australian State library.

SMH, 16 Nov 1872. The Trans-Continental Telegraph. Volume *The Sydney Morning Herald*.

Smith, T. F., 1870–71. *Diary of Thomas Frederick Smith, Overland Telegraph Construction Party.* Adelaide: State Library of South Australia, PRG 198.

Solomon, V., 1885. *NT Times Almanac for 1886.* Palmerston: Northern Territory Times and Gazette.

Spencer, B., 1896. *Report on the Work of the Horn Scientific Expedition.* Adelaide: cited in http://www.ntlis.nt.gov.au/heritageregister/heritage_register.

Spencer, B. & Gillen, F., 1912. *Across Australia.* 2nd Edition, Vol. 2 ed. London: MacMillan and Co.

Strehlow, T. G. H., 1969. *Journey to Horseshoe Bend.* Sydney: Rigby, Seal Books.

Stuart, J. M., 1862. *Explorations in Australia: The Journals of John McDouall Stuart During the Years 1858, 1859, 1860, 1861, When he Fixed the Centre of the Continent and Successfully Crossed It from Sea to Sea.* Online: http://www.gutenberg.org/ebooks/8911 accessed December 2020.

Sweet, E., 1870. *Early Experiences in the Northern Territory: the pilot of the Roper.* Public Service Review, South Australia.

Symes, G. W., 1969. Babbage, Benjamin Herschel (1815–1878). [Online]
Available at: https://adb.anu.edu.au/biography/babbage-benjamin-herschel-1550
[Accessed 9 March 2021].

——, 1976a. Ross, John (1817–1903). [Online]
Available at: https://adb.anu.edu.au/biography/ross-john-4507/text7371,
[Accessed 12 April 2021].

——, 1976b. Todd, Sir Charles (1826–1910). [Online]
Available at: [Online] http://adb.anu.edu.au/biography/todd-sir-charles-4727/text7843 [Accessed 3 March 2021].

Thompson, D., 2008. *The Australian Telegraph Network 1854–1877*. Melbourne: Museum of Victoria.

Thomson, A., 2000. *The Singing Wire*. London: Vintage.

Todd, C., 1 Jan 1873. *Adelaide and Port Darwin Telegraph: report by C. Todd on the construction and completion of the Adelaide and Port Darwin line of telegraph*. Adelaide: Govt. Printer.

——, 1872. *Family Letters 1855–1897*. https://www.catalog.slsa.sa.gov.au/record=b2188794 ed. Adelaide: State Library of South Australia.

——, 1884. *South Australian Parliamentary Papers 191/1884*. Adelaide: SLSA.

Todd, L., 11 Dec 1952. *'Telegraph Todd' And The Overland Line*. Adelaide: Chronicle.

TPAS, no date, Telegraph Pole Appreciation Society. [Online] Available at: https://www.telegraphpoleappreciationsociety.org/images/userImages/oz/the-overland-telegraph1.pdf [Accessed 11 June 2021].

Traynor, S., 2016. *Alice Springs: From singing wire to iconic outback town*. Adelaide: Wakefield Press.

Venus, R., 2013. *Charles Todd's Middle Name*. Adelaide. Journal of the Historical Society of South Australia.

Wallace, L., 2004. *Cape York Peninsula: A history of unlauded heroes 1845–2003*. Brisbane: Queensland University Press.

Warburton, P. E., 1875. *Journey Across the Western Interior of Australia*. 1981, Facsimile edition, Hesperian Press ed. London: Sampson Low, Marston Low and Searle.

Wilson, A., 1983. *Report on the Relics of the Overland Telegraph Line from Batchelor to Pine Creek*. https://territorystories.nt.gov.au/10070/460820/0/0 ed. Darwin: NT Division of the Institute of Surveyors and the Northern Territory Government.

Wilson, B., 2000. *A Force Apart: A History of the Northern Territory Police Force 1870–1926*. Darwin: A thesis submitted in fulfilment of the requirements of the Northern Territory University for the Degree of Doctor of Philosophy.

Woods, A., 1871. *Journal of Alfred Woods*. Adelaide: State Library of South Australia GRG 154/6.

Twenty to the Mile

Index

A

Abareeka 149

Abbott, William 30–2, 36, 276, 232

Aborigines 21, 85, 91–2, 124, 128, 130–1, 133, 137, 139–40, 144, 149–50, 156, 165, 173, 182, 220, 235, 246, 250

Adcock's Store 262

Adelaide vii, ix, xvii, xviii, xix, xx, 2–12, 15–17, 23, 25, 29–31, 35–6, 40, 49, 54, 57, 59, 63–4, 66–7, 69, 71, 73–4, 83, 87, 9–3, 95, 97–100, 102–5, 109–10, 112–13, 118, 122–3, 130, 133, 135, 137–8, 143, 150, 156–9, 164–5, 174, 177–9, 181, 196, 199, 202, 209, 212, 232–4, 257, 264, 272–3, 277

Adelaide–Port Darwin Overland Telegraph Line Exploring Party 20, 223

Adnyamathanha 197

'Advance Australia' message viii, 58, 264

Afghan cameleers xv, 34, 175, 178, 199, 204

Aldinga 4, 74, 273

Aldridge, Jim 143, 271–3

Alice Creek 48

Alice River 42

Alice Springs viii, xi, 2, 44–5, 47, 49–53, 109, 113, 115, 125, 127, 137, 156–9, 168, 175, 178, 185, 193–4, 202, 215, 220, 224, 227, 229

Alice Springs Telegraph Station viii, ix, x, xi, 42, 47, 49, 113–4, 137, 151, 167–70, 225–7, 269

Alkngulura 217

Allchurch, Ernest 113

Andado Station 219

Anderson, James 234

Andrews, James (Jimmy) 186

Anmatyerre 21

Anna Creek Station 205, 210

Antipodes 75

Apatula/Finke 224

Arltunga 50

Arlyernpe 217

Arnhem Land xi, 206

Arrernte 220

Ashburton Ranges 89, 91–2

Atalante 27

Atherreyurre viii, 45

Attack Creek 54–5, 91, 95, 132, 141, 164, 166–7, 229, 235, 239

Ayers Rock
    see Uluru

B

Babbage, Benjamin Herschel 30–2, 36, 276

Bacon, Harley 35, 182, 276

Bagot, Charles 93, 272, 273

Bagot, Edward Meade viii, 19, 30, 32–3, 39, 196

Bagot, John 211

Banjoewangie
    see Banyuwangi
Banyuwangi viii, ix, 56, 58, 69, 94, 162–3
Barkly Tablelands 173
Barngarla 194
Barrow Creek ix, x, 2, 49–52, 93, 133–4, 136–7, 143–4, 193, 220, 228, 230
Barrow Creek outrage 135
Barrow Creek Roadhouse 230
Barrow Creek Telegraph Station xviii, 51–2, 130, 133, 228–30, 233
Barrow Street, Southport 261
B.A.T. viii, 8–10, 15, 57–8, 62–3, 66, 69, 162–3, 268–9
B.A.T. Ball 162
Batchelor 71, 276
Batten, William 148–9
Bayfield 97
Beltana 2, 32–3, 126, 178, 186–7, 193, 196–200, 204, 210, 229
Beltana Telegraph Station 197
Bengal viii, ix, 15, 18, 57, 62, 72–7, 198, 275
Benjamin Head 23
Bennett, J.W.O. 53
Blackmore River 120, 261

Blackwell, Doris 157
Blood, John Henry 31, 33, 181, 212, 276
Blyth, Minister Arthur 66, 71
Boucaut, Ray 32, 47–8, 89, 92–3, 95, 220, 276
Bowley, Joseph 142
Bradshaw, Atalanta Hope 157
Bradshaw, Doris 115
Bradshaw, Mrs. 157
Bradshaw, Thomas 113, 156, 170, 227–8
Brisbane 3, 4, 11, 243
British Australian Telegraph Company
    see B.A.T.
Brock's Creek 101
Brock, William 101
Bromley, E.R.C. 27
Browne, Dr William James 189
Brunette Downs Station 131
Buchanan, Nat 173
Burke and Wills 6, 174, 178, 199
Burketown 7, 8
Burrundie xi, 120–2, 189, 253–7, 263
Burton, Robert 60–1, 63, 69, 77, 88–92, 93–5
Byng, Harry 149
Byrne, Patrick (Paddy) 155–6, 221–2

C

cameleers
    see Afghan cameleers
camels xv, 21, 29, 35, 40, 45, 125–6, 153, 159, 171, 175–9, 185, 186, 187, 198–201, 215, 217
Carew, Bob 127
Carmichael, Samuel 181, 182
centenary monument 266
Central Mount Stuart ix, xviii, xix, 21–3, 40, 51
Central Mount Sturt 21,
Chambers Bay 5, 6
Chambers Creek 34, 36

Chambers Pillar ix, 43, 180, 186, 193, 223–4
Chambers Pillar graffiti 224
Charley 177
Charlotte Waters 2, 36, 39–40, 45, 47–9, 51–3, 99, 138, 142, 154–6, 176, 179, 181–2, 185, 193, 216–22, 224
Charlotte Waters Telegraph Station 154–55, 218, 220
Chawner 90–2, 172
Chinatown 263
Christopher Pinnacle 155
Clarke, Benjamin viii, 47–49

Index

Claud Hamilton 277
Claymore 100
Cobourg Peninsula 93
'Coolies' x, 16
Coward Springs 206
Cox, Matthew Dillon 87, 100–1
Crawford, Lindsay 188
Crawford, Miss 151
Creaghe, Harry 188–9
   Emily 173, 188–9
Crispe, Thomas 20, 277
Crowder, William A. 74–7, 80–2, 84–7, 89, 90, 92–3, 95–6, 100,–1, 164, 274, 276
Cullen River 142
Curtis, George 138–40

D

Daer, Abram 143–4, 146, 149, 151, 245
Dalhousie Springs 40, 154, 206, 216
Dalwood, William Trevett 19–20, 28, 59, 60–1, 63–6, 69, 273
Daly, Daniel 61, 63, 87
   Harriet 264
Daly Waters 2, 87, 89–91, 94, 114, 121, 126, 129, 143, 148, 151, 153–4, 165, 167, 171, 193, 241, 243–5
Daly Waters Cemetery 245
Daly Waters Telegraph Station 69, 122, 144–5, 188
Darwent, Joseph 19–20, 28, 57, 59–60, 63–6, 69, 273
Deane, George 101
de Grey Station 179, 191
Delamere Station 189
de Latour, George 149
Dolphin 74–6
Douglas, Captain William Bloomfield viii, 11, 15–17, 61–3, 65–6, 71, 72, 73, 97, 100, 101, 165, 258
   Harriet viii, 61–3
   Mrs Ellen 61, 63
Dunmarra Roadhouse 241
Dyke, Thomas 77, 138–9, 141, 274, 276

E

Eastern Extension Telegraph Company 268, 269
Easther, William 85
Edinburgh 56–8
Edith River 142
Elder, Thomas 25, 45, 177–8, 187, 197, 199, 200
Elsey 193
Elsey Creek 148, 245–6
Elsey River 92
Elsey Station 246, 248, 251
Elsey Telegraph Camp 139
Elsey Telegraph Station 189, 246
Elvoy, Leonard 172
Emungalan 251
Engineers Australia xvii, 83, 267
Enterprise 83, 277
Escape Cliffs 6, 19, 20, 42, 73, 199, 206
Estelle 263
Eureka Stockade vii, 1
Explorers 171, 194

F

Farina x, 193, 201–4
Farina Post and Telegraph Office 201
Farina Restoration Group Inc. 202
Farina Station 202
Favenc, Ernest 188
Fergusson Ranges 22
Fergusson River 94, 128, 142, 189, 253, 256
Finke Depot 42–4, 182, 219, 224

289

Finke River 40, 42, 159, 182
Finniss, Colonel 19–20, 58, 73, 206
first message ix, xviii, xix, 92, 97, 110, 265
First Northern Territory Expedition 6, 19, 42
first phone call 198
first pole 11, 59, 63, 264
first pole, Harvey's 54
first pole memorial 266
first telegram vii, ix, 36, 58, 97
Fitts, George 255, 257
Flinders, Matthew 29
Flinders Ranges 29
Flint, Ernest Ebenezer x, xi, 47–9, 113, 130, 134–5, 137, 226, 228–30
Florence 137

Flying Cloud 72, 83, 149
Flynn-of-the-Inland 187, 199
Foelsche, Inspector Paul 16, 63, 259, 234
Forrest, Alexander 189–90, 191
Forrest, John x, 177, 189–90, 200, 212
Franks, John ix, 135, 137, 230, 231
Freeling Springs (Yardiya) 162, 210
Freeman, Miss 118, 122
Fremantle 4, 178
Frew's Ironstone Ponds ix, xvii, xix, 54, 87, 89, 90, 94, 96, 97, 181, 194, 241–2
Friends of Mound Springs 206, 212

G

Galle 4, 11, 57
Gason, Mounted Constable Sam 134, 136
Geelong vii, 1
George de Latour 148
Ghan xi, xii, xv, 162, 195, 200, 213–4, 224
Ghan Heritage Trail 194
Ghan Railway 194–5, 200, 213–4
'Ghans' 199
'Ghantown' 204
Gibson, Alfred 186, 187
Giles, Alan McFarlane 130–2, 231–2, 234–5, 274
Giles, Alfred 20, 21, 22, 84–6, 128, 155, 189, 223, 247, 248
Giles, Christopher 47, 154–5, 176, 222, 271–2, 276
Giles, Ernest ix, x, 155, 175–6, 179, 180–7, 200, 212, 217, 224
Gillen, Francis (Frank) James 113, 156–7, 221–2, 239–40
gold x, xi, 7, 17, 50, 63, 70, 100–1, 117–9, 133, 171, 179, 196, 220, 252, 257, 263
gold rush 50, 95, 117, 250, 252, 257–9, 261
Gore's boat 262

Gosse, Dr Francis 135
Gosse, William Christie ix, x, 174–5, 176–8, 185–6
Goss, Fred 114, 129, 151, 165–6, 188
Gothenburg disaster x, 27, 85, 272, 273
Government Gums x, 200, 201
Goyder, George vii, 19, 25, 40, 42, 44, 50, 53, 63, 70, 73, 140, 154, 162, 206, 250, 261, 267, 276
graffiti 224
Great Artesian Basin 206
Great Northern Hotel 204
Great Sandy Desert 179
Great Victoria Desert 187
Gregory, Augustus 16, 24
Gulf of Carpentaria 4, 6, 7, 74
Gulnare viii, 15, 17, 28, 62, 64–6, 71–3, 75, 275
Gumen 131–2
Gunn, Jeannie xvii, 246, 247, 251–4

Index

H

Hablett, George 207
Hack, B 77, 96–7, 275
Halleem 177
Halpin, Captain Robert 58, 264, 268
Hamilton 136
Hammer and Gad Eating House 211
Hammond, Walter 234
Hanley, Tom 49, 156
Harris, Ted 47–8
Harry the Camel 199
Harvey, William 20, 22–3, 25, 39, 45, 53–4, 223, 272–3
Hassell, Thomas 143, 144
Head, Benjamin 235
Hearne 20, 224
Heavitree Gap 45
Hergott Springs 202, 204, 216
Hermannsburg Mission 52, 159
Hewish, Albert 207–9, 215
Hewish, Andrew 209, 215–16
Hewish, Mary 207
Hibernia 56–8
Hocking, Stanley Percival 220
Holtze, Maurice 121
Holtze, Waldemar 121
Honeymoon Gap 45
Horn, Austin 27
Horrigan, Jack 173
Horrocks, John Ainsworth 178, 199
horse express ix, xix, 92–3, 95
Horseshoe Bend 44, 159, 216
Howley, Andrew 60, 63, 88, 93, 97, 133, 273, 276
Hübbe, Samuel 52
Hughes, Sir Walter 177
Hugh River 22, 35, 42–4, 48, 216, 276
Hume, Andrew 138, 140
Hummel, Captain 15, 73, 76
Hussey, James 130

I

Ildracowra 223
Inspector Foelsche 147
Investigator xix, xx, 56–8

J

Jarvis, Stephen 51, 272–3, 277
Jemmy 134, 135, 147
Jervois, Governor Sir William 187
Johnston, Charles Henry x, xviii, 18, 84, 86, 88–9, 92, 101, 133, 138–49, 155, 191, 240, 245, 249, 274, 276
Johnston, Joseph [Joe] McLean William 47, 119, 122, 155, 181, 222
John Urquardt 249
Joining Point 241–2

K

Kamran 175, 176
Katherine xi, 2, 23, 69, 83, 188–91, 193, 234, 245–6, 252–34, 257
Katherine Telegraph Station x, 74, 132, 142, 189, 191, 256
Kaytetye ix, 130, 134, 136, 228
Kaytetye spear 228
Kekwick, William Darton 23, 235
Kelsey, Dudley Evan 11, 117–20, 122, 128, 259, 261
Kelsey, John George (Jack) 113, 117, 121–3, 151, 153
Kersley Street, Southport 120, 263
Kidman and Co 206

Kidman, Sidney 202
Kimberley 173, 231, 249
King, Stephen 2, 19, 20, 60, 63, 69, 71, 84–7, 88–92, 94, 96, 273, 276
Knuckey, Richard Randall x, 27, 39–41, 84, 85, 92, 95, 143, 172, 217, 220, 250, 271–2, 277–8

Kohinoor viii, 11, 73
Kraegen, Carl 47–9, 220, 229, 276

L

Lake Amadeus 176, 182
Lake Christopher 155
Lake Eyre 32, 35, 51, 213
Lamond, Barney 173, 231
lancewood (*Acacia shirleyi*) 90, 91, 96, 241–2
Larrakeeyah 74, 77, 275
Larrakia 8, 53
Leichhardt, Ludwig 16, 24, 73, 138, 186
Leichhardt's Bar 72, 148
Levi, Philip 36, 211
Lewis, John xix, 87, 92–4, 97
Lewis, J.W. 177
lightning 36–7, 124, 141
Limmen National Park 248
Limmen's Bight 246

Lindsay, David xi, 158
Little, John Archibald Graham viii, x, xvii, xix, 17–18, 67, 74, 77, 80, 97, 119, 122, 124, 144, 148, 155, 164–6, 230
 Blanche 165
 Edith 165
 Egbert 165
 Matilda (Mattie) 144, 165
 Maud 171
Liverpool vii
London ix, xix, xx, 4, 7, 8, 11, 12, 15, 69, 109–10, 112–3, 138, 264, 268
Lord Ashley 277
Loudon, John 49
Lowrie, Captain 80, 82–3
Loxton, Bill 138, 140, 144
Lucy 94

M

MacDonnell Ranges 22, 36–7, 40, 42, 45–7, 53, 175, 182, 215
MacDonnell, Sir Richard 5
MacNamara, Patrick 246
Madely, Florence xi
maintenance 101, 124, 128, 143, 190, 207
maintenance crews 99, 123, 207
malaria 19, 88, 92, 142
Maria Island 74, 100–1
Marree 202–4
Marree Hotel 203–4
Marshall, Barry 250
Marshall, Jennifer 250
Marsh, Captain Henry 72, 149–50
Mataranka 245, 248

McArthur River 188
McClure's Springs 49
McGowan, Samuel 3, 156
McKay, John 113
McKenzie, Scotty 219
McKinlay, John 6, 20, 24, 73, 178, 199, 206
McKinlay's exploration party to Arnhem Land 206
McLachlan, George vii, 9, 15, 16, 62–3, 72, 100
McMinn, Gilbert Rotherdale viii, xi, 25, 39, 42–5, 49, 65–6, 133, 175, 182, 271–2
McMinn, William 27, 60, 63–4, 66, 273
Meidinger Cells 114–5
Melbourne vii, 1–4, 11, 74, 110, 181, 186

Index

Millner, Dr James Stokes xviii, 25, 58, 73, 97
Mills, William Whitfield viii, 22, 25, 27, 39, 44–5, 47, 271–2
Milner, John 87
Milner, Ralph 86–7
Mitchell, Alexander 26, 27, 50, 94, 96–7, 100
Monck, Viscount Charles 10, 13
Montagu, Corporal George x, 147, 149
Moonta vii, 44, 154
Morse code xviii, 11, 116–7, 135, 195, 227
Morse, Samuel vii, 115
mosque 204
Mound springs 202, 206, 209

Mount Connor 176
Mount Gwynn 22
Mount Liebig 176
Mount Margaret 32
Mount Margaret Station 36, 51, 93
Mount Olga 186
Mueller, Johannes [John] Ferdinand x, 47–50, 113, 156, 220, 229
Murphy, Bernard 251–2
Murray, Robert McKellar 74, 191, 189, 191, 255–7
Musgrave, Charles William x, 27, 272
Musgrave Ranges x, 176, 186

N

Nash, Charles 27, 249
Nation, William 171–2
Newcastle Waters 37, 87, 90–1, 96, 137, 144, 172–3, 239, 277
New Crown Station 219
New South Wales xiv, 3, 9, 93, 179

New Zealand 2, 151, 163, 268–9
Norman River 7, 8, 74
Norman River Post Office 7
Normanton viii, 3, 7–10, 15, 66, 74, 77, 275

O

O'Brien, Jim 204
Omeo viii, ix, 17, 25, 59–62, 67, 74, 77, 80–1, 100–1, 273, 275
Oodnadatta xi, xii, 35, 49, 126, 159, 162, 167, 208–9, 212–6
Oodnadatta Track 194, 202, 206, 213

Oppenheimer poles x, 40, 41, 70, 127, 190, 201, 214, 233, 243, 253, 264, 266, 277
Osborn, Noel 9–10
O.T.L. cost 112
Overland Telegraph Line managers 26

P

Packard, Harrison 73, 76, 100, 275
Palmer, Charles 229, 273, 277
Palmer, Colonial Secretary Arthur Hunter 7–8
Palmerston viii, ix, x, xi, xvii, xviii, 8–9, 11, 16, 40, 42, 44, 58–60, 62, 67, 71, 97, 101, 106, 108, 112, 117, 120–2, 146, 148, 150–1, 161–5, 172, 193, 230, 261, 268
Palmerston Book of Deaths 75
Palmerston District Council 117

Palmerston, District of 76
Palmerston Overland Telegraph office 107
Palmerston Telegraph Offices 58, 265
Palmerston to Pine Creek Railway 120, 263
Pamayu 239
Pangi Warrunha 204
Paqualin, W. A. 19, 59, 60, 62–3, 273
Paterson, Mary 208

293

Patterson, Robert Charles xvii, xix, 26, 66–9, 71, 73–7, 79–80, 86–8, 95–7, 143, 165, 193–4, 242, 273, 275

Perth x, 4, 6, 175, 187

Phillips, George 130, 132

Phillips, James 30, 196

Pine Creek xi, 2, 118, 122–3, 193, 253–5

Pine Creek and Burrundie 253

Pine Creek Telegraph Station 254–5

Port Adelaide 80, 90, 99, 101, 105

Port Augusta viii, x, xvii, xviii, 6, 10, 12, 17, 19, 29, 30–4, 50, 62–3, 114, 129, 194,–5, 198–9, 269

Port Augusta Heritage Trail 193

Port Augusta Telegraph Office 30–1, 196

Port Augusta to Government Gums (Farina) railway x

Port Darwin vii, viii, ix, xi, xvii, xix, 2, 8–13, 15, 19, 20, 23, 30, 44, 57, 59, 60, 62, 65, 67, 69, 71–2, 74, 80, 87–9, 92–5, 97–8, 99–100, 109–10, 114, 117, 120, 122, 126, 149–50, 164, 191, 232, 261–2, 273

Powell's Creek 2, 19, 90, 92, 121–2, 126, 130, 133, 138–9, 142–3, 153, 166–7, 173, 188–9, 193, 209, 233–4, 239, 241, 247, 276

Powell's Creek Telegraph Station 121, 139, 141, 188, 237–9

Price, Frederick 107, 113

Pybus, Alfred 123, 241, 274

Q

Queensland x, xiv, xvii, 3, 7–10, 15, 17, 25, 77, 87, 93, 100, 148–9, 171, 173, 178, 181, 188, 199

R

Randall, Walter David 208

Rangatira 277

Rawlinson Ranges 187

Readford, Henry (Harry) 131–2, 234

Read, William 75, 76

Red Lily Lagoon 86

Rees, John 130

Renner, Dr Frederick Emil 69, 90–1, 233–4, 250

Renner family 233, 250

Renner Springs 90, 140–1, 193, 233–5, 239, 250

Reynolds Ranges 45–7

Rickards, Charles 144–7, 149, 151, 245

Ringwood, Alexander 69, 87, 89, 91–2, 96, 100, 276

Rix, Dr Edward Cecil 90, 275

Roadmasters Museum 267

Robinson, Alec 181

Roper Bar 71, 73, 77, 80, 83–4, 86, 145, 245

Roper Bar Crossing 249

Roper River viii, ix, 9, 15, 41, 63, 66–7, 72–5, 82, 84, 88, 90, 94, 97, 141, 143–4, 148–9, 245–6, 248–9

Roper River Depot ix, 79, 81, 84–5, 100, 138, 248, 258, 276

Roper River Police Station 249

Roper Store 248

Ross, George 207

Ross, John 20–1, 23, 25, 32, 52, 54, 136, 186, 211, 223, 247, 272, 276

rum 22–3, 71, 80, 96

Rum Jungle 70–1, 276

Rutt, Walter 69, 75, 84, 88, 94, 96–7, 273–5

Ryan, Ned 52, 206

Index

S

Sahleh 177
Scar, Frank 173
Scott, George Byng x, 150
scurvy 23, 83, 87, 112, 142, 155, 222, 274
Searle, Henry 251–2
Second Northern Territory Expedition vii, 20, 44, 92, 250
Semaphore 3
shackle 118
Shirley, Mounted Constable John Charles x, 130–2, 231, 234, 239
Si Jin 134
Singapore xii, 4, 6–7, 11, 13, 94, 164
Skinner, Joseph 113, 156
Skull Creek 136
Smith, Thomas Frederick 33, 35–6, 229, 277–8
Sourabaya 57
South Australian government 1, 9, 12–13, 17, 31, 57–8, 62, 179, 187, 204
Southport 2, 28, 53, 59, 118–22, 124, 126, 153, 188, 193, 255, 261–4
Southport Chinatown 120
Southport jetty 263
Southport Telegraph Station 255, 262
Spencer, Baldwin 156, 219–1, 239–40
Spencer Gulf 29, 32, 194

Spicer, Leslie 115
Sportsman's Hotel and Pioneer Cash Store 251–2
Springvale Station 189
Stapleton, James Lawrence ix, 60, 63, 88, 93, 101, 118, 132,–5, 137, 142, 144, 230–1, 273, 275
Stewart, Mounted Constable 216
Stott, Constable Robert 120, 234
Strangways, Henry 10, 204
Strangways Ranges 22, 46–7
Strangways Springs 2, 22, 193, 204, 207–9
Strangways Springs cemetery 208
Strangways Springs Telegraph Station 142, 205
Strehlow, Bertha 222
Stuart 2, 5, 6, 9, 12, 20, 21–4, 39, 41–3, 46, 51, 54, 55, 63, 87, 159, 186, 194, 211, 223–4, 230, 235, 239, 247
Stuart (Alice Springs) 47, 159, 215
Stuart Town Memorial Cemetery 50
Sturt 24
Supple, Bernie 207
Sweet, Captain Samuel White 2, 15, 17, 8, 57, 62–3, 66, 7–3, 75–6, 80–1, 83 Elizabeth 17
Sydney vii, 2–4, 11, 138, 181, 268, 277

T

Tapscott, Robert 74, 275
Tararua 80–2
Tasmania vii, xvii, 3, 69, 93
Tassie Street 30
Tate, Professor Ralph 220-1
Taylor Creek 136
Telegraph Fleet 56
telephone 198
Temple Bar Gap 45
Tennant Creek 2, 49, 53–5, 83, 89, 92, 95, 121, 140, 173, 193, 231–2, 234, 239

Tennant Creek Telegraph Station 134, 141–2, 173, 231–2, 234
termites 44, 70, 90
The Explorers' Way 194
The Peake x, 19, 25, 30–3, 35–7, 45, 47, 134, 153, 157–8, 162, 184, 186–7, 193, 210–13, 215, 217, 272, 276
The Peake Telegraph Station 162, 172, 181, 187, 190, 210–11
The Residency 57, 59, 73, 161–2, 206
The Shackle 44, 117–8, 120–2, 151, 153, 257–61

The Shackle Telegraph Station 118–9, 257
Tietkins, William Henry 186
Timor 6, 62
Tjingilli (Jingili) 240
Todd, Charles vii, ix, xii, xi, xvii–xix, xxii, 1–4, 6, 9, 12, 18–20, 22–24, 26, 32, 36–7, 39–40, 44, 47, 49, 53–4, 58, 61, 64,–6, 68–70, 80, 88, 92, 94–5, 98, 101, 112, 116, 124, 126, 130, 133, 135, 137–8, 148, 155, 162, 164, 193, 196, 211, 229–30, 241, 245, 250, 257, 265, 273, 271

Alice Gillam (nee Bell) 2, 45
Lorna 2, 4, 13
transit of Venus 3
Tucker, Charles 143
Tuckwell, Ned 63
Tymn, Charles 63, 64

U

Uhr, D'Arcy 100
Uluru x, 176, 186
undersea cable ix, xii, xix, xx, 3, 6–10, 15, 57, 69, 94, 109, 162–4, 268

Ural 148–51
Urquardt, John 249

W

Wadlata Outback Centre 195, 269
Walkman, Mounted Constable W. 222
Warburton, Peter Egerton ix, 32, 175, 177–9, 185, 200
Warlirra ix, 241
Warloch Ponds 139, 148, 245, 247, 276
Warumungu 239
Watson, Richard 47–9, 130, 133, 144, 220
Wells, Bob 158–9
We of the Never Never 246

White, Dennis 177
Williamstown vii, 1
William Willshire, Mounted Constable x, 132, 224
Wilson, Aveling 138
Winnecke, Charles 220
Women on the Line 151 ff.
Wood, Dr. 234
Woods, Alfred Thomas 25, 27, 37, 39, 50–1, 53, 91, 175, 190 39, 271–3
Woolwonga massacre 259

Y

Yam Creek 2, 17, 44, 100–1, 118–9, 120, 124, 144, 155, 193, 252, 257–9, 261

Young Australian ix, 80–3, 100, 248
Young, Thomas 48

CPSIA information can be obtained
at www.ICGtesting.com
Printed in the USA
LVHW051844170222
711394LV00014B/462

9 780648 142195